INSIDE THE ARAB STATE

MEHRAN KAMRAVA

Inside the Arab State

جامعة جورجتاون قطر
GEORGETOWN UNIVERSITY QATAR

Center *for* International *and* Regional Studies

OXFORD
UNIVERSITY PRESS

OXFORD
UNIVERSITY PRESS

Oxford University Press is a department of the
University of Oxford. It furthers the University's objective
of excellence in research, scholarship, and education
by publishing worldwide.

Oxford   New York

Auckland   Cape Town   Dar es Salaam   Hong Kong   Karachi
Kuala Lumpur   Madrid   Melbourne   Mexico City   Nairobi
New Delhi   Shanghai   Taipei   Toronto

With offices in

Argentina   Austria   Brazil   Chile   Czech Republic   France   Greece
Guatemala   Hungary   Italy   Japan   Poland   Portugal   Singapore
South Korea   Switzerland   Thailand   Turkey   Ukraine   Vietnam

Oxford is a registered trade mark of Oxford University Press
in the UK and certain other countries.

Published in the United States of America by
Oxford University Press
198 Madison Avenue, New York, NY 10016

Library of Congress Cataloging-in-Publication Data is available
Mehran Kamrava.
Inside the Arab State.
ISBN: 9780190876043

Printed in India on acid-free paper

CONTENTS

ACKNOWLEDGMENTS

This book grew out of a research initiative I undertook under the auspices of the Center for International and Regional Studies (CIRS) at Georgetown University in Qatar. As one of the first steps in the research, CIRS held a two-day brainstorming session in which a number of renowned scholars of the Arab world shared their ideas on the overall direction this volume should take and the questions it should ask and answer. I am deeply grateful to my colleagues at CIRS for organizing the working group, and to the working group participants—Fateh Azzam, Michaelle Browers, Juan Cole, Stephanie Cronin, Ahmad Dallal, Steven Heydemann, Michael Hudson, Rami Khouri, Beverley Milton-Edwards, and Adham Saouli—for so generously sharing their thoughts and ideas of what I should explore in this volume.

Thanks to the efforts of Abdelaziz Sebaa, the Algerian Ambassador to Qatar, a number of colleagues in Algeria met and shared with me their insights and perspectives on developments in the country. They included Zouaoui Benhamadi, Liess Boukra, Farouk Ksentini, Abdellaoui Laid, and Amina Mesdoua. I am grateful for their kindness and the generosity of their spirit.

Mohammad Almasri patiently explained to me the methodology used by the Arab Center for Research and Policy Studies in collecting annual public opinion surveys in twelve Arab countries. I have relied on this data extensively in Chapter 5. Appendix 1, which explains the methodology used in the annual survey, was kindly provided to me by Mohammad.

At different stages of working on the book, I was assisted by a number of superb research assistants, including Mohammad Abu Hawash, Noof Al-Thani, Safa Babikir, Emma Mogensen, and Erika Thao Nguyen.

ACKNOWLEDGMENTS

Once an initial draft of the book was completed, I had the good fortune of having a second brainstorming session, this time to have the different chapters read and reviewed by another distinguished group of colleagues and friends. They included Osama Abi-Mershed, Zahra Babar, Daniel Brumberg, Steven Cook, Kristin Diwan, Daniel Esser, Desha Girod, Islam Hassan, Suzi Mirgani, Irfan Nooruddin and Marina Ottaway. I feel extremely fortunate and honored to have had early feedback on my writing from such an esteemed group of scholars. The book no doubt still contains many shortcomings. But I am convinced that it is much improved from its earlier drafts because of their feedback.

Grateful acknowledgment also goes to the Qatar Foundation for its support of research and other scholarly endeavors.

Finally, my colleagues at CIRS, where the project was conceived and completed, were instrumental in helping to create a most supportive and intellectually stimulating environment in which to write the book. Their support and assistance, as with everything else I have written since 2007, is most deeply appreciated.

1

STUDYING ARAB POLITICS

The world watched with eager anticipation as old autocrats collapsed one after another across the Arab world in the early weeks and months of 2011. Dictators whose grip on power seemed firm and unshakable not long ago, and entire regimes well-entrenched and considered powerful, were either pulled down by the power of public protests or were shaken to their core. It was generally assumed that age-old vestiges of authoritarianism would soon collapse. Old, familiar names—Ben Ali, Mubarak, Qaddafi, Saleh—soon became synonymous with "deposed dictators." Domestic Arab politics, often perceived as stale and immobile, or downright dangerous and brutal, suddenly became exciting, hopeful, filled with possibilities.

But this was not to be. At least not yet. What was optimistically called the Arab Spring, the start of a new era, turned out to be, in Steven Cook's words, a "false dawn."[1] Before long, politics had become business as usual. For many of the less fortunate Arabs, politics as usual would actually have been a blessing as their countries descended into the abyss of civil war and chaos. Overnight, countless middle-class Iraqis, Libyans, Syrians, and Yemenis were turned into homeless refugees.

This book traces the fateful odyssey of domestic Arab politics starting in the early 1950s, when most modern institutions of the state were established, up until today. The account presented here is only loosely chronological. The periods lasting up until 2011, the challenges to states that fateful year, and the responses of the states to these challenges are each examined in separate chapters. But they are presented here less as a narrative and more through the analytical lens of state–society interactions, highlighting the importance of the causes, processes, and consequences of the nexus between, and the contests among, states and societies in each period.

The essence of politics boils down to state–society relations. But these relations are far from mechanical. There are cultural, ideological, and normative dimensions to the interactions as well, and such factors as legitimacy and citizenship are also instrumental in shaping politics. The issues of citizenship, legitimacy, and political Islam, especially after 2011, are also examined here.

To say that 2011 has thrown the Arab world's regional and domestic orders into turmoil is only to state the obvious. In the aftermath of the Arab Spring, the established order in the Middle East partially collapsed. In the new reality that emerged, state and non-state entities intermingled, and at times the tension between the two redefined Arab politics and geography.[2] After the uprisings, we see the emergence of new actors and the reproduction of old problems, new settings, and old patterns. We also see the emergence of "flexible linkages between states and non-state actors."[3] States are not about to disappear or dissipate any time soon, earlier neoliberal assumptions about the end of history and the consequences of globalization notwithstanding.[4] In this book, I have placed the state at the center of political analysis, critically examining it in relation to society in general and social actors and social dynamics in particular.

The central argument

This is a book about state–society relations in the Arab world, focusing on the institutional makeup and composition of Arab states and how they have sought to establish coercive and "ideological apparatuses" enabling them to rule over society.[5] Through the lens of historical institutionalism, I maintain that critical junctures provide a window of opportunity for state leaders to craft institutions and institutional arrangements that enable them to rule over society. Once these institutional arrangements are in place, two sets of dynamics begin to occur. At one level, as institutions mature, and as their operations become routine, they begin to develop lives of their own. Slowly, they assume internal dynamics that move them in one direction or another. The actors who created these institutions, however, may not always approve of the direction in which they are moving. Thus, a potential area of tension develops between agency and structure—what state actors wish to see of the institutions of the state and how these institutions actually behave.

A second dynamic has to do with the growing gaps in the efficacy of the coercive apparatuses of the state as compared to its ideological apparatuses. All states rely on a combination of coercive and ideological apparatuses to govern. In the Arab world, as the efficacy of the ideological apparatus of the state eroded in the 1970s and the 1980s, greater emphasis was placed on its coercive apparatuses. By 2011, even these coercive apparatuses could not function properly, becoming susceptible to challenge and overthrow through a series of loosely connected social movements.

The social movements of 2010–11 presented another critical juncture in Arab politics. Made possible largely through self-organized, spontaneous mass mobilizations, the results of the social movements that swept across much of North Africa and the Levant could be clustered into three broad categories. Some social movements, as in Morocco and Kuwait, fizzled on their own as their demands were partially but proactively met by the state. Other social movements, especially those occurring in societies with multiple fractures, and the heavy intervention of external actors, degenerated into civil wars as they weakened or altogether overthrew state authority without establishing alternative systems of rule. Libya, Syria, and Yemen belong to this unfortunate category.

A third category of social movements actually succeeded in overthrowing existing centers of political authority and in establishing new ones in their place. Most notably this occurred in Tunisia and Egypt. The outcomes, while greatly different, do not change the fact that in both countries social movements gathered sufficient pace and scope to force long-reigning rulers to step down. To the chagrin of purists, I maintain that these two admittedly very different cases of social movements ushered in revolutions.

For most, but not all, states of the Arab world, 2011 marked another historical critical juncture, when an opportunity was presented to reorganize the basis of state–society relations. These critical junctures came about because the power balance between state and society began to change in favor of the latter. By the late 2000s, most Arab states had lost most or all vestiges of the legitimacy they once had, at best retaining support among a narrow group of die-hard regime cronies and affluent oligarchs. As mass mobilization tipped the scale in society's favor, the states' coercive apparatuses scrambled to retain existing networks of power and authority. In each individual case, context-specific dynamics, along with the agency of the actors involved, shaped processes and outcomes.

In Algeria, the memory of the country's bitter civil war, which had ended only a decade earlier, played an important role in keeping the impulses of both state and social actors in check and in ensuring that the potential for instability and chaos was minimized. In Morocco, the monarchy retained enough of its ideological legitimacy, and was sufficiently proactive to placate the demands of the February 20 Movement. The possibilities for drastic ruptures in state–society relations were thus undermined. In Tunisia, by contrast, the state had exhausted its legitimacy for some time, and its politically marginalized military displayed little appetite for keeping existing structures of power intact. What followed was a pacted transition, one in which newly branded soft-liners from the two sides embarked on a process of mutual accommodation and consensus as they tried to craft a new order.

No such accommodative process got underway in Egypt, Syria, or Yemen. In each case, all or parts of the armed forces, as *the* key institution of the state, refused to give up their position of power and privilege in the face of mounting popular demands for change. Each of the ensuing transitions acquired its own dynamics and its own character. At the broadest level, in Syria and Yemen, state responses exacerbated societal divisions along pre-existing fault lines and plunged the two countries into civil wars. The Libyan polity also suffered from pre-existing cleavages, but the civil war that followed Qaddafi's overthrow was less a result of state responses to the uprisings than the absence of meaningful institutions, and the inability of social actors to agree over how to go about constructing them from scratch.

The outcome of the Egyptian uprising was decidedly different. The social movement that began in 2010 quickly mushroomed into a successful revolution in early 2011. But the revolution was aborted before it had a chance to take its course, victim to a combination of path dependence, with the army unwilling to let go of its privileged political position, and agency, with the incompetence of President Morsi and the ambitions of General el-Sisi proving decisive in the unfolding of events. Egyptian society, meanwhile, featured a fair amount of ethnic, religious, and sectarian homogeneity that prevented it from sliding into civil war, enforced by the many institutions of the state (such as the civil service, banks, schools, and the military) which kept functioning as President Mubarak's authority was being dismantled.

Regardless of how the post-uprising Egyptian state envisions itself, it is neither revolutionary nor democratic. In fact, it is bereft of most forms of legitimacy, propping itself up almost entirely through its coercive apparatus. In this sense, the Egyptian state is hardly unique. Most post-uprising Arab states are perceived as illegitimate by their populations, at times more so than the regimes they replaced. Now that the dust of the 2011 uprisings is slowly settling, Arab politics has once again become a contested terrain. State–society relations in the Arab world remain conflictual, reliant not on the ideological apparatus of the state but on its coercive arms.

The Arabian Peninsula deserves a separate treatment as compared to North Africa and the Levant. To be clear, I do not subscribe to the idea of "Arabian exceptionalism." Nevertheless, states and societies in the Arabian Peninsula have indeed had patterns of change and nonlinear evolution that are different from those in North Africa and the Levant.[6] In the Arabian Peninsula, national and contextual differences notwithstanding, states grew mostly organically from society, with tribes and family clans as key elements in the nexus between the rulers and the ruled. Multiple means of overlap and connection between state and society were solidified over time through the flow of oil revenues into the coffers of the state, thereby significantly enhancing state capacity. This enhanced capacity enabled the oil-dependent states to ride through the Arab Spring upheavals relatively unscathed.

For these oil states, the year 2011 was not a critical juncture; 2014 was. Beginning in 2014, sudden and steady collapses in oil prices precipitated declines in state capacity. Declines in state capacity in turn prompted changes, or at least modifications, to prevailing social contracts underlying state–society relations. In other words, politics in the Arabian Peninsula began to see qualitative changes after 2014.

In constructing my arguments, I have employed a number of concepts, two of which, *institutions* and *critical junctures*, need to be defined at the outset. *Institutions* are generally defined as those "structures and organizations that regulate human interactions,"[7] or the "non-technologically determined *constraints* that influence social interactions and provide incentives to maintain regularities of behavior."[8] Along similar lines, Elinor Ostrom defines institutions in terms of "prescriptions that humans use to organize all forms of repetitive and structured interactions." She maintains that "individuals interacting within rule-structured situations face choices regarding the actions and strategies they take, leading to consequences for themselves and for others."[9]

Insightful as these definitions are, they do not distinguish clearly between *formal* and *informal* institutions. Whereas informal institutions may be seen as "socially shared rules, usually unwritten, that are created, communicated, and enforced outside officially sanctioned channels," formal institutions are those "rules and procedures that are created, communicated, and enforced through channels that are widely accepted as official."[10] There are, of course, different varieties of formal and informal institutions—educational, social, political, etc.—and my focus here is on formal political institutions. Briefly, political institutions are those structures and practices, such as constitutions and other formal regulations, through which the state seeks to establish connections with and influence over society. They are, in other words, the primary instruments through which state power is formulated and projected, both domestically and internationally.

In Douglass North's study of institutions and institutional change, he makes a distinction between "institutions" and "organizations," viewing the latter as political, economic, social, or educational "bodies" of one kind or another (political parties, firms, churches, universities, etc.).[11] This important distinction is often left blurred in much of the literature on path dependence. Based largely on insights offered by North, political institutions may be conceived as those formal and informal rules and procedures as well as the organizations that states employ to maintain themselves in power.[12]

Critical junctures, as already mentioned, can be especially determinative of the perseverance of, or changes to, institutions. Critical junctures are those instances during which structural constraints on political action—chief among them economic, cultural, ideological, and organizational influences—are significantly relaxed for a relatively short period of time. During this time, "the range of plausible choices open to powerful political actors expands substantially and the consequences of their decisions for the outcome of interest are potentially much more momentous."[13] These windows of opportunity enable actors to take actions, such as crafting institutions, that can have longer-term consequences. Some historical "junctures are 'critical' because they place institutional arrangements on paths or trajectories, which are then very difficult to alter."[14]

Institutions shape incentives and disincentives, but in politics, and especially in Arab politics, individual decisions are also important.[15] The interaction between institutions and agency occurs through various processes. These three interconnected domains—institutions, agency, and processes—form the core of the analysis here. More specifically, my focus here has been on the means through which Arab states have asserted power before and after the 2011 uprisings through interplays of institutions, agency, and processes.

This book's primary objective is to present an account of the political causes, processes, and consequences of the dynamics underway in the Arab world over the last several decades. While I reach as far back as the 1950s and the 1960s, my primary frame of reference is the present day. My goal here is not to propose a grand theory of Arab politics. More modestly, I present an account of the transformations and transmutations of Arab politics before and after 2011, exploring the timing and features of the outcomes that have been produced out of the interactions of institutions, individuals, and processes.

The scope of the book

The book begins with an overview of Arab politics beginning in the 1950s and the 1960s. It traces the transformation of Arab politics from the populist corporatism of earlier years through to the personalist authoritarianism of the 2000s. In the process, despite a proliferation of multiple institutions that incorporated increasing numbers of urban professionals into the orbit of the state in one form or another, Arab states underwent a steady atrophy whereby they lost much of their political, ideological, and even economic nexus with society, save for paying monthly salaries to the civil service. Well before the twenty-first century, Arab states had already become overwhelmingly dependent on the element of fear in order to force their populations into submission and to stay in power. By the 1990s and 2000s, authoritarianism in much of North Africa and the Levant featured little of the carrot it once used, and instead relied more and more on the stick of repression. "Republics of Fear" became the norm. Jails were bursting with political prisoners. Torture was rampant.

Chapters 3 and 4 focus on the state, that collection of officially recognized instruments of power through which societies are governed, national borders are protected, and power and influence are projected beyond internationally recognized boundaries. Chapter 3 examines the dynamics that brought about the collapse of Arab states in late 2010, early 2011. The chapter looks at the underlying dynamics that fostered social movements in multiple Arab countries, many of which ultimately succeeded in overthrowing sitting authoritarian leaders. The chapter's specific focus is on the underlying causes, processes, and extent to which the 2011 uprisings led to, or alternatively obstructed, institutional change in the Arab state.

Chapter 4 zeroes in on the exercise of power, looking specifically at the means through which post-2011 Arab states project power within their borders and protect their sovereignty, how they go about policing, and the relationships they feature with their armed forces and military. In examining post-uprisings politics, the chapter looks at why and how old patterns of political rule, and politics more generally, re-emerge after the uprisings, paying particular attention to the role of individuals and the decisions they made at key junctures during and immediately after the uprisings.

States do not operate in a vacuum but do so in relation to other states and, even more elementally, in relation to their societies. Any examination of the state—any state—is incomplete without attention to its manifold and complex relations with the society over which it governs. The institutional means of power and control are by themselves insufficient to ensure the resilience and efficacy of the state even on a temporary basis. States also need legitimacy to be able to govern, no matter how brittle and narrowly-based that legitimacy may be. The 2011 uprisings impressed upon Arab leaders that they cannot ignore normative bonds between instruments of power and the people. Politics cannot simply be mechanical. Chapter 5 therefore looks at three key non-mechanical dimensions of politics in the Arab world after 2011, namely citizenship, legitimacy, and religion. By analyzing public opinion data collected in twelve Arab countries since 2011, the chapter demonstrates that post-uprising Arab states suffer from a deficit of legitimacy. They are generally perceived by their populations as corrupt, inefficient, and unable to deliver on basic goods and services. With their legitimacy largely in question, Arab states have little option but to rely increasingly on coercion and brute power to stay in office.

Chapter 5 also explores the rise of the Islamic State. Despite its efforts to portray itself as a purely religious enterprise, the Islamic State has nothing to do with theological developments in Islam and everything to do with power: the powerlessness of the Iraqi and Syrian states to prevent its emergence and expansion, the power of its leaders to attract new recruits and to conquer new territory, and their power to hang on to what they have captured. By the same token, it is only power dynamics that will determine the Islamic State's future.

Chapter 6 focuses on the politics of the Arabian Peninsula. A combination of abundant oil resources, relatively small population sizes, and the evolution of tribal clans into ruling families has bestowed on the countries of the region comparatively high levels of state capacity. This capacity enabled the oil-rich states to ride through the 2011 uprisings without the need for extensive institutional adjustments. Saudi Arabia, in fact, soon embarked on a campaign aimed at spearheading a regional counterrevolution, and Qatar and the United Arab Emirates also did their share to ensure that the uprisings served their own national purposes in far-flung places such as Libya, Syria, and Yemen.[16] It was not until the collapse of oil prices in 2014, which if not a critical juncture for these states was at least an important watershed year, that each of the oil-rich states of the region undertook significant changes to their operations. In the end, rentierism was not abandoned but tweaked in order to be prolonged, and the fundamentals of state–society relations stayed the same as before, though slightly altered.

Contestation, as this book shows, has been a recurrent and endemic feature of power and politics in the Arab world. Leaders have consistently shown little appetite for holding themselves accountable for their actions or their expenditure of the public purse. They have treated demands for transparency as a nuisance, manipulated the ballot box, spewed false promises, fattened the pockets of relatives and oligarch supporters, and accused those questioning them of treason and sedition. The year 2011 offered a glimmer of hope and optimism, and that sense of the possible may still come to fruition in a country like Tunisia. For now, however, Tunisia stands as a lone example of the politics of consensus and compromise in an otherwise sea of conflict and repression. Qualitatively, today's Arab politics is little different from what it was before the Spring that shook its core; and, sadly, few indications point to a tomorrow that could offer something better.

2

STATES, INSTITUTIONS, AND POLITICAL ATROPHY

After the Second World War and the dawn of independence, following Egypt's lead, the Arab states generally adopted regimes of governance that relied on a social contract on the one hand and the incorporation of various social strata into the orbit of the state on the other. The ensuing corporatist populism was derived from and based on the state's imposition of a social contract on society. This was complemented by a corporatism that included the incorporation into the state of industrial workers, a burgeoning civil service, and, through the official state party, other middle-class urban professionals.

By the early to mid-1970s, this corporatist populism had turned increasingly authoritarian. The state shed its pretenses to street democracy and became steadily more exclusionary. It also abandoned its ideological zeal in all but name, instead adopting generic slogans such as "national progress" and "development." Ruling generals and colonels, now in office for a decade or so, wore suits and adopted civilian outlooks, and, instead of the national liberation army of yesteryears, the state became more reliant on the police forces and the fear they incited among the people in order to stay in power.

The state's mutations continued into the 1970s and the decades that followed. By the 1980s, exclusionary authoritarianism began to acquire increasingly personalist dimensions, with presidents assuming their tenures in office to be unending and their reelections as mere pro forma. This personalism at the top occurred simultaneously with a proliferation of institutions at the various levels of the state designed to guide the country's supposed march toward progress. This institutional proliferation also provided convenient venues for the employment of high-school and university graduates, and hence their continued dependence on the state. But at its core, or rather its apex, the state continued to rot, and neither the growth in number of its salaried employees nor its institutional configuration could mask its larger structural atrophy. Aged leaders surrounded themselves with crony capitalists. Patronage provided clientelistic ties within and among successive layers of functionaries throughout the state machinery and the bureaucracy. As the economy declined, the bonds frayed and grew increasingly tenuous. Bereft of electoral, ideological, or developmental legitimacy, repression became pervasive. Fear became the state's biggest sustaining element. If and when that fear no longer existed, as it ceased to do so in 2010–11, the state could hardly sustain itself.

This chapter provides a snapshot of the Arab state before the start of the Arab uprisings. By looking specifically at processes of state-building, I focus on the underlying causes and the broader consequences of the institutional transformations that Arab states experienced from the 1950s into the first decade of the 2000s. Since state-building is a *process*, it is inherently dynamic and changeable. I argue here that two interrelated developments were responsible for the institutional transformations that comprised the state-building process in the Arab world. First, state-builders set out to create and then change state institutions in ways they deemed appropriate. Although not unencumbered by historical antecedents, the state-builders' leeway in creating or reconfiguring institutions was greatest during historic critical junctures, of which the Middle East has had a fair number. Their logic, meanwhile, was all too frequently informed by the imperative of power maximization.

A second factor resulting in institutional change is the phenomenon of path dependence, through which institutions, their functions, and the constellations in which they are arranged and configured assume their own inertia and patterns of change. Once established and in operation, institutions can develop a life of their own. Internal patterns and rhythms emerge within the institution, moving it in directions that may not necessarily be consistent with the vision and intentions of its original crafters. Agency is not the only cause of institutional change; even without external stimuli, institutions change over time because of their own internal operations.

The institutional changes that the Arab state underwent simultaneously made it larger in size and less efficacious in function. As the state morphed from its corporatist populist beginnings into exclusionary authoritarian and personalist molds, partly by design and partly on its own, it became steadily more fragile and brittle, so much so that its long-term viability became increasingly untenable. All that was needed was a spark, a push, to topple what appeared to be an impressive and fear-inspiring edifice which was nonetheless rotten and weak at the core. The fateful spark appeared near the end of 2010.

Institutions and institutional change

In recent years, students of comparative politics have paid considerable attention to the question of institutional change and evolution. The studies that have been produced as a result tend to fall into the two broad categories of rational choice on one side and historical institutionalism on another. On occasion, there have been some fruitful crossovers.[1] For the most part, however, the two schools tend to see the processes of institutional change either through the prism of rational and intentional decisions made by political actors, or, alternatively, through the inner workings and inertia of institutions themselves that lock them into a more or less identifiable path of change.

Here I will address two issues in the burgeoning literature on institutional change, one theoretical and another empirical. Theoretically, I argue that at different points in the life of institutions, different logics may be called to the fore. Briefly, I maintain that state-related and other formal institutions of power are initially created and established through deliberate crafting and the rational choices of state actors. From then on, institutions tend to assume a life of their own and are subject more to path dependence rather than deliberate decisions made by state actors. Things change, however, if and when state leaders determine that institutional adjustments are needed, at which time purposeful decision-making by those involved once again tends to become the norm. In sum, both rational choice and path dependence are important—or, conversely, neither is unimportant—though each tends to be prominent at different times in the life of institutions.

A second area of analysis addressed here is the study of institutional change in the Middle East. Significant strides have been made in recent years toward the study of institutional analysis in the United States, Europe, Asia, and Latin America.[2] The Middle East, however, has for the most part fallen below the radar for most scholars of institutional change, with only a few studies devoted specifically to the analysis of the causes and consequences of institutional change in the region.[3] I hope to fill some of this analytical vacuum by focusing here on the causes, processes, and, more specifically, the consequences of the timing of institutional change in the Middle East.

To elucidate the arguments made here, I have divided the lives of states into three ideal-type phases: an initial phase of political institutionalization; a subsequent phase of political consolidation; and a third phase of corrective actions, precipitated by crises or a simple desire to enhance political efficacy and staying power. Each of these phases corresponds roughly with one set of causal variables for institutional change: rational and intentional choices in the institutionalization phase; path dependence in the consolidation phase; and a mix of rational choices and path dependency to remedy emerging institutional deadlocks or to attenuate crises. In the Middle East, sometime beginning in the 1980s and 1990s, a fourth, context-specific phase appeared, namely that of institutional atrophy.

Of particular importance to the start of the state-building process are historical critical junctures, during which political leaders are faced with a range of critical choices before them, and whichever of these choices they adopt will have a lasting impact. "These choices close off alternative options and lead to the establishment of institutions that generate self-reinforcing, path-dependent processes."[4] As Mahoney argues, "junctures tend to be 'critical' because once a particular option is selected it becomes progressively more difficult to return to the initial point when multiple alternatives were still available."[5] At different periods in the establishment and evolution of each of the Arab states, one or more specific determinants have shaped the nature and the processes of political institutionalization and consolidation. At the beginning, throughout the 1950s, when most Arab states were initially being formed, new state institutions were established and operationalized through creative and deliberate political crafting, with little or no regard to preexisting institutional arrangements. This process of political institutionalization was a product of institutional crafting, rational and intentional choices, the usage of ideological blueprints for institutional design purposes, the articulation of constitutional arrangements, bargains and compromises, and, eventually, the actual construction and establishment of a vast majority of the key institutions of the state.

Once this initial phase was over, institutions began to change and evolve mostly according to internal logics of their own. Guided by the logic of "increasing returns,"[6] path dependence sets in, and a process of political consolidation began to take place, whereby the state sought to enhance its capacity in relation to domestic and international actors and to ensure its own longevity. As limited and non-comprehensive as it might be, political consolidation tends to constrain the range of options open to existing or aspiring political actors. With time, existing political institutions reproduce themselves in different guises that are often dictated by the logic of survival strategies. Unless prompted to do so by a need for corrective action, or by exogenous shocks of one sort or another, state actors tend to allow path dependence to continue on its course, allowing the state to deepen and solidify its roots in relation to society as much as possible.

Institutional deadlocks and actual or perceived shocks, however, can prompt state leaders into action, forcing them to assume more proactive postures in relation to the institutional makeup, roles, and efficacy of the state. This is especially the case with nondemocratic states, whose continued survival depends on frequent adjustments to the rules of the game in relation to the social actors they seek to keep compliant. State leaders often keep watchful eyes over the pattern and direction of institutional change, allowing and even enabling institutions to reproduce themselves, through layering or changes initiated from within the institutions themselves, so long as that institutional change is in a direction consistent with the leaders' broader agendas and vision. If at some point state leaders assume that emerging institutional arrangements are moving in a counterproductive direction, or that the state itself must respond to actual or perceived threats, they begin to employ a variety of defensive mechanisms. These corrective actions are usually made up of a combination of deliberate, rational planning on the one hand and institutional path dependence on the other.

Reinvigorated agency often transpires within an established and, by now, entrenched set of institutional patterns, thus resulting mostly in measured institutional tinkering rather than wholesale replacement. This accounts for the simultaneous initiation of seemingly contradictory and confused measures by the state in much of the Arab world, namely the start of liberalization processes in the early 1990s and then clamping down on political activists within a few years. These contradictions are actually manifestations of competing impulses emanating from within the state: its own desire to continue operating as usual, and its leaders' efforts to make adjustments necessary to prolong their survival.

During the initial period of political institutionalization, state actors are able to choose from a wider menu of institutional choices that are available to them than is the case as time goes by. In fact, it is often at this initial critical juncture that state-crafting occurs, when state institutions are created with little or no regard to historical precedent or existing patterns of institutional evolution. *Political institutionalization* refers to the establishment, arrangement, and codification of the various institutions of the states, often through constitution-making or other constitutional mechanisms . Once this initial phase is over and as political consolidation sets in, path dependence steadily takes over and institutions tend to develop a life of their own. *Political consolidation* refers to the operationalization of the institutions of the state both domestically and internationally. It revolves around the degree to which state capacity is developed in relation to domestic non-state or international actors, whereby the state can independently and successfully articulate and carry out its agendas in both the domestic and the international arenas.[7]

Path dependence tends to continue during the phase of political consolidation unless and until state leaders perceive that deliberate institutional reengineering is needed in order to resolve unintended consequences resulting in institutional deadlock or inefficiency, or to address some impending or unfolding crisis. In these instances, state leaders once again step in and try to come up with creative solutions that will remedy the situation and will enhance their chances of political endurance. Under such circumstances, agency and deliberate crafting become the norm again. But this time, state leaders are not creating institutions from scratch and are not working with a blank canvas. For the most part, they make adjustments and modifications to existing institutions and the roles they play—or to existing institutional arrangements—rather than engage in the wholesale creation of institutions anew. Their decisions, in other words, are somewhat constrained this time as compared to their first attempt at institution-building. As North argues, if and when institutional change becomes necessary, "secondary institutional arrangements will be innovated at a much lower cost than changing the fundamental institutional arrangements" of the system.[8] Nevertheless, if the efforts of state leaders are successful, once the institutional adjustments are over, old patterns of path dependence tend to return.

The menu of institutional choices available is bigger, and the scope for maneuvering and negotiating among political actors is wider, when starting with a clean slate. Especially in the initial phases of the state-building process, existing rules and procedures that constrain behavior are often either nonexistent or, as is commonly the case in the immediate aftermath of revolutions and wars of national liberation, are deliberately abrogated and targeted for change. In these circumstances, the architects of the new state bring with them different priorities to the table, and also different levels of know-how, power, and skill. In the jockeying for positions that ensues—sometimes through negotiations and maneuvers, sometimes through forced elimination and purges—those leaders left standing then proceed to implement their institutional designs and priorities as the new blueprint of the whole state. What matters here is power politics: who wins, who loses, and who is able to outsmart or outmuscle others in the bid to institutionalize newly-won powers. Their agendas then become the agendas of the state.

In terms of the constraints exercised by preexisting (or extra-territorial) institutions, insights from historical institutionalism, and more specifically path dependency, can be very helpful. In broad terms, historical institutionalism explores "the role of history in institutional emergence, perpetuation, and change; it is comparative in its attempt to gain insights through comparative studies over time and space; and it is analytical in its explicit reliance on context-specific micro models for empirical analysis."[9] As its designation implies, historical institutionalism is concerned primarily with the evolution and change of institutions, and, more specifically, with how the direction of institutional change is influenced and constrained by preexisting institutional patterns and processes. Avner Greif, for example, makes the following argument:

> A society's institutions are a complex in which informal, implicit institutional features interrelate with formal, explicit features in creating a coherent whole. These interrelations direct institutional change and cause this institutional complex to resist change more than its constituting parts would have done in isolation. Hence, this institutional complex is not a static optimal response to economic needs. Rather, it is a reflection of an historical process in which past economic, political, social, and cultural features interrelate and have a lasting impact on the nature and economic implications of a society's institutions.[10]

This "path dependence," as Mahoney argues, "characterizes specifically those historical sequences in which contingent events set into motion institutional patterns or event chains that have deterministic properties."[11] Thelen warns against deterministic explanations that imply some sort of "institutional 'lock in.'"[12] But she does maintain that "once in place, institutions do exert a powerful influence on the strategies and calculations of—and interactions among—the actors that inhabit them."[13] Institutions are not static but constantly adapt and respond to shifts in the larger environments within which they find themselves.[14] These shifts, or, more precisely the direction of change, are guided by the logic of "increasing returns," whereby:

> the probability of further steps along the same path increases with each move down that path. This is because the *relative* benefits of the current activity compared with other possible options increase over time. To put it a different way, the costs of exit—of switching to some previously plausible alternative—rise. Increasing returns processes can also be described as self-reinforcing or positive feedback processes.[15]

Increasing returns often result in "institutional layering," which "involves the partial renegotiation of some elements of a given set of institutions while leaving others in place."[16] Another process of change is through "institutional conversion," which occurs when "existing institutions are redirected to new purposes, driving changes in the role they perform and/or the functions they serve."[17]

Historical institutionalism in general and path dependence in particular—along with notions such as increasing returns and institutional layering—explain processes of institutional change once institutions are already in place. They are particularly apt in describing processes of institutional change in polities that are relatively more stable and developed, where adaptations and renegotiations tend to be subtler, gradual, and often evolutionary. There are instances, however, especially in the developing world and in relatively underdeveloped and unstable polities, where institutions suffer complete breakdowns due to what one observer has termed "society-rooted politics,"[18] resulting in failed states of one form or another (Lebanon from 1975 to 1990, Iraq since 2003, Syria since 2011, and Yemen since 2014).

More common than failed states in the developing world are instances when institutional change tends to be sudden and abrupt. In many such political systems, in fact, the emergence of institutional incoherence and dysfunctionality, as well as internal and exogenous shocks, necessitate institutional reengineering and crafting, thus ushering important changes to existing patterns of institutional conduct and arrangement. Especially in the developing world, not all institutional change is layered or even a product of conversion. Sometimes state leaders are prompted into action by massive, sudden, and fundamental shocks to the system, like attempted coups or popular demands for change. More often, however, state leaders are simply motivated by a desire to enhance the efficacy of the institutions through which they rule, or, at most, to ensure that institutional change and evolution does not slip from under their control. At any rate, agency and deliberate actions play a determining role here in influencing the makeup, arrangement, and roles of institutions.

Along the same lines, historical institutionalism seems to ignore the moment of inception at which institutions are born, particularly during critical junctures, and the process of birth that initially gives rise to institutions. Instead, historical institutionalism implies that existing institutions—or some previous mutation of them—have always been around, albeit under radically different forms and configurations. The important questions of how critical junctures come about, and the possible role of ideas in their development, remain largely unanswered in path dependency perspectives.[19] Theoretically, one can always point to some preexisting patterns or sources of behavioral constraints that have shaped or influenced one or more existing institutions. But this line of analysis can be stretched beyond its analytical utility. At the same time, we cannot ignore the inertia that institutions and institutional patterns exhibit and retain over time, often even after major shocks and changes. Instead of an either/or scenario, we must determine what set of explanatory factors are predominant and outweigh the others, and at which particular junctures in the life of institutions.

In basic terms, at any given time, both the rational choices of the actors involved and path dependence are responsible for institutional change. At some points in the life of an institution, agency and deliberate choices are more determinative of change, while at some other points the primary cause is path dependence. When institutional formation is at embryonic stages and institutions have yet to become settled, as in the initial phases of state-building and political institutionalization, the rational choices of the actors involved, coupled with pure power politics, determine the overall configuration of institutions and the direction of their change. Once these same institutions have had time to settle and have resumed routine operations, they develop internal rhythms and dynamics of their own—an internal logic driven by increasing returns, which in turn motivates them to reproduce in ways that are familiar and are perceived to entail the least amount of risk. Insofar as formal political institutions are concerned, this process of steady institutional reproduction, often through layering, frequently occurs during processes of political consolidation.

At this point institutions assume more or less a life of their own, and, if left on their own, provide blueprints and an increasingly narrow range of options for further institutional production and reproduction. Ian Greener maintains that once institutions are in place, path dependence is "likely to emerge where both structural and cultural vested interest groups are dependent upon one another to hold power."[20] After the period of production, he writes, "a period of reproduction" ensues in which increasingly entrenched institutions and ideas "lock out" other, competing ones and "the opportunity cost for challenging the system" steadily rises.[21] The resulting set of institutions and their arrangements continue operating unless and until they become threatening to leaders, or outlive their utility or prove to be dysfunctional, or, worse yet, face some type of crisis from within or from the outside. Such circumstances often prompt state actors to initiate defensive or corrective measures.

This is particularly the case in "sultanistic" and other personalist regimes,[22] when state leaders create institutions for the specific purpose of maintaining themselves in power, and when leaders remain paramount and institutions act as power auxiliary. While not "sultanistic" as theorized by Chehabi and Linz, in the 1980s and 1990s many Arab states became increasingly personalized, with leaders treating institutions as instruments of power aggrandizement at best and as political irritants at worst. Under such circumstances, so long as institutions do the job they were designed for—i.e. keeping the leaders' powers intact and perpetuating them—they are left alone and, in fact, operate more or less based on their own inertia. If they outlive their utility, or worse yet become a source of liability, or perhaps become a little too independent and a potential source of competition to the leader, then they have to contend with the deliberate, calculated decisions of the state's leaders.

This has been the overall pattern of institutional inception and change across the Arab world since the 1950s, especially in North Africa and the Levant. History, of course, does not move in a linear path; it often entails fits and starts, reversals, and stagnation. It may even feature radical ruptures in one direction or another. Nor do any two countries, much less entire regions, move along similar or parallel trajectories simultaneously. Nevertheless, in many instances, certain broad trends, occurring pretty much along the same time-horizon, with similar causes and consequences, can indeed be detected. In North Africa and the Levant, we see political leaders starting processes of state-building in earnest, beginning in the 1950s, by establishing manifold political institutions and attempting to consolidate them through a variety of means. These methods of political consolidation included the incorporation of allies and broader strata of society, especially workers, urban bourgeoisie, and middle-class professionals. This was done primarily through four key institutions: the parliament; the mass-based, state-sponsored political party; the civil service; and the armed forces, which served as a critical mechanism for recruitment into and promotion within the state, as well as, of course, the exercise of power.

Over time, each of these institutions changed in ways that in the long run only undermined their efficacy. The parliament soon turned into a rubber stamp for the power elite and failed to provide any meaningful nexus between state and society, much less to watch over and balance the executive. The political party became similarly hollow in significance, becoming instead an elite conduit into the upper echelons of the state machinery and yet another arm of the bureaucracy staffed by career apparatchiks. At the rank-and-file level, many individuals from lower-middle-class backgrounds joined the party in the hope of upward political mobility. The civil service grew in size and, paradoxically, inefficiency. It also became rife with corruption, nepotism, and patronage. A similar expansion occurred in the numeric size of the military and its hardware, a quantitative growth that failed to translate into qualitative development. Whatever efficiency the state exhibited was usually limited to isolated pockets within the vast bureaucracy or to state-controlled enterprises, a notable example being the civilian police force, which relied on repression and fear to keep opponents in check.

Overall, what state leaders assumed to be the consolidation of institutions they had created decades earlier, and on which they relied to rule, entailed a simultaneous degeneration of those very institutions. This lack of political efficacy did not necessarily mean vulnerability to collapse. The state's sheer size and its institutional makeup gave it a certain amount of built-in adaptability. At times of crisis or pressure from below, the state could use the parliament for purposes of broadening its social base through co-option and concession, as was often the case in Morocco and Egypt. This ensured that the oligarchs within the state's orbit remained loyal, as in Egypt and Syria. At other times, the state blamed some of its own functionaries and promised to clean house, as the Jordanian monarchy is fond of doing. The other option, often adopted simultaneously, was increased repression and clamping down on those who did not buy into the state's cosmetic openings. By 2010–11, the carrot-and-stick combination of concession and repression no longer worked in Tunisia, Egypt, Libya, and Syria. But it did work, and so far has proven effective, for the states of Morocco, Algeria, Jordan, and those in the Arabian Peninsula.

Authoritarian state-building

The year 1952, in which a group of military officers in Egypt overthrew the country's monarchy and took over the Egyptian state, is generally considered a landmark date for the start of the modern state-building processes both in Egypt and in much of the rest of the Arab world. Egypt's Free Officers revolution inspired military takeovers and the launch of parallel processes of state-building in Syria (1954), Iraq (1958), and Libya (1969). Tunisia's independence from France in 1956, and Algeria's in 1962, although acquired through very different means, resulted in similar state-building trajectories.

The extent to which political leaders start with a clean slate in their state-building efforts depends on the specific contexts within which they find themselves. No matter how hard they try, nevertheless, it is doubtful whether they can completely free themselves of various historical antecedents and legacies of the past. Practices, assumptions, and even institutions can linger on and continue to influence new political arrangements. Preestablished patterns of behavior and expectation, identities, and ways of relating to institutions of power do not simply change overnight just because some revolutionaries want or demand them to change. For Arab revolutionary state-builders, as much as they may have desired it, the year they came to power was not "year zero." They still had to contend with the institutional and relational legacies they inherited, especially those left over from the colonial period.[23]

While historical antecedents influenced and perhaps even constrained the range of choices before them, incoming Arab military rulers viewed themselves as revolutionaries imbued with a sense of historic mission, charged with dragging their countries out of colonial subjugation and underdevelopment, and propelling them into independence and modernity. To do so, they generally assumed, required buy-in from the broader masses in general and from certain key social strata in particular. They therefore devised institutions of mass political inclusion, namely official political partners and parliaments, that at once enabled the incorporation of targeted audiences and the generation of ideological means of mobilization and visions of the future. Officially sanctioned mass demonstrations, usually in support of one state-sponsored campaign or another, became part of the regular modus operandi of the state. The guiding principles of these campaigns, meanwhile, were informed by an overarching ideology, whose basic tenets were fairly uniform across the board: nationalism and defense of the motherland; solidarity with other Arab brethren, and especially with

Palestinians; nonalignment in international affairs; state-guided economic development; and secularism.

Significantly, those social actors or groups that were not in one way or another within the state's orbit were intentionally omitted, at times brutally, from the state-building process. A prime example of such groups was the Muslim Brotherhood, local variations of which were founded first in Egypt (in 1928) and subsequently in Mandatory Palestine (1938), Jordan (1945), Syria (1945), Iraq (1960), and other parts of the Middle East. In almost every single case, despite its rabid anti-colonialism and its stated goal of contributing to the national project, the Muslim Brotherhood was brutally suppressed and excluded from the state-building process. The state-centric narrative of nationalism that emerged saw no room for such organized groups, or even ideological currents, that did not share the leadership's narrow definition of the national interest.

Centralized leadership did not necessarily mitigate the state's need to resort to populist mobilization. In fact, the institutional configurations that emerged as a result featured strong combinations of populism and corporatism. The early reliance of the state on the incorporation of the broader masses, and especially of certain social strata, into its orbit made political leaders beholden to popular demands and to the choreography of street democracy. The state as a whole and political leaders in particular had to cater to popular demands; in fact, they often *created* popular demands, by chasing some soon-to-be-reached "liberation" in order to appear as if they were responsive to the demands and wishes of the people. Sacrificed in the process were the developmental capacities of the state, as addressing the structural economic exigencies that demanded politically taxing decisions gave way to the imperative to secure immediate and short-term economic returns.[24]

The military, meanwhile, was never far from the ruling apparatus. In fact, the armed forces formed the spine of the regime, often becoming, as Eric Nordlinger first articulated, direct rulers and viewing themselves as long-term fixtures within the power structure.[25] In Nasser's Egypt, for example, the period from 1952 to 1970 witnessed eighteen different cabinets, of which only the first one—in power for less than two months—was headed by a civilian. Also, approximately

37 percent of the last fifteen cabinet members were military officers, many of whom occupied the most important ministerial portfolios.[26] As Imad Harb observes:

> throughout the years of transformation, the Egyptian military was there to protect the regime and participate in governing. Staffing the cabinet, ministries, and state machinery with military personnel was a constant practice for two reasons: the military's belief that it alone had the bureaucratic organizing skills to run the affairs of the state and assuring control over a traditionally independent bureaucracy.[27]

While the armed forces constituted the regime's institutional backbone, as well as its muscle internally and externally, state leaders sought to enhance their legitimacy further through a multitude of grand promises designed to catapult their populations out of the dark ages and into modernity, thereby fostering economic wealth and progress. Thus emerged a series of social pacts, or ruling bargains, that formed the basis of an implicit understanding between the rulers and the ruled. The ruling bargains were essentially "a set of norms or shared expectations about the appropriate organization of a political economy in general."[28] In reality more a product of imposition from the top rather than the organic growth of an understanding between the state and social actors, these ruling bargains were premised on the state's delivery of certain essential goods and services in return for society's political compliance and, when needed, enthusiastic loyalty.

The broad parameters of these shared expectations were as follows. The state was the sole and ultimate defender of the national interest, as defined by the president and his inner circle, and also the guarantor of the nation's success and progress. In doing so, the state took on the task of providing free public education, ensuring large-scale employment for graduates through the provision of jobs in the public sector, instituting subsidies for foodstuffs and other basic goods, and fostering industrialization by importing factories and other heavy industries. These goods and services, and the benefits accrued from them, were targeted toward certain key groups that the state saw as particularly important stakeholders: small farmers, "national" capitalists, workers, the urban middle classes, and the military.[29] In return, the state expected the population's political gratitude and compliance during ordinary times and its loyalty and devotion in times of crisis. When compliance and loyalty were not forthcoming, the element of repression was ever-present. That the state was seldom able to make good on its end of the bargain reduced little of its impulse to resort to coercion whenever it deemed necessary.

The combination of benevolence and repression inherent in social pacts gave Middle Eastern authoritarian systems a fair amount of adaptive capacity that was rooted in their formal and informal modes of governance.[30] For states like those in Morocco, Algeria, and Jordan, this built-in adaptability meant weathering the crises of the Arab Spring relatively unscathed. Moreover, because they were premised on state control over and involvement in various facets of social and political life, the populist ruling bargains that emerged in the 1950s and 1960s impeded the development of civil society organizations and political parties.[31] Although the state was not quite capable of becoming, or even aspiring to become, similar to the totalitarian regimes of the former Soviet bloc, its extensive reach into society made political organization outside its orbit exceedingly difficult. This was compounded by the state's manipulation of social and cultural norms that it used instrumentally for political purposes, with its abuse of religion and patrimonialism as the most glaring examples.[32] Ruling bargains, in sum, undermined society's potential for independent, non-state sponsored, political mobilization. They also provided little breathing room for the emergence and development of nongovernmental organizations. And, what energy was left in society to engage in politics, the state made sure was directed only toward those goals that it alone supported.

Adaptability and cultural manipulation notwithstanding, the Arab states of the 1950s and 1960s suffered from several structural contradictions. By the 1970s and 1980s, through a combination of path dependency on the one hand and crafting by increasingly authoritarian leaders on the other, the states became steadily more exclusionary in order to stay in power. Of the structural contradictions plaguing them, three stood out and over time became especially problematic for the state to manage. One such contradiction revolved around the institutions of legitimation in general and elections in particular. For purposes of inclusion and incorporation, and also to maintain a façade of democracy, literally all Arab states by now—save for those in the Arabian Peninsula—had national parliaments of one sort or another. But, as we saw earlier, seldom did parliaments actually matter, and the parties that occupied them were often equally irrelevant. With the possible exception of Morocco, political parties in the Middle East were not allowed to develop a tradition of meaningful activism or popular support.[33] Most Arab republics were at any rate practically single-party states, in which the party, with a generic platform of nationalism and economic development, was seen as essential to the task of nation-building and ensuring the regime's legitimacy.

The state also contradicted itself in that it was at once centralized and yet it adhered to a regular schedule of presidential and parliamentary elections and the need to abide by the constitution.[34] However, given its inability or unwillingness to let elections be free and fair, the state often mismanaged them, at times overmanaging and at times leaving them too unfettered and therefore with uncomfortable results.[35] Not surprisingly, the tepid steps toward liberalization that appeared in the early 1990s in countries like Egypt, Yemen, Algeria, and Tunisia were quickly reversed.[36]

The state's own flirtations with controlled liberalization only deepened the contradictions it faced. Throughout the early 2000s, for example, Hosni Mubarak's son and presumed heir Gamal steered the ruling National Democratic Party toward "liberal" ideals, aided by a few well-known public intellectuals, such as Alayeddin Hilal, Abdel Moneim Said, and Hossam Badrawi. The younger Mubarak and the state intellectuals around him began using terms such as citizenship, transparent administration, civil society, government efficiency, and women's rights.[37] With the state's authoritarian impulse intact, however, such empty rhetoric was seen by most Egyptians as downright insulting. As elections became more farcical, a typical example of which were the 2010 parliamentary elections, they turned into one of the biggest sources of political grievance against the state.[38]

A second structural contradiction had to do with the functional and institutional incongruities resulting from the changing role of the armed forces in the political system. As ruling colonels and generals increasingly identified themselves as civilians to international and domestic audiences, and as the military's political role became more complex, the evolving nature of civil–military relations posed challenges for both civilian leaders and for the armed forces. The military remained central to the modus operandi of the state, with the state's survival ultimately boiling down to the military's willingness to crush popular dissent or demands for reforms from below.[39] At the same time, however, whereas increasingly civilianized leaders continued to depend on the military to stay in power, the military did not always see its own fortunes tied to the fortunes of those in power.

In general, the stronger a regime's record of satisfying political and socioeconomic demands, the more likely the armed forces will prop it up. Also, generous pay and perks for the armed services are likely to result in increased and continued military support for the state. Those armed forces that do not have internal cleavages are more likely to stay in support of the regime. Similarly, militaries with extensive records of human rights abuses are also likely to continue backing authoritarian leaders.[40] In Egypt and Tunisia, as popular pressure for change gathered momentum in late 2010, the regime's poor record of satisfying political and socioeconomic demands made it easier for the armed forces to abandon civilian rulers. By contrast, the comparatively more repressive nature of the state in Syria and Yemen gave military leaders there much less reason to abandon the regimes.

This is largely also because in Syria and Yemen, the military's interest and survival also remained tied to the fate of the civilian leadership. In Syria especially, while the country is technically in a state of war with Israel and its territory is under occupation, the military never quite detached itself from the destiny of the regime.[41] And in Yemen, various strategic units of the armed forces, numbering about 15 to 20 percent of the country's total uniformed force, were led directly by members of the ruling Saleh family.[42] But this was not the case in Egypt and Tunisia, where over time the military establishment developed its own corporate identity and interests apart from the rulers. In the Egyptian case in particular, although the military remained closely integrated into the regime, it had developed multiple economic interests, had been largely depoliticized over time, and was susceptible to American pressure.[43] In Tunisia, in an attempt to keep the political aspirations of the armed forces in check, both Bourguiba and Ben Ali had kept the military small in size and with a low budget. Over time, military commanders saw increasing distance develop between them and Ben Ali's oligarchic rule. When the popular protests of 2010 erupted, both the

Tunisian and Egyptian militaries sought to protect their own interests by jettisoning the leaders.[44]

In all cases, fear remained the ultimate guarantor of the state's rule, exercised through a wide array of state intelligence agencies, or the *mukhabarat*. The intelligence organizations appeared fierce and were greatly feared, but they were also largely ineffective.[45] This ineffectiveness notwithstanding, in Egypt and elsewhere state security reached deep into society and spread fear, terror, and a general perception of omnipresence.[46] In Tunisia, by Owen's account, some 10 percent of the population was in one way or another sustained through employment in the state security machinery.[47] This helped foster a "deeply rooted culture of fear" as the state actively sought to instill fear among the people.[48] Ironically, the state feared the people as much as the people feared the state.

The state's management of the economy constituted a third contradiction, or challenge, for the Arab states. Populist corporatism necessitated continuous and generous state expenditure, especially on sunk costs such as a steadily growing civil service, military hardware for the armed forces, and inefficient state-owned enterprises. By the 1970s, the same levels of expenditure proved untenable across the board. As part of their economic survival strategies, in the 1980s and 1990s many Arab states began implementing several economic reforms, including partial privatization, limited stabilization and minor reductions in subsidies, trade reforms designed to raise foreign exchange and exports, the provision of managerial autonomy, and the encouragement of foreign investments.[49] In many cases, as in Egypt and Tunisia, the World Bank and the International Monetary Fund required the implementation of structural adjustment programs that were meant to address external debt obligations and mounting trade deficits.[50] Painful as they were, however, the ensuing adjustments failed to integrate the states into the global economy. Instead, they led to precipitous declines in foreign direct investments, deepened dependence on migrant labor remittances, and increased brain drain.[51] They also deepened corruption and further facilitated the rise of state-tied oligarchs.[52]

Moreover, structural adjustment programs not only failed to address but further deepened shortcomings and challenges involved in the state's delivery of key social services, particularly in education, healthcare, and social welfare. Across the MENA region, educational systems suffered from inadequate curriculum development, teacher training and pedagogy, and insufficient financial resources. They also remained—and continued to remain—out of line with the labor market, making the public sector the main source of employment.[53] The national health systems were also fragmented, mismanaged, and inefficient, problems compounded by underfunding and lack of government commitment to mobilizing resources.[54] To help keep inflation in check, meanwhile, a disproportionately large part of the social welfare expenditure continued to be spent on food and fuel subsidies, severely straining the social security system in its coverage of public sector employees, while providing little maternity leave insurance and leaving out those in the private sector altogether.[55]

These structural contradictions were compounded by the increasing personalization of the state at the very top. In addition to an elaborate state security system, as well as some attention to republican forms such as elections and parliament, the states came to rely increasingly on the leader's cult of personality, with presidents acting as monarchs and seeing themselves as wiser and more farsighted than the people they ruled.[56] These presidents-for-life believed in their own unique political skills and in the indispensability of their historical role. Most importantly perhaps, they had uncanny survival instincts, as well as a voracious appetite for both power and cruelty, which enabled them to outwit and outmuscle potential opponents and to hold on to office.[57]

Structurally, the presidency sat at the apex of the state, followed by small circles of senior army officers, crony capitalists, and intelligence agencies, the main agencies of civilian administration, and then the main centers of ideological legitimation, such as the educational and religious establishments, followed by a pliant and tame judiciary.[58] The presidents, often with insurmountable power, surrounded themselves with people who could be trusted for their loyalty and their ability to manage the mammoth bureaucracy, interlocking intelligence agencies, and the official party. But the person of the president, and his immediate family members and small inner circle, remained at the core of the system, and their priorities, as well as idiosyncrasies, frequently had system-wide reverberations. Given the increasing personalization of politics, the president's personal temperament, health, mental state, and individual political skills often stood, and in some cases still stand, at the center of political life. This, naturally, did not serve the system well, especially in moments of crisis, as in 2010, when the state could no longer survive through the sheer wiliness of one individual. As the crisis neared, "the big man, the 'boss,' began to make big mistakes."[59]

The president's relatives, meanwhile, were part of a team meant to protect family interests. In both Syria and Egypt, this family interest was thought to be best protected through holding on to the presidency from one generation to the next. The leader's cult in fact encouraged a belief in the importance of his son. Not surprisingly, two of the central priorities of the monarchical presidencies included a smooth succession to their designated heirs, and the legitimation of the succession through elections.[60] But the oxymoron of a presidential monarchy, however carefully stage-managed, was not lost on the population, for whom the state's theatrics—of an energetic son continuing the mantle of his wise father—merely added insult to injury. These states had begun to weaken long before they actually crumbled.

Its best efforts notwithstanding, by the early 2000s the state's atrophy was well underway. Whether it was through "soft authoritarianism" designed to co-opt opposition forces, as in Egypt and Tunisia, or through informal means of inclusion and consultation in the policy-making process, as was the case in Syria, the state sought to hang on to power and to ameliorate the political and economic grievances of the urban middle classes.[61] In Egypt, the state had even effectively "deinstitutionalized" workers and their once robust tradition of trade unionism, by both eroding their social status and by fostering the demise of trade unionism.[62] In the last years of his rule, Mubarak also used and abused the religious card to divide and rule.[63]

In one form or another, all prerevolutionary states co-opted the public sphere, relied on the security forces, and excluded the citizenry from the political process. But they also invariably fostered social contestation by isolating the political and economic elites from the people and excluding the middle classes from most if not all decision-making processes.[64] And their increasing reliance on fear as a primary pillar of rule made them innately susceptible to acts of defiance and valor. By 2010, social conditions facilitated the transformation of individual acts of heroism into collective action. But social conditions by themselves do not make a revolution. Revolutions occur within a context of state weakness and atrophy, something from which Arab states, to one extent or another, all suffered.

Republican atrophy and monarchical persistence

It was no accident that the Arab states which succumbed to the revolutionary wave of 2010–11 were all republics, or, as Roger Owen has more aptly described them, monarchical republics.[65] At least in name and cosmetic form, with the exception of Algeria, by and large it was the Arab world's presidential republics and not its monarchies that experienced the Arab Spring. Morocco and Jordan, of course, were not immune to instances of popular unrest in 2010–11, and in Bahrain a nationwide uprising was only stopped through military intervention by Saudi Arabia and the United Arab Emirates. But the five Arab states in which mass-based revolutions succeeded in toppling long-time rulers, or in Syria's case have come close—the others being Tunisia, Egypt, Libya, and Yemen—were all republics. More specifically, all were exclusionary authoritarian autocracies.

Autocracies by nature suffer from a number of disadvantages that make them vulnerable to being overthrown. For them, information is scarce, and what is available is unreliable. Citizenship in autocracies is also a politically contested notion and competes with other identities such as kinship, region, religion, and ideology. The state demands compliance from its subjects, while it lacks accountability and responsibility. And the public treasury and the ruler's purse are indistinguishable.[66]

Within these broader limitations, across the Arab world presidential security systems suffered five inherent basic weaknesses. These included problems of political management; a large crony sector; inability to incorporate the young into the state's political or ideological projects; limited capacity to respond to crises; and preoccupation with stability.[67] Throughout the 2000s, mounting economic difficulties and the growing potential for protests led to a narrowing of political space throughout North Africa and the Levant.[68] At the same time, because of the increasing personalization of the political system—not just by the president, but by members of his family and the oligarchy surrounding him—what was perceived to be "the regime" offered a readily identifiable target for popular anger, protests, and demands for change. In fact, as political power rested on familial, social, or state-sponsored exclusion, the resistance it provoked followed and targeted the state along these very lines.[69]

Much of the discussion over the persistence of authoritarianism in the Middle East in general and in the Arab world in particular has, correctly, focused on the importance of the robustness of the coercive apparatus of the state.[70] As the analysis above also suggests, the armed forces and their relationship with the civilian leaders of the state remained, and continue to remain, key to the latter's hold on power. But besides the military there are other institutional and structural factors that, at least in 2010–11, enabled the Arab monarchies to cope better with pressures from below.

This of course has not always been the case, and it would be inaccurate to assert that monarchies in general are better equipped to deal with mass-based uprising as compared to presidential republics. Within the Middle East itself, the monarchies of Egypt, Iraq, and Iran all lacked staying power. These were all monarchies whose legitimacy rested on contrived "civic myths" that, in the absence of political and economic efficacy, failed to generate long-term popular support for the regime.[71] Of this category of monarchies, only Jordan and Morocco have managed to hang on. The Moroccan monarchy's civic myth tends to be less of a myth and rests on a more robust history of patronage and legitimacy, rooted in the king's position as *Emir Al-Momenin* (Commander of the Faithful) and the phenomenon of the *Makhzen*.[72]

Nevertheless, even in the case of these two remaining monarchies outside the Arabian Peninsula, which are not in a position to buy off the population's compliance through rentier political economies, the remaining Arab monarchies display a number of structural features that enhance their political resilience. Sean Yom and Gregory Gause point to a combination of three factors: coalitional support; control over natural resources and the rents accrued through them; and foreign backing.[73] Monarchies also tend to rely upon crosscutting coalitions that link different strata of society to the ruling family.[74] Of particular importance in this regard are entrepreneurs and the big merchant families. Over time, the mutual dependence between the ruling family and the entrepreneurial classes has shifted in favor of the former, who control the country's petrodollars and the contracts on which the merchants rely.

The Arab world's surviving monarchies have also proven themselves to be comparatively more adaptable to changing social and political circumstances. All authoritarian regimes in the Middle East have featured a certain level of what Steven Heydemann calls "bounded adaptiveness." This bounded adaptiveness enables them to adjust and accommodate to circumstances through the interaction of formal and informal modes of conflict resolution, bargaining, and managing coalitions.[75] It also enables regimes to have different, and at times competing, sets of rules of the game. Adaptation, in the form of controlled opening without sacrificing elite cohesion, helps autocrats expand ruling coalitions as necessary and thereby maintain power.[76] Morocco's two last kings, Hassan II (r.1961–99) and Mohammad VI (r. 1999–), have been particularly effective at co-opting potential opposition actors through controlled and measured reforms from above.[77] In the 1990s, King Hassan II went so far as to adopt the slogans of "democratic series" and "the government of alteration" in his efforts to co-opt members of the opposition.[78]

What could best be described as "pluralized authoritarianism" was, and remains, the preferred system of rule for some of the republican systems as well, most notably in Yemen under former president Saleh and in Syria under the Assad dynasty.[79] The ways in which the elites use and interact with other elites depends on the institutional makeup and features of the state. In both Yemen and Syria, internal competition among the elites restricted the elite's ability or willingness to defect from the ruling coalition. In Syria in particular, the elite cannot afford to defect from the ruling coalition because of the existential threat this would pose to them.[80] Since the beginning of the country's civil war in 2011, the limited level of decentralization that characterized the Syrian state has helped Bashar al-Assad to cling on to power. Assad's assumption of full control in June 2005, and subsequent replacement of the old guard with his own cronies, did not change the informal process of policymaking and consultation that informed the way in which the regime had operated since the early 1970s. In the process, Bashar al-Assad, just like his father before him, has played more the role of a chief coordinator, much like a chief operating officer, rather than a strictly authoritarian leader.[81] In one form or another, the regimes that fell in 2011 were all "highly centralized, hierarchical, and [featured] tightly regulated corporatist structures of interest representation."[82] But Syria's comparative institutional decentralization has made elite concessions risky and difficult, and elite defections all but impossible. The ruling coalition has therefore largely held together despite the severest of institutional crises.

Conclusion

Processes of state-building in the Middle East have been generally divided into four interrelated phases. In the initial phases, beginning in the 1950s and 1960s, key state institutions were created in order to give shape and substance to the state's ambitious agendas of development and modernity. These institutions included a modern bureaucracy, a powerful military, expansive healthcare and educational systems, and factories and modern industries. This creation of institutions was followed by a second phase beginning in the mid-1960s, during which state leaders sought to consolidate their rule. Doing so often entailed tinkering with the institutions of rule they had created earlier. Parliaments became more pliant. Mass-based political parties turned more bureaucratic. Opposition parties were banned, and elections assumed a more cosmetic nature. The space once allowed for political contestation was contracted.

Within a span of a decade or so, this was followed by a series of corrective measures meant primarily to enhance the state's management of the economy. Thus began the so-called open-door policies of the mid-to late 1970s, designed to enhance private market operations and to attract and facilitate the flow of foreign direct investments into the economy. Nearly two decades later, in the early 1990s, a series of limited political liberalizations was instituted to open up political space in a tightly controlled fashion. Although for state leaders the economic liberalizations of the 1970s and the limited political openings of the 1990s were not intertwined, the two developments did constitute the same continuum of institutional corrections designed to prolong the state's longevity.

Neither economic nor political liberalization were sufficient to reverse the state's slide toward institutional atrophy, perhaps largely because both efforts lacked political commitment and meaningful substance. The economy continued to deteriorate, its performance chronically hampered by an obtrusive, inefficient, and often corrupt state machinery. And politics remained fundamentally authoritarian, with an ever-narrower space for political expression and participation.

Starting with the initial phase of the state-building process, corporatist populism became the modus operandi of newly established republican systems across the Arab world. By the mid-to late 1970s, the authoritarian ruling bargains that had emerged in the process had degenerated into rule by fear and sheer coercion. These exclusionary, authoritarian systems became increasingly personalized, with presidents more and more reliant on a narrow inner circle of close family members and wealthy and corrupt oligarchs. As such, they offered ready targets for popular anger and resentment as the regime could hardly deliver on its economic and political promises, as elections became more farcical, and as the intelligence services became more repressive. The armed forces, meanwhile, became steadily more professionalized, in the process strengthening their corporate identity. In Tunisia and Egypt, when popular protests threatened the interests of both civilianized leaders and those of the armed forces, the state's defection by military leaders paved the way for its overthrow. In Syria, elite cohesion has so far held through a bloody civil war, a product of an informal, consultative system of elite interdependence first inaugurated in the 1970s.

As authoritarian regimes, the Arab republics typically all politicized state institutions through a ruling party and the political control of the military. They consolidated power and curtailed freedoms through wars and military conflicts, and used elections and referendums as means of staying in power. The state invariably infringed on the daily lives of its citizens and collected massive amounts of information on both the general population and especially on its opponents. State leaders managed and exploited the economy as a means of increasing support and allocating resources to allies. Decision-making was centralized, and fear permeated both society and the machinery of state, including within the state bureaucratic apparatus.[83] The system mistrusted the masses as much as the masses mistrusted the system.[84]

Regardless of their institutional makeup, all Arab authoritarian systems possessed a certain amount of adaptability, although the republics were on the whole far more rigid and inflexible as compared to the monarchies. The twentieth century was not particularly kind to Middle Eastern monarchies, with the Egyptian monarchy overthrown in 1952, Iraq's in 1958, and Iran's in 1978–79. But the ones that have survived into the present century seem institutionally better equipped to weather crises rooted in popular protests. They incorporate into their orbit wider and more influential social strata; they are comparatively more adaptable; and, for those in the Arabian Peninsula, they have access to more direct and more lucrative sources of rent.

Given the richness of institutional diversity across the Arab world, it is difficult to classify the states that were overthrown in 2011 into one ideal-type category.[85] Before the Arab Spring, most Arab states experimented with various forms of soft authoritarianism through elite co-option and by opening up or narrowing political space as required by changing circumstances. This hybridity between corporatist authoritarianism and limited liberalization enabled them to stay in power for as long as they did. But for most, neither liberalization experiments nor authoritarian retrenchment was sufficient to give them the capacity to resist popular protests in late 2010. Thus began the revolutions of the Arab Spring.

3

CHALLENGING THE STATE

By all accounts, the events that shook the Arab world in the closing weeks of 2010 and early 2011 were seen as revolutions by those who took part in them. At least initially, these events followed a pattern seen most recently and dramatically in Iran, first in 1977–78, and, just prior to the Arab Spring, in 2009. Iran's Islamic revolution, and its short-lived corrective in 2009, followed a pattern first witnessed in France in the late 1780s in the lead-up to the great French Revolution. As in France, the collection of events in Iran that grew into a revolution did not initially start out as such. The events were, instead, largely uncoordinated and haphazard acts of open defiance against a state that was, unbeknownst to the perpetrators, woefully unprepared to deal with the unfolding uprising. As these events snowballed into an increasingly coherent and coordinated movement, and as the state's hurried and bungled responses further weakened its grip on power, what had at first started as a series of scattered acts of defiance and heroism soon emerged as a revolution.

This was, broadly, the genesis of the French and Iranian revolutions. It also characterizes the overall pattern of what transpired in Tunisia and from there Egypt, Libya, Syria, Bahrain, and Yemen. The 2011 Arab uprisings started out as acts of political defiance and protest. Before long, these largely uncoordinated acts coalesced into revolutions. In each country, the revolution followed a different path. Tunisia's revolution has ushered in a generally orderly, negotiated transition. Egypt's transition, comparatively disorderly and chaotic, was reversed relatively soon after it succeeded. The Libyan, Syrian, and Yemeni transitions ended up in civil wars, and Bahrain's was brutally repressed before it had any chance of growing into something bigger.

This chapter traces the causes, processes, and consequences of the 2011 uprisings. The broad outlines of the arguments here are as follows. As we saw in the previous chapter, by the 1980s and 1990s the Arab states of North Africa and the Levant had managed to squander whatever legitimacy had been left of their corporatist populism and instead relied increasingly on repression and the element of fear to stay in power. In late 2010, a series of developments coalesced to result in revolutions first in Tunisia and then in Egypt, Libya, Bahrain, Syria, and Yemen. These revolutions first started out as social movements, movements that emerged not in vacuums but as a result of everyday acts of resistance and defiance that had come to be features of life in the Middle East for several decades. Not all revolutions start out as social movements, and not all social movements end up in revolutions. But in 2010–11, the social movements sweeping the Arab world did grow into something different, in some cases into revolution and in others morphing into civil wars.

A revolution is a very specific kind of a political event, comprising three separate but intimately connected developments. These are 1) structural changes in the state's institutional makeup; 2) changes in the ways in which the state and society interact and interface; and 3) changes to the political culture, which informs popular values and assumptions about politics. Not all revolutions are alike, of course, and they tend to fall into one of three ideal types: those that start out as deliberate, planned campaigns to overthrow and replace regimes, broadly called *planned* revolutions; those that are more *spontaneous* and emerge with less initial planning and in a more uncoordinated and haphazard manner; and those that are *negotiated*, in which the only way out of a negative balance of weakness between state and society is for representatives from the two sides to negotiate a way out of the deadlock, usually using popular elections as a way of doing so.[1]

The 2010–11 uprisings began as social movements that quickly mushroomed into spontaneous revolutions. The Tunisian and Egyptian revolutions succeeded in overthrowing the *ancien régime* and ushering in a new order, in the latter case only temporarily. In both instances, the revolution succeeded because of the defection from the state of perhaps its strongest component, namely the armed forces. Such defections did not occur, at least not on the same scale, in Syria, and thus the Syrian revolution soon devolved into a civil war between the state's opponents and its supporters. The bloodbath that ensued was only prolonged by the meddling of outside actors. In Libya and Yemen, the *ancien régime* did succumb to popular pressures from society, but the fractiousness of social actors vying for newfound power prevented them from agreeing on how to forge a new political order. Hence Libya and Yemen also descended into civil wars. And in Bahrain, what was beginning to emerge as a nationwide social movement calling for political reforms was quickly suppressed and then placed in a sectarian framing meant to narrow its appeal and to vilify its proponents.

All revolutions necessarily involve state weakness and its institutional vulnerability to pressures by social actors. What differs from one kind of revolution to another is the timing of the state's weakness in relation to the mobilization of groups with revolutionary objectives. In planned revolutions, institutional vulnerability is forced on the state through the deliberate efforts of individuals who consider themselves to be revolutionaries dedicated to the cause of overthrowing the state. In their campaign, they often adopt specific ideological blueprints for their goals and objectives, and follow thought-out tactics and strategies for bringing about the state's defeat. These were the paths followed by the Russian Bolsheviks in October 1917 and by communist guerrillas in the lead-up to the Chinese and Cuban revolutions.

In broad terms, in planned revolutions revolutionaries appear first and through their efforts they precipitate state weakness and ultimately its collapse. In spontaneous and negotiated revolutions, state institutional weakness appears first, providing the space within which social actors can voice their opposition to the state. These revolutions germinate within society and begin as efforts by individuals who express opposition to the state of affairs in relation to one or more issues. If these issues find enough salience among others to compel them to oppose political targets as well, and if the state intentionally or inadvertently provides space and opportunity for the growth of these sentiments, then a mass-based, largely spontaneous revolution ensues.[2]

41

There are always individuals and groups in dictatorships who call for the state's violent overthrow. But these are often voices in the wilderness, the state's impulse for repression making the costs of joining such groups en masse prohibitively high. Only when the state eases up on its repression—somehow providing actual or perceived opportunities for expressions of political sentiments—can social actors start campaigns that may grow into social movements. How the state responds to these social movements, both intentionally and inadvertently, and how actors within social movements capitalize on or squander the opportunities and challenges presented to them along the way, determine whether they end up as revolutions—and if so, what type of revolutions—or degenerate into civil wars. It is to this last category of spontaneous movements that the Arab uprisings belong, ending up either as spontaneous revolutions or as civil wars, or, as in Bahrain, crushed in their infancy.

Collective action and social movements

The 2011 uprisings all began as social movements.[3] A social movement is a popular movement that starts within one or more social strata in order to achieve specific social or political goals. Social movements often seek to change government policies or traditional patterns of political behavior.[4] As such, they are based on common purposes and social solidarities and are outgrowths of what many have called "contentious politics."[5] Those who take part in social movements not only demand change but also operate within the context of "inherited understandings and ways of doing things" and the "boundaries of constituted politics, culture, and institutions."[6]

Similar to other collective action processes, social movements are shaped and influenced by dynamic interaction and intersection between opportunities and threats.[7] They are interactive campaigns that "consist of interactions between temporarily connected (and often shifting) groups of claimants."[8] Social movements depend heavily on political entrepreneurs for their scale, durability, and effectiveness. Leaders can create social movements only when they tap into and expand deep-rooted feelings of solidarity and identity.[9] For social movements to emerge and grow, actors must find ways of organizing themselves and sustaining their mobilization through reliance on existing social networks and building internal capacity. Social movements require strategic employment of a repertoire of collective action, capitalizing on cleavages in society, bringing people together around inherited cultural symbols, and utilization of and reliance on dense social networks and connective structures.[10]

Social movements combine three kinds of claims—program, identity, and standing—and assert popular sovereignty.[11] It is important to see how those demanding change interact with those within the larger body politic. Also important is to look beyond political contestation and change, and to see how institutions like firms, schools, churches, and others change as a result of social movements.[12] Social movements, in sum, need to be studied in relation to the institutional and structural contexts within which they form and operate.

In recent years, the spread of social media has facilitated the formation and steady spread of demands for social and political change, and, in some instances, subsequent mass mobilization. In the twenty-first century, advances in communications technology have lowered the costs of coordination among actors and, at the same time, have more definitively excluded those without access to communication means.[13] Social media and communication technology—cell phones, Twitter, and blogging—facilitate the emergence of virtual networks that enable activists to communicate and mobilize. They have made the scope of mobilization broader, but also more unpredictable.[14] As we shall see shortly, social media, Facebook in particular, played a highly significant role in sustaining the social movement that turned into Egypt's spontaneous revolution.

Narratives and stories also play important roles in animating the imagination of those involved in social movements, and the spread of these narratives through social media can help facilitate the growth and maintenance of collective action.[15] Ultimately, however, social movements are about mass mobilization, and, depending on their internal dynamics and the context within which they find themselves, they may disappear altogether or mutate into some other form of politics.[16]

Equally significant in shaping collective action are the role and importance of space. Collective action processes are influenced by the arena in which they unfold, which in the context of the Middle East have generally been cities. As primary sites of politics, cities invariably shape and influence patterns of rule, state authority, and governmentality. They also influence the forms and patterns of political contestation. As Asef Bayat correctly observes, cities "leave their spatial imprints on the nature of social struggles and agency," and provide particular kinds of politics at different levels.[17]

Authoritarian states often use public space as arenas for demonstrating their actual and symbolic power. Sidewalks, streets, major thoroughfares, and squares all become sites where the state's claim to eminent domain extends to its proactive demonstrations of power and its reach into personal and private lives. Tensions between the state's agendas and the impulse toward the natural rhythm of urban life are inescapable. In the Arab world in particular, the transformation of urban space into public space in cities as diverse as Tunis, Cairo, Manama, Daraa (Syria), and elsewhere has been especially contentious.[18] Not surprisingly, the uprisings featured massive occupation and reappropriation of public space by the people as shows of defiance and opposition to the state and its authority.[19] Many sites of the physical powers of the state, and even many ordinary city squares without overt political significance, were turned into arenas of disorder and of people power.[20]

The social movements that emerged in parts of the Arab world in late 2010–11 grew out of demands for more effective citizenship and more equitable social and political orders.[21] They featured information-rich politics, imagined communities and distributed authority, and demands for personal dignity, political accountability, and transparency.[22] The uprisings were not necessarily inspired by ideological or religious sentiments, but instead by demands for the rights of citizenship. As with Iran's 2009 Green Movement, the social movements that led to the Arab uprisings were post-ideological.[23] They were motivated by "the retrieval of some quintessential cornerstone of civil life" taken away first by colonial masters and then by local despots.[24] According to Hamid Dabashi, "the Arab Spring is not the final fulfillment of a set of ideologies but the exhaustion of all ideologies, a final delivery from them all."[25] This post-ideological character paved the way for the non-ideological nature of the revolutions that set out to overthrow the region's existing states.

Said Arjomand has called Iran's 1978–79 revolution the last of the great ideological revolutions.[26] In 2010–11, due to a number of ideological and tactical reasons, Islamist movements remained largely marginal to the start of the Arab uprisings.[27] Islam played at best a small role in mobilizing protesters, despite the fact that across the Arab world the religious establishment represented what Bahgat Korany calls the "deep society."[28] In fact, given the social function of mosques and other religious institutions in a society like Egypt's, the Muslim Brotherhood was best positioned to foster mass mobilization. But throughout the Arab world, formal Islamist groups had sought to accommodate rather than actively undermine and oppose ruling states. In Egypt, Jordan, and Yemen, the Muslim Brotherhood was in fact reluctant to spearhead the overthrow of the regime, which they viewed as entailing great risks. Moreover, many Islamist activists tried to present themselves as having become more pragmatic and less ideological, therefore often adopting the language, strategies, and modes of contestation of nonreligious groups. This "post-Islamism" characterized even the Egyptian Muslim Brotherhood, which had all but abandoned the slogan "Islam is the solution."[29]

This diminished role of Islam in the initial phases of the uprisings was the result of two complementary developments. First, more radical and extremist Islamists by and large stayed away from the uprisings in their early phases. In fact, whereas politically moderate Islamist activists emerged as significant actors working within and through existing political institutions, radical Islamists showed less inclination to participate in elite-challenging collective behavior.[30] This was reinforced by a second development, namely the Islamists' deliberate de-emphasis of their religious identity and agenda in order to widen their appeal among diverse groups in society. When the uprisings got underway, Islamist movements sought to broaden the scope of their mission by adopting the slogans of "dignity, freedom, and social justice." Once they did so, they could no longer dictate the outcome of their movements.[31]

The Egyptian Muslim Brotherhood in particular appears to have been keenly aware of its limited ability to mobilize street protests. In fact, the Muslim Brotherhood appears to have had at best minimal success in mobilizing one of the most restive classes in Egyptian society, namely industrial workers. Worker mobilization in Egypt has often been largely secular, whereas the mobilization of the lumpen intelligentsia may be either secular or religious.[32] At best, the Brotherhood's mobilizational capacity seems rather limited. As it turned out, this lack of institutional backing from Islamist movements did not adversely affect the outcomes of the popular uprisings.[33]

Before turning to the revolutions of 2010–11, it is important to note that the social movements that gave rise to them occurred within the context of highly receptive societies in which profound processes of social change, and political unease, had already been percolating for some time. Resistance to power is not only physical but also takes everyday forms. Bayat, in fact, cautions against an uncritical adoption of notions of social movement that focus largely if not exclusively on outward, public manifestations of what are more subtle, complex processes of change in society. Instead, Bayat points to the importance of "contentious politics and social 'nonmovements' as key vehicles to produce meaningful change in the Middle East."[34] Real change, he maintains, happens at the subaltern level. Since authoritarianism has rendered mass mobilization nearly impossible—especially of the scale of Iran's 1978–79 revolution—much collective action takes place through the efforts of non-collective actors, through what Bayat calls social non-movements. In the Middle East, these non-movements represent the mobilization of millions of subalterns.[35] Throughout the Arab world, in fact, it has been professional associations and syndicates that have carried out their goals as well as secured important political objectives, usually through the medium of Islam.[36]

In addition to syndicates and professional associations, informal networks played a critical role in recruiting and mobilizing adherents. These networks were composed of workers and unemployed or underemployed professionals, as well as university students, and emerged and operated within local contexts tied to existing structures of power.[37] Although these groups had the rage and the class consciousness of the revolution, they lacked its political vision or organization.[38] In Tunisia and Egypt, in fact, along with the mobilization of the unemployed and the efforts of the oppositional intelligentsia, working-class consciousness constituted an important factor in the uprisings.[39] But neither the workers nor the intelligentsia saw themselves as foot soldiers in a revolutionary movement, or, for that matter, capable of acting on their anti-state sentiments. Unbeknownst to them, what they were taking part in was turning out to be a full-blown revolution.

CHALLENGING THE STATE

Revolutions and civil wars

By 2010, societies across the Arab world had developed conditions that transformed individual demonstrations of heroism into collective action. Not all social movements transform into spontaneous revolutions. But those that began in Tunisia and Egypt did. Social movements are often animated by demands for specific objectives that may or may not be strictly political. If these demands grow to include overtly political objectives that run contrary to those of the state, and if the state cannot successfully address such demands or withstand the force of the collective pressure being placed on it, then it will succumb to a popular, spontaneous revolution.

The works of professional syndicates, socially rooted (non)movements for change, and persistent and spreading demands for citizenship rights all combined to make social movements possible. Violent and armed opposition to the state has been a common feature of Arab politics for some time, a product of the state's repression, the moral bankruptcy of political leaders, and the resonance of violent narratives and experiences among the population.[40] State violence had always elicited violent and brutal opposition. And state co-option had created a social and political fabric of collusion and collaboration, prompting some opponents to view violence as the only way to break the order of subjugation.[41] The 2010 social movements had few options open to them: either peter out or be crushed at the hands of the state; or grow in scope and evolve into a full-blown revolution that overthrows the state; or morph into a prolonged armed resistance to the state and devolve into a civil war. Bahrain's social movement was crushed by the state, Tunisia's and Egypt's became revolutions, and Libya's and Syria's degenerated into civil wars.

Let us first turn to the case of revolutions. For our purposes here, we can adopt Sydney Tarrow's definition of revolution as "a rapid, forcible, durable shift in collective control over a state that includes a passage through openly contested sovereignty."[42] Revolutions are made possible through a confluence of several factors, namely economic and social dislocations resulting from dependent capitalist development, the political vulnerabilities of dictatorship, and favorable conditions in the world system where outside powers will not interfere on the side of the state. Revolutionary movements give people a sense of hope, and, over time, feelings of empowerment and eager anticipation. The emergence of radical, revolutionary political culture can legitimize causes around which people mobilize and rally.

Spontaneous revolutions, and the social movements that can give rise to them, are notoriously unpredictable in their direction and outcome. It is virtually impossible to predict the eruption of mass protests in authoritarian regimes, given that they are usually the product of "short-term events that unexpectedly redraw the informational landscape of mass politics."[43] Since authoritarian regimes demand compliance and conformity, preference falsification is rampant and can result in the unpredictability of popular outbursts.

The timing of the transformation of a social movement into a revolution is also blurry at best. During the course of the social movement, the first use of the word "revolution" is often for symbolic purposes, more a metaphor rather than an actual blueprint of what is about to happen. The word is often used not only to arouse passions about a better, ideal future but also to evoke symbolism, sometimes mockingly and sometimes as a historical reference. It is only slowly that the word gets widespread currency, develops actual and substantive meaning, and starts to refer to a process and an objective rather than a symbolically evocative but substantially hollow figure of speech.[44]

The steady shift in the language of social movements signifies deeper, more profound changes in popular perceptions across broad strata of society. "Revolutions are ultimately about passionate commitment and great willingness to sacrifice."[45] Eric Selbin describes revolution as a "Sisyphean journey from the impossible to the possible to the plausible to the probable."[46] "Resistance, rebellion and revolution are made to seem possible when people articulate compelling stories" that provide them with the belief that such a revolutionary change is possible, with the energy to do so, and in some cases even with the strategies and tactics of doing so.[47] Increasingly, the popular narrative focuses on the emergence or creation of revolutionary situations and the struggle for control of the state, which would then foster fundamental and far-reaching efforts to transform the political, economic, and cultural systems.

This shift in the self-perceptions of the social movement and its narrative occurs at the same time as, and reinforces, the role and significance of violence as an inescapable facet of what is now commonly seen as a *revolutionary* uprising. While violence is never planned and is not a deliberate part of spontaneous revolutions, it becomes an important aspect of the revolution's highlight—symbolically, emotionally, and practically.[48] This violence often becomes inescapable as the state, weak and dying as it may be, is unwilling to be simply pushed aside. Revolutions, in fact, are often paradoxically helped along in their journey to success by the very efforts of states determined to defeat them.

As the 2010 social movements turned into full-blown revolutions, they retained their mass-based, largely leaderless character. This is where they differed markedly from Iran's 1978–79 revolution, during the course of which the country's clerical class was propelled to the leadership of what also became an increasingly ideological uprising. The Arab revolutions were not devoid of intellectual content; they simply lacked what may be called "revolutionary intellectuals."[49] Throughout the 1990s and 2000s, Arab states showed little tolerance for meaningful and substantive intellectual activity, even by those who defended law and order, called for small and incremental changes, and generally endorsed the status quo. Thus when the uprisings broke out, they lacked intellectuals, especially revolutionary thinkers and ideologues whose job it is to advocate revolutions before they erupt and who join in once the revolution gets going.[50]

Why did the uprisings break out in the first place? The uprisings were, of course, manifestations of longer-running politics of resistance at both the subaltern and formal levels.[51] But the specific sparks that precipitated them were both more immediate and longer-term. The immediate cause of the uprisings were two horrific developments. One was the spread on the internet of photos of the bloodied, broken body of a young Egyptian named Khaled Mohamed Saeed, who had died in Alexandria at the hands of the police in June 2010.[52] The second catalytic event was the self-immolation of a despondent Tunisian fruit seller, Mohamed Bouazizi, on 17 December 2010. An act of desperation, Bouazizi's sacrifice set off demonstrations first in his hometown of Sidi Bouzid and then in other Tunisian cities. Heartened by what they saw unfold in Tunisia, Egyptians soon joined in, and from there the contagion spread over to Libya, Syria, Bahrain, and Yemen.

These anti-government demonstrations occurred within the context of societies rife with political resentment and anger aimed at the state and its leaders. These sentiments were greatly aggravated in 2010 by sudden rises in the price of foodstuffs. In general, there is little evidence that unrest correlates with popular pressures, poverty, unemployment, or ethno-religious heterogeneity.[53] There is also no evidence that unrest correlates with internet access, cell phone use, or the permeation of social media such as Facebook and Twitter.[54] Arab Spring countries, in fact, did not display significantly higher levels of unemployment or digital connectivity at the time of the uprisings. Nevertheless, whereas various measures of economic hardship such as unemployment and income inequality do not correlate with unrest, inflation and corruption do.[55] In fact, perceptions of high levels of corruption and sudden price increases correlate directly with higher levels of unrest. Coincidentally, sharp rises in the prices of wheat—from $157 per metric ton in June 2010 to $326 per metric ton in February 2011—directly affected Egypt, the world's largest importer of wheat.[56]

Sharp price rises did more than just fuel popular anger against the state. They also contributed to the increasing weakness and fragility of the state, especially in Syria and Egypt, in the lead-up to the 2011 uprisings. The price of wheat and other foodstuffs had grown because of severe, adverse changes in the climate, drought, and the mismanagement of natural resources by the government. From 2007 to 2011, for example, Syria experienced the worst long-term drought and crop and livestock devastation in its modern history, resulting in a massive exodus of rural inhabitants to the country's urban areas and severe strains on state resources and services.[57] The inability of the Egyptian and Syrian states to deal with the adverse effects of the drought, combined with the dramatic rise in prices and strains on state resources and services, directly contributed to their fragility and weakness in the face of steadily rising demands for change.[58]

The scale and intensity of the unrest caught state actors by surprise. Most of these state elites were detached from and largely unaware of the reality around them, believing, for example, that the protests were the actions of foreign agitators.[59] But the initial dismissiveness, combined with frequent and severe overreactions, only helped further fuel popular passion against the state. As the protests gained momentum in Tunisia and Egypt, there was a steady crumbling of power at the apex of the state. Once the military's leadership defected from civilian autocrats, the latter's fate was sealed. Elsewhere, in places where the president's family was in command of units in the military—in Libya, Syria, and Yemen—protracted civil war ensued. In Libya and Syria, in fact, state actions directly contributed to making the uprisings bloody.[60]

What began as social movements ended up as spontaneous revolutions in Tunisia and Egypt and as civil wars in Libya, Syria, and Yemen. The deciding factor between the two outcomes was the nature of the pre-uprising state and its responses, both structural and in terms of policy, to the uprisings as they unfolded. But uprisings, successful or not, did not occur uniformly across North Africa and the Levant, and, as we have seen, their outcomes were far from uniform. It is to the causes of these variations that the chapter turns next.

The 2011 uprisings

The uprisings involved the eruption of nonviolent mass protests over many days. The protests spread across multiple geographic locations, and the protesters gained control over major public spaces such as landmark squares, roundabouts, and avenues. These events, as we shall see shortly, represented an evaporation of *haibat al-dawla* (awe of the state) that power-holders had for so long cultivated. Conversely, an awe of the people (*haibat al-sha'b*) was generated, with state actors fearing the power of the people. Although neither of these types of fears had staying power and they did not last long, the uprisings signified a large-scale rejection of "the overarching myths of patriarchal benevolence" that state leaders had long used to justify their hold on power.[61]

Once localized protests broke out in Tunisia over the death of Mohamed Bouazizi, it was only a matter of time for the contagion to spread among social classes within Tunisia and across national boundaries over to Egypt and elsewhere. More than anything else, this contagion was facilitated through the internet. The internet has changed the ways in which political actors communicate with one another, especially in political systems in which information flows and communication are highly restricted. Earlier, in 2004, the internet had been decisive in the mobilization of Ukrainians during the country's Orange Revolution—perhaps the first revolution in history to have been organized largely online.[62] During the Arab uprisings, the battle between the state and the people was fought in streets as well as in digital space, as protesters tried to disseminate information and organize protests while the state sought to block access to the digital media.[63] Digital media also helped spread and strengthen cross-national linkages, further facilitating the eruption of copycat protests from one country to the next. Ironically, at a time when the Arab states were eager to distinguish themselves from each other, a drive for Arab unity from below, a desire to emulate the social movement next door, emerged and spread from one country to another.[64] Satellite television, the internet, and the digital media played pivotal roles in the spread of the uprisings.[65]

The uprisings entailed the empowerment of society in two distinct but interrelated spaces, one physical the other virtual. In the same way that streets and squares were turned into sites of protest and people power, the internet and social media were turned into arenas of contestation. They were used for collecting and disseminating information, expressing opinion, voicing outrage against the government and solidarity with the protesters. This virtual state was far easier for the protesters to capture, and, at the same time, much more difficult for the state to control and repress.

The Arab uprisings may have had similar geneses but, as we have seen, they had decidedly different processes and outcomes. These differences were largely shaped by three independent variables. The first independent variable was the nature of the preexisting regime. More specifically, differences in pre-uprising levels of centralization of power proved decisive in shaping different outcomes of the events. When power was centralized, as in Egypt and Tunisia, the transition was relatively smooth. But when power was not centralized, as was the case in Syria, the transition resulted in a protracted conflict between state elites and social actors, eliciting violence on both sides.[66] In all cases, the role of the military was central to the success or failure of the uprisings. The armed forces were key to the nature and outcomes of the transitions.[67] They either facilitated transitions, as in Tunisia and Egypt; or fostered their implosion, as in Libya; or repressed and prevented them, as in Bahrain; or fractured them, as in Syria and Yemen.[68]

A second independent variable at work in shaping different outcomes was "strategic value," or the extent to which the country experiencing the uprising was considered strategically significant for other international stakeholders. Bahrain's uprising was crushed by Saudi Arabia and the United Arab Emirates because a) they could, and b) they simply did not want an anti-state uprising in their neighborhood. In Tunisia, where Western security stakes had a relatively lower priority, the French, the Americans, and the Arabs more quickly abandoned Ben Ali. In relation to Egypt, however, there have been more incentives for external actors to securitize their relations with Egypt, especially since the country can serve as a bridge between the Persian Gulf and Central Africa and because of the strategic importance of the Suez Canal.[69]

The third independent variable contributing to different outcomes of the uprisings had to do with the role of agency. Structures may shape the context within which grievances take shape and are formulated. But collective action is, ultimately, a human enterprise subject to the initiatives of individuals, their priorities and objectives, and their preferences and idiosyncrasies. The transitions were informed by the structural and institutional features of the states under duress, but also by the skills of incumbent rulers and those of their opponents.[70]

In the final analysis, "agents, not structures, drove the uprisings… the Arab uprisings did not come, they were made."[71] As we shall see shortly, Rachid Ghannouchi's role in shaping the direction of the Tunisian transition cannot be overstated, and, by the same token, neither can the roles played by President Abdelaziz Bouteflika and King Mohammed VI in preempting prospects for similar developments in Algeria and Morocco respectively.

Tunisia led the way. Throughout December 2010 and into early January, protests against the regime continued and gained momentum. As the demonstrations gathered steam, President Ben Ali's increasingly personalist rule and the infamously corrupt coterie of oligarchs and family members that constituted his inner circle made for readily identifiable targets of popular anger. A narrative of "us" (the people) versus "them" (al-sulta, the authorities) had by now gained widespread currency among the people.[72] On 12 January, the president ordered the deployment of army troops in the streets of the capital as a sign of force and ostensibly to frighten away the protesters. When the president ordered the army to use force to disperse the demonstrators, senior army commanders refused and pulled their troops back into their barracks on 13 January. In a last-ditch effort to salvage his rule, Ben Ali delivered a televised address to the nation the same day. "Now," he said, "I understand you."[73] But by then hardly any of the protesters were willing to hear him out. And the army commanders had also decided that continued support for Ben Ali would subvert their core organizational interests.[74] The next day, on 14 January 2011, Ben Ali fled Tunisia.

It took only twenty-eight days of popular protests to depose Ben Ali. The commission that was formed after the president's departure made some key decisions that proved highly consequential for the post-Ben Ali transition. In fact, in many ways those decisions appear to be facilitating a transition to democracy: taking a process-first approach (unlike Egypt); holding elections for members of a Constitutional Assembly charged with drafting a constitution and presenting it to the people for their approval; having an anti-majoritarian proportional representation system; and ensuring male–female parity.[75] Throughout, Tunisian political actors have exhibited a spirit of coalition-building, with the Islamist Ennahda party engaging in confidence-building and reaching out to the other parties and actors. Ennahda has not been unique in this respect, and other parties have also sought to engage in partnerships and coalitions, seeking to place compromise as the centerpiece of the country's nascent democratic experiment.[76] As a result, Tunisia's transition has been remarkably, and rather uniquely, smooth and free of violence.

Despite a number of significant similarities with Tunisia, Egypt's transition was decidedly different. Throughout the 2000s, Egypt's authoritarian system had given rise to a "culture of protest" among intellectuals, students, and urban professionals.[77] Nevertheless, similar to Tunisia, in Egypt in the 2000s neither the intellectuals nor the workers thought that Mubarak's overthrow would be a realistic objective.[78] In fact, when a group of opposition activists launched the *Kefaya* (Enough) movement in 2004, their goals merely consisted of pressing for free and fair elections, demanding that opposition parties be allowed to contest parliamentary seats, and making sure that President Mubarak's son Gamal did not succeed him in a hereditary fashion. The movement also sought to redress Egypt's diminished international influence and profile.[79] But soon after the 2005 parliamentary elections, *Kefaya* became ridden with internal ideological squabbles and leadership splits, and quickly found itself increasingly marginalized and irrelevant to the country's political life. But the sentiments that had given rise to it in the first place still remained. In fact, given the absence of such a comparatively moderate outlet, these sentiments only grew in force and ferocity.

The street protests in Tunisia had a direct, heartening effect on the Egyptians fed up with Mubarak's authoritarian regime. Khaled Mohamed Saeed's horrific death, graphically remembered thanks to the internet, gave Egyptians added impetus to turn city streets and squares into arenas of political protest. Similar to in Tunisia, the president, his inner circle, and the security forces provided ready, and increasingly despised, targets for the protesters. As the internet activist Wael Ghonim put it, "with every passing day I became more convinced that the police force was the chain that the regime tied around our necks; if the police force could be neutralized, the regime would be paralyzed."[80]

In its early days, the uprising featured a generational divide, with most of the protests being led by the young.[81] Soon they grew to include Egyptians from all ages and all walks of life. "We all craved an alternative," Ghonim recorded later. "We needed a savior, and we were ready to pour our hopes into any reasonable candidate."[82] For many Egyptians, in the final weeks of 2010 and early 2011, that savior seemed to be Mohamed ElBaradei, a legal scholar and one of the country's most experienced diplomats, with name recognition and respect both at home and abroad. Self-ascribed "revolutionary" activists often cluster around a perceived "leader," a savior—in Egypt's case ElBaradei. But seldom do these initial leaders end up being victors in the emerging movement, and they are even less likely to be the heirs of what is rapidly growing to become a revolution.

It was actually only on 14 January 2011, the day that Ben Ali fled Tunisia, that the word "revolution" became widespread in Egypt.[83] What was once unthinkable was now seen as possible, indeed probable. Explicit in calls for Mubarak's removal was the demand that the state live up to its end of the bargain and that dignity (*karama*) and freedom (*hurriya*) be observed.[84] Daily protests now took place across Egypt, though none quite as massive and as determined, and symbolically as important, as the ones in Cairo's iconic Tahrir Square. A sense of solidarity prevailed in which Muslims and Christians, men and women, were all united in their desire to overthrow the political order.[85] The regime, meanwhile, did not really know how to respond to protests. By now even the Egyptian State Security knew that it was vulnerable.[86]

By far the most massive protests took place on 25 January, intended to commemorate Police Day but called Day of Rage by the protesters. Soon 25 January came to symbolize the start of Egypt's 2011 revolution. Defections from the regime helped shatter Mubarak's façade of invincibility. The institutions of rule either proved ineffective or unwilling to help Mubarak retain power. For some time, the official National Democratic Party and the parliament had sought to co-opt elites and to serve as a means of elite nexus with the state. Despite seemingly successful attempts at co-option, once the uprisings erupted the business elite and government intellectuals were quick to abandon the state.[87] The NDP and the parliament soon proved ineffective and inconsequential, and even the army began to waver. As scattered clashes between protesters and regime supporters continued, calls for Mubarak's departure grew louder, eventually causing the president to resign on 11 February. He handed over power to the army.

Agency and the choices of post-transition leaders, as well as the country's authoritarian past, were instrumental in shaping the course of events in Egypt after Mubarak's fall.[88] From the start, the Egyptian military saw itself as the guardian of the transition, which it saw as an opportunity to enhance its popular standing. In the immediate aftermath of Mubarak's departure and the political vacuum that ensued, a 28-member Supreme Council of the Armed Forces (SCAF) was formed and took control of state affairs until new presidential elections were held in June 2012.

From February 2011 to August 2012, through the SCAF, the Egyptian military emerged as the most powerful stakeholder in the transition. Whereas the Tunisian military adopted a legalistic approach and returned to barracks, the Egyptian military sought to shape the rules of the game in the post-Mubarak era.[89] Mubarak had handed over power to the SCAF because the military wanted to protect its economic interests and also to hide its weaknesses and inefficiencies.[90] It soon became apparent, however, that the SCAF's objective was to protect the corporate interests of the military and to control the transition process. By the second half of 2012, the SCAF was facing a prisoner's dilemma: it was unwilling or unable to give up power, and yet its continued rule was weakening its position.[91] It finally opted, with some reluctance, to hold popular presidential elections in May and June 2012.

By now, the Egyptian Muslim Brotherhood, once a bastion of political opposition to the regime but a latecomer to the 25 January revolution, had regained its bearing and was vying for political power. The party took part in the presidential elections, and its candidate, Mohamed Morsi, won by securing a slim majority of the votes cast. But success at the ballot box actually turned out to be a kiss of death for the Brotherhood, as neither the party nor Morsi proved particularly effective at governing.

In post-transition Egypt, there was no broad agreement among the elites over the rules of the transition, and the elections never delivered authoritative results that the losers could not reject.[92] Despite much popular yearning for change, in its early months the country's post-transition system continued to operate as an authoritarian–democratic hybrid. The military continued to remain a dominant force in the political system, now having come out of the shadows to which it had retreated over the course of the previous decades. While Morsi sacked some prominent generals, he appointed many others to key state institutions and state-related agencies, such as the Suez Canal and the civil aviation authority, and retired military men continued to be appointed to provincial governorships.[93] Neither the military nor the Muslim Brotherhood showed any appetite for dismantling the country's legacy of political authoritarianism.

This authoritarian legacy directly contributed to the direction of the post-transition system in three ways. First, authoritarian leaders held over from the *ancien régime* continued to play key roles in the new system. Second, authoritarian political infrastructures, such as the State Security Court, remained in operation and continued to function as if nothing had changed. Finally, authoritarianism had fostered an unbalanced political scene, one in which the various political forces, both Islamists and non-Islamists, did not trust each other. This widespread suspicion and mistrust continued in the post-transition period among both political actors and the electorate at large, and there was little consensus over the rules of the game and even the electoral process.[94] In fact, given its nearly 50–50 split, the 2012 presidential elections actually appeared to have deepened rather than lessened popular polarization across the country.[95]

Of these, the military's continued, and now overt, presence in the political process was most immediately consequential insofar as the course of events was concerned. Upon assuming office, Morsi forced the retirement of dozens of military officers, including some well-known allies of Mubarak. But the SCAF's taste for power appears to have prompted Morsi's own defense minister, General Abdul Fattah el-Sisi, to launch a military coup in July 2013 and to take over power. Morsi and many of his cabinet members were imprisoned, and, in a move reminiscent of the old regime, the Muslim Brotherhood was legally banned and its assets were seized. Promising new elections in the near future, el-Sisi, through the military, launched a violent crackdown on Brotherhood supporters and other protesters who took issue with the coup and the repressive direction that the revolution was beginning to take. State repression reached heights seldom seen before, even after el-Sisi's rule was given a gloss of legitimacy in presidential elections in May 2014, in which he supposedly received 97 percent of the votes cast. The Egyptian revolution, it seemed, had come full circle.

The day after Egypt's 25 January revolution, scattered protests began appearing in a number of small Syrian towns. Slowly these protests gathered pace, culminating in major demonstrations in the town of Daraa in March following the arrest by the police of six students writing anti-government graffiti on the wall. The police's harsh response to the protests in Daraa backfired, and before long there were other anti-government rallies across Syria, including in Damascus itself. The government initially responded using a carrot-and-stick approach, unleashing its security forces on the demonstrators while also promising to lift the state of emergency, which had been in effect since 1963. By the end of April, however, little that the authorities did placated or deterred government opponents. The state relied increasingly on the armed forces to quell the uprising. As the protests continued, however, unlike Tunisia and Egypt, the Syrian army did not defect from the state, and defections by other state allies were also comparatively few. Before long, the country was plunged into civil war.

As discussed in the previous chapter, the Assad regime built a state that had multiple centers of authority. The elites cooperated together across institutional lines and operated in a relatively decentralized system.[96] This gave members of the political elite—including military commanders, Ba'ath Party leaders and high-ranking state functionaries, and members of the business oligarchy—a vested interest in the state and therefore incentive not to defect to the opposition. War-making also compelled the Assad regime to reconfigure its social base, tighten its dependence on global authoritarian networks (including greater reliance on the Hezbollah), restructure its military and security apparatus, and to adapt its mode of economic governance. The state also reemphasized its role as an agent of economic redistribution and a provider of economic security.[97] In Syria, war has been a catalyst for authoritarian restructuring.[98]

Libya's uprising, meanwhile, began in February 2011, when government security forces opened fire on a group of protesters in Benghazi. The first anti-government demonstrations broke out in Libya on 14 February 2011, just three days after Mubarak's ouster from power in Egypt. Demonstrations soon spread to other cities, and Qaddafi's farcical attempt to claim the mantle of what he called the "people's revolution" found no takers. Before long, the entire country was in rebellion, one driven by three larger dynamics. First, over the preceding decades, Libya's rentier political economy had failed to create sufficient and adequate employment opportunities for the country's youth and to modernize the economy. Secondly, the country's eastern region of Cyrenaica, where Benghazi is located, remained underdeveloped, increasing the potential for popular resentment against the Tripoli-based state. In the lead-up to the conflict, in fact, Libyan society had witnessed steady polarization, and most Libyans had begun identifying with one side or another. Finally, there were the domino effects of the Tunisian and Egyptian revolutions.[99]

One of the distinguishing characteristics of the Libyan uprising was the early intervention of external actors. Outside powers had also become involved in the Syrian uprising, but only after the country's civil war was already underway. In Libya, within two weeks of the outbreak of the first demonstrations, both the United Nations and NATO started initiating measures designed to weaken Qaddafi's hold on power and to expedite his departure from office, including the imposition of a no-fly zone over Libyan skies. Qaddafi's rule was weakened, but he still commanded enough support, especially among die-hard, armed loyalists, to resist leaving office until the following August, when his compound in Tripoli was overrun. Before long, what had started as a popular uprising had turned into a full-blown armed rebellion, with multiple militia groups fighting one another and vying for the capture of Qaddafi. Both the rebels and Qaddafi loyalists saw the conflict as a zero-sum game, whereby the survival of one meant the destruction of the other.[100] On the run, Qaddafi was finally captured on 20 October 2011 and shot on the spot.

The transition that followed was, and as of this writing still is, fraught with conflict and uncertainty. Soon after street protests broke out in Benghazi, a National Transitional Council (NTC) was formed to direct the country's emerging revolution. Over the course of his 42-year rule, Qaddafi had carefully avoided the establishment of any viable political institutions that might have potentially challenged his personal hold on power. As the uprising spread, therefore, his rule crumbled quickly. At the same time, however, the NTC found itself unable to reconstitute a national military to coordinate Qaddafi's overthrow and to establish its authority at the local level. Instead, the Council funded and encouraged local communities to have their own militias and to maintain law and order on their own.[101] With weapons and other forms of military assistance now pouring into the country from the likes of Saudi Arabia, Qatar, and the UAE, which were in search of local allies in the post-Qaddafi era, national reconciliation was made exceedingly difficult. Even after popular elections were held in July 2012 for a legislative body tasked with drafting a constitution, the country's centrifugal forces could not be brought back together, their fractiousness fanned all the more intensely by international intervention. As of this writing, Libya's civil war continues to rage unabated.

The outcome of Yemen's uprising has been similarly tragic and bloody. Major demonstrations took place in Sana'a in January 2011, with the protesters initially demanding improvements to the economy and an end to pervasive government corruption. Quite spontaneously, in February 2011, a "tent city" grew outside Sana'a University, giving birth to Change Square.[102] Well into the initial weeks and months of 2011, the Yemenis were only demanding the establishment of a "civil state" (*dawla madaniyya*).[103] Heartened by the toppling of dictators in Tunisia and Egypt, however, the demands of Yemeni protesters soon escalated to include an end to President Ali Abdullah Saleh's 34-year rule. The following month, one of Saleh's former allies, General Ali Muhsin, defected from the regime and joined Change Square with his troops, resulting in the square's militarization.[104] From the start, Yemen's transition assumed military dimensions, with Saleh finally forced out of office in February 2012.

In Yemen, deep-seated elite rivalries revealed themselves during the course of the uprising, thereby affecting the outcome.[105] Many Yemenis initially saw the country's transition as an empty affair "run by a gaggle of reshuffled old-regime elites."[106] Before long, outside actors, principally Saudi Arabia, became involved, and power was passed between the elites through the efforts of Yemeni politicians, foreign powers, and the UN. The revolutionary youth who had started the uprising soon found themselves marginalized and outside the transition process.[107]

The Saudi government has long considered Yemen to be the geostrategic extension of the kingdom's security. Its efforts to direct the course of events in Yemen, largely through General Muhsin and other tribal leaders, further complicated an already volatile and increasingly militarized transition. The wily Saleh, meanwhile, once again proved his skills as a tenacious survivor, allying himself with Yemeni Houthis in an effort to regain power. With alleged help from Iran, the Houthis and Saleh loyalists took over Sana'a in September 2014, forcing the president, Abdrabbuh Mansour Hadi, to flee. By now Yemen had plunged into a full-blown civil war. Hadi, who had previously served as Saleh's vice president, found ready allies in Saudi Arabia and the UAE, which invaded Yemen in March 2015 and, amid much carnage, installed Hadi back in power. As of this writing, in early 2018, Yemen's bloody civil war, and the Saudi and Emirati invasion that fanned its flames, show no signs of abating.

The very same day that protests broke out on the streets of Benghazi against Qaddafi's rule, 14 February 2011, Bahrainis gathered in the streets of Manama and other cities in what had been billed as a Day of Rage. The protests remained mostly nonviolent and orderly, and their demands were decidedly nonrevolutionary. They sought instead the rewriting of the constitution, which many felt gave the royal court undue powers over the parliament, an end to arbitrary arrests and police repression, an end to nepotism and corruption, and the dismissal of the country's notoriously corrupt prime minister, Sheikh ifa bin Salman bin Khalifa, who has been in office since 1971 and who also happens to be the king's uncle. Even as they converged on and camped out at Manama's Pearl Square, pretty much in the same way that Egyptians and Yemenis were doing in Tahrir and Change Squares respectively, the protesters remained largely orderly and kept their demands relatively moderate. But the government's response was harsh and violent. Within a month, as the protests continued, a military force of 1,000 Saudi and 500 Emirati troops entered Bahrain and took up positions around government buildings in Manama. Bahraini security forces were then free to partake in "a binge of repression."[108]

Similar to Yemen, Bahrain has always had strategic and political significance for Saudi Arabia. In fact, prior to 2011, the comparatively open nature of Bahraini politics had been a source of considerable worry for the Saudis. Despite cycles of protest and political repression, Bahrain had long had a vibrant civil society, of which the Saudis did not always approve.[109] The Saudis have also long been highly wary of truly participatory politics in Bahrain and what a freely-elected parliament in Manama could mean for Saudi Arabia itself, especially for the restive Eastern Province.[110] Not surprisingly, the Saudis have long sought to maintain various forms of influence in Bahraini politics.

One of the ways in which this influence is maintained is through Bahrain's multifaceted dependence on Saudi Arabia. The bulk of Bahrain's oil comes from an offshore field it has shared with Saudi Arabia since the 1950s, operated by Saudi Aramco. The majority of Bahrain's tourists come from Saudi Arabia, many using the causeway between the two countries that is the island's sole land link to the Arabian Peninsula. Bahrain also receives extensive amounts of Saudi foreign aid. Saudi authorities have been known to remind the Bahraini monarchy occasionally of its continued need for and dependence on Saudi goodwill.[111]

Almost immediately, Bahraini and Saudi authorities framed the small island state's national uprising in sectarian terms, portraying it as the work almost exclusively of the country's Shia population acting on behalf of Iran. For the ruling Al-Khalifas, resort to sectarianism was seen as the most effective way of preventing the formation of a broad political alliance between the country's largely disenfranchised Shia and its Sunni opposition groups. This sectarian framing has had dramatic consequences not just in Bahrain but in reverberations across the Middle East. It dramatically altered the nature of state–society relations inside Bahrain and well beyond. Internally, through a policy of alternating repression and concession, the state has deepened preexisting social cleavages, giving rise to mutual mistrust among the country's traditional opposition groups, and has sought to lure away more amenable opposition figures through co-option and promises of reform.[112]

The sectarian framing has had consequences for the rest of the Middle East. Justin Gengler's observation in this regard is worth quoting at length:

> Beyond the utter undoing of Bahrain's social fabric, this sectarian stratagem has had the equally disastrous effect of exporting the country's internal political conflict abroad. The swift labeling of the February 14 uprising as an Iranian-backed coup attempt, followed by the decisive military intervention by Saudi Arabia to end mass protests, transformed a fundamentally domestic event into a new regional cold war. Incited by governments to take up the fight against the Shiite enemy, many Gulf Sunnis ultimately accepted the challenge in places like Syria, Iraq, and later Yemen, including several Bahraini nationals who would assume important positions within the Islamic State group.[113]

The serious challenge that the demonstrations posed against the monarchy's legitimacy prompted stern police and legal responses from the state. In addition to detention and imprisonment of suspected activists, the government has also sought to redraw the country's sectarian balance by taking away citizenship rights from a number of Shia opposition figures, while at the same time granting citizenship to Sunni residents from Pakistan and elsewhere. Some of the other monarchies in the Middle East also experienced street protests, but nothing of the scale and magnitude of Bahrain's. In the other monarchies that experienced some unrest in 2011, by and large the protesters did not question the legitimacy of the person of the monarch or the monarchy as a system of rule. Instead, they mostly called for reforms—such as freedom for the press and the right to establish civil society organizations—and the removal of corrupt or incompetent ministers. Most of the protests were, in fact, relatively small, generally peaceful, and mostly non-confrontational.[114] State behavior was also key in diffusing what could have become a series of crises. Political leaders skillfully deflated public protests by blaming and then sacrificing individuals within the state.[115] In addition to dismissing unpopular politicians, all of the three other monarchies that witnessed expressions of mass discontent—Morocco, Jordan, and Oman—responded swiftly and effectively by calling for national dialogue and expanding the scope of those co-opted into the regime. In Jordan and Morocco especially, groups with capacity for collective action became even more invested in the status quo.[116]

As we saw in the last chapter, a number of scholars offer structural explanations for the persistence of monarchy in the Middle East in the face of the Arab Spring and point to a combination of three factors: domestic coalitional support; state control over natural resources and the rents accrued through them; and foreign backing.[117] These dynamics were indeed key in enabling the monarchies of the Arabian Peninsula to ride through the Arab Spring uprisings relatively unscathed, as discussed in Chapter 6 below. But the uprising in Bahrain, street protests in Oman, and, a few decades earlier, the Iranian revolution of 1978–79 all demonstrated that monarchies are not necessarily structurally immune to the start or evolution of social movements into something bigger.

Regardless of its form and style of rule, whether republican or monarchical, the success or failure of a political system in staving off a popular revolution depends on two key variables, one structural and the other revolving around agency. Structurally, the effectiveness of institutions through which corporate groups in society are co-opted into the political system and become vested in its maintenance is a central factor in undermining the potential for its overthrow. At the same time, the skills of the political leadership in addressing or placating demands for change are central to the state's resilience. In Bahrain, the monarchy refused to meet the demands of the protesters even halfway, promised reforms that were only cosmetic and superficial, and doubled down on its repression and its dismissal of protesters as supposed puppets of Iran. As a result, the protests only grew in scale and ferocity. In Morocco, by contrast, the monarchy acted quickly and decisively to head off mass protests as soon as the first signs of popular unrest appeared. In early 2011, all was not quiet in Morocco. But the institutional adjustments made by the state, and the actions of the king himself, quickly prevented the unrest from growing into a larger anti-state movement. In the republican system next door, in Algeria, the state's similarly decisive and nuanced response, comprising both personal initiatives by President Bouteflika and institutional adjustments by the state, also undermined possibilities for the emergence of a social movement.

Let us examine these two cases in some detail. Major protests erupted in Rabat on 20 February 2011, with protesters chanting slogans against autocracy and in favor of a new constitution that would impose limits on the powers of the monarch. Other demonstrations soon followed in Casablanca, Marrakesh, Tangiers, and other big cities. Morocco has long featured a vibrant political scene, with a number of long-established political parties. But political parties and their leaders have often been isolated from the public and knew little about popular yearnings for change, instead having preoccupied themselves with narrow, electoral politics and parliamentary maneuvers.[118] The 2011 protests were largely the work of new actors and new voices in the polity, principally self-organized youths, who had new demands and wanted to foster real, meaningful change.[119] The youth used the term *alhogra*, from the Arabic word for contempt, to denote the conditions of suffering and difficulty, injustice, humiliation, and scorn by the ruling class. The "February 20" movement, which was subsequently born out of a loose coalition of several different youth groups, was different from its predecessors because of its boldness and its demands for meaningful change. The movement's demands might have been bold, but they were not revolutionary: a new constitution that would guarantee sovereignty to the king and the right to rule to the people; accountability and the punishment of the corrupt; release of political prisoners; and acknowledgment of Amazigh as Morocco's second official language.[120]

The state's response was swift, with the king moving quickly and skillfully to deffuse tensions and placate the emerging opposition. The monarch convened a commission charged with drafting a new constitution, which was subsequently approved in a popular referendum in July 2011. The new constitution increased the executive powers of the prime minister and the cabinet, removed the king's power to dissolve the parliament, enshrined freedom of the press, introduced significant reforms to the judiciary, and made Amazigh one of the country's official languages (along with Arabic and Arabic-Hassani, spoken by Morocco's Sahrawi population).[121] The status of the king changed from having been "sacrosanct" in the previous constitution to being "duly respected" in the new document. And, instead of the king appointing 1,200 state officials, the number of royal appointments have now been reduced to about 250.[122]

The king also pardoned a number of political prisoners, and parliamentary elections, scheduled for the following year, were brought forward by a year and were held in November. When the Justice and Development Party, with its Islamist platform, won a plurality of seats in the parliament, it was allowed to form a cabinet.

In Morocco, the monarchy is seen as a unifying factor for all Moroccans and a central pillar of Moroccan national identity. Moreover, the monarchy's historical pedigree equips it with a certain amount of flexibility that enables it to adapt itself to the winds of change.[123] But the region-wide span of the 2011 uprisings, and their ability to topple long-reigning rulers, required special attention and skill. This was no ordinary protest by a group of disenchanted, disillusioned youth. But Mohammed VI proved himself to be up to the challenge. He was able to impose his own rules of political engagement in order to hold the consequences of the Arab Spring at bay.[124] The king determined the pace, scope, and limits of political reforms. He managed to anticipate the political reforms needed and to respond to them beforehand, engineering and choreographing Morocco's own version of an Arab Spring. In a series of tactical moves, the king also found new political partners needed to widen his base.[125]

If in Morocco it was the king's deft response to the protests that prevented them from growing into a revolution, in Algeria it was the bitter memories of the 1990s civil war that resulted in what one observer called "rebellion in installments."[126] In late 2010 and early 2011, Algeria saw scattered protests, acts of civil disobedience, and workers' strikes, all of which were contained by a combination of police action, concessions, and built-in restraint. Similar to their Moroccan counterparts, Algerian protesters did not call for revolution but for reforms, and their demands elicited several responses from the authorities aimed at appeasing them. Specifically, food subsidies were increased, loan conditions were eased, the state of emergency that had been in place since 1992 was lifted, special courts meant to try terrorists were abolished, and a series of "national consultations" with leading public figures took place. The state also introduced a number of constitutional amendments and reforms designed to make the political system more democratic, promised more media access to the opposition, and allowed the establishment of new parties.[127] At the same time, it widened its already extensive patron–client networks and co-opted more figures into its orbit, thereby further helping its maintenance of power and its stability.

President Abdelaziz Bouteflika, in office since 1999, continues to retain some of the popularity and goodwill he had garnered in fostering national reconciliation in the wake of the country's bloody civil war in the 1990s. This relative popularity, along with fears that the country might slip back into the fratricide of the 1990s, and the state's apparent receptiveness to demands by the protesters, prevented protests in Algeria from gaining much popular traction. But the state's impulse for maintaining the status quo since then, by repeatedly amending the constitution to keep the ailing Bouteflika in office, is likely to backfire. In fact, in 2014 a new movement named *Barakat* (Enough) began asking for meaningful openings in political space.[128] In the past, such developments have been undermined by a combination of upgraded authoritarianism on the one hand and tactical concessions on the other. If the same pattern is to be repeated in the future, the prospects for a major uprising in Algeria, of the kind that occurred in Tunisia and Egypt, seem highly unlikely.

Conclusion

Seldom is history marked by a rupture that frees political actors from preexisting constraints and enables them to act as they please. Antecedent power relations are as constraining on actors in society as they are on state elites, although the latter's hold is comparatively loosened during disruptive episodes such as social movements and revolutions. The role of agency, in fact, is particularly pronounced in social movements and revolutions. Those partaking in a social movement may decide to expand the scope of their campaign to press for a total change of regime. In revolutions, some leaders may outsmart and outmaneuver their competitors within the revolutionary movement and in the state. And state leaders themselves need to decide how to respond to social movements or revolutions: dismiss and ignore them and let them run their course; meet their demands halfway and hope their sails are deflated; combat and repress them so that they are contained; or employ any other combination of options that alleviate the threat posed.

Ultimately, what we have in 2010–11 is a series of structural developments, precipitated by the institutional weakness of the state, which opened the space and opportunity for social agents to act and to place demands on the state. In the social movements that ensued, agency had much to do with the direction the movements took, with decisions by state leaders on the one side and by the movements' participants on the other leading to alternative outcomes. Those outcomes, discussed here and in the next chapter, included lack of meaningful political change and business as usual, or civil wars, or, in a couple of instances, revolutions.

The 2010–11 Arab uprisings invariably began as social movements that had been sparked by acts of individual sacrifice and heroism, both deliberate and unintentional. These movements were united more in what they did not want—more of the same—rather than by what they wanted, which remained largely unarticulated and unspoken but was broadly understood. In Tunisia and Egypt, social movements confronted states whose elite cohesion cracked under pressure, in turn facilitating the emergence and eventual success of spontaneous revolutions. In Syria, state actors remained vested in the maintenance of the state as control over parts of the decentralized system gave them incentives for its preservation. Defection from the state was kept to a minimum and a civil war ensued. This civil war was largely facilitated because of the intrusion of external actors soon after the start of the protests in March 2011. Saudi Arabia and Qatar pursued Bashar al-Assad's overthrow with uncommon zeal and poured money and hardware into the conflict and in support of groups hoping to overthrow him—groups that prided themselves on their violent extremism and employment of terrorist tactics. Before long Russia and Iran also got involved, this time to prop up the Assad regime and defeat his opponents. Turkey also involved itself, and sought to make sure that it remained a relevant, if erratic, player in the Syrian crisis. Syria has since become a bloody battleground.

Foreign intervention also turned Libya's regionally-originated social movement into a nationwide civil war. Once protests began in Benghazi, NATO sought to hasten Qaddafi's overthrow by imposing a no-fly zone over Libyan skies. Qaddafi was indeed soon overthrown. But the absence of preexisting state institutions, which he had systematically dismantled over the course of four decades, left the fractious rebels with little of an institutional basis to build on. Once foreign actors, this time Qatar and the UAE, tried to win over the loyalty of the different rebel factions through money and logistical support, civil war was all but inevitable.

The outcome of Yemen's social movement has been equally fraught, again largely because of foreign intervention. What started in Sana'a's Change Square developed enough steam to force the immovable President Saleh eventually out of office. But the fractiousness of those fighting him, and the efforts of outside powers trying to influence outcomes to their own liking—this time Saudi Arabia and Iran—soon plunged the country into civil war.

Bahrain's social movement was crushed before it had any chance of growing into something bigger, or, for that matter, just pursuing its initially modest goal of a more equitable, less discriminatory system. As soon as anti-state protests began to grow in force and scale in early 2011, Saudi Arabia—in whose economic, diplomatic, and political orbit Bahrain firmly belongs—ensured that the dissidents were hammered into submission and had no chance of pressing even modest demands against the state. Just as the Syrian state has deepened its dependence on Iran and Russia (as well as on the Lebanese Hezbollah) as a last-ditch survival strategy, the Bahraini monarchy has done the same in relation to Saudi Arabia and to a lesser extent the UAE.

By way of summary, the above analysis yields four main conclusions. First, elite cohesion is critical in determining the strength or weakness of the state as it encounters pressures brought to bear on it through socially-generated movements for political change. If elite unity cracks under pressure, as it did in Tunisia and Egypt, then it becomes exceedingly difficult for the state to continue to retain power.[129] If defections are kept to a minimum, ostensibly because different elite groups have vested interests in maintaining the status quo, as has been the case in Syria, then the state can linger on even despite ferocious military assaults.

Second, in the face of state weakness and collapse, an absence of relative social cohesion and comparatively lower levels of social homogeneity appear to be positively correlated with civil wars. In Syria, Libya, and Yemen—the countries in which anti-state uprisings ended up in civil wars—preexisting sectarian, regional, and ideational cleavages were polarized during the course of the uprisings and, within the context of weakened or nonexistent state authority, pitted groups and communities against one another. It would not have been surprising for Bahrain's social movement to have had a similar outcome had it not been crushed early on.

Polarization of social heterogeneity during uprisings touches on a third conclusion, namely the potentially decisive roles played by outside actors in influencing and shaping outcomes. All states draw strengths and weaknesses domestically *as well as* internationally. The overthrows of Ben Ali and Mubarak were largely domestic affairs. If anything, they were facilitated through a *lack* of international intervention, ostensibly by the United States. In the opposite direction, Iranian and Russian interventions have kept the Syrian state from collapsing. And Saudi Arabia's regional activities have been consequential in directly shaping outcomes in Bahrain, Syria, Yemen, and, later on in the process, in Egypt. Not to be left on the margins, at different times Qatar and Turkey have also tried to direct the uprisings' outcomes in ways supportive of their own objectives.

Finally, as the examples of Morocco and Algeria clearly demonstrate, agency matters. Social movements, state responses, political maneuvers, street protests, and the litany of other efforts that make up politics are, in the final analysis, initiatives undertaken by individuals. As a general rule, institutions may indeed shape the limits and range of individual initiatives. But in most political systems in the Middle East, individuals continue to retain their primacy over institutions. In the episodes under discussion here, the Moroccan king's decision to call for early elections in 2011, and repeated constitutional amendments in Algeria to keep President Bouteflika in office, are cases in point. How social movements evolve and affect the body politic often depends on the state and its resilience, and frequently how the state responds depends on the initiatives of its leadership.

Elite solidarity and institutional unity, social cohesion and cleavages, foreign interventions, and agency—all variables influencing the outcomes of uprisings in 2010–11—have also shaped the nature of the Arab states that emerged in the post-2011 period. It is to the analysis of these states that the next chapter turns.

4

NEW SETTINGS, OLD PATTERNS

Early hopes that the 2011 uprisings, optimistically called the Arab Spring in the early years, would usher in an era of democracy across the Arab world and the rest of the Middle East did not come to pass. Soon, in fact, it became painfully obvious that the uprisings mirrored not so much the velvet revolutions of 1989 in Eastern Europe, but the rebellions that rocked Europe back in 1848. Ironically, those earlier rebellions, which similarly ended up in the reassertion of power by repressive political systems and the disillusionment of those who had fought in them, were also called the "Springtime of Nations."[1]

Given the magnitude of the apparent changes underway across the Arab world in the final weeks of 2010 and early 2011, and the hopeful optimism that characterized the collapse of long-reigning autocrats from Tunisia to Egypt and Libya, it was only natural for scholars of the region also to be optimistic about the prospects of their outcomes. One scholar confidently declared that "the Arab world that emerges from the Arab Spring will be fundamentally different."[2] In the new Arab order, he argued, there would be decreasing significance attached to the role of individual persons and leaders as key decision-makers.[3] Another observer reasoned that since the uprisings were forms of decentralized, "inter-linked nodal points" of "post-modern resistance" with "universal aspirations for freedom and democracy," their outcomes "could institutionalize those norms systematically and for the long run."[4]

But such was not to be. Within a couple of years of the 2011 uprisings it became evident that they resembled those of 1848 rather than 1989. In 1989, the broader context within which the revolutions of Eastern Europe occurred was much more supportive of political liberalism and democracy. This context included the ideational and practical bankruptcy of communism as a system of rule, US support for democratic transitions, and promises of greater integration into NATO and the European Union if Eastern Europe adopted the ways of Western Europe.[5] In 2011, instead of pressing the authoritarian governments of the Middle East to liberalize, many external actors, both in the West and inside the region, did their best to ensure that the outcomes of the uprisings were not democratic. There were, of course, other differences. In 2010–11, unemployment in the Arab states was higher than it was in Eastern Europe in the 1980s, civil society was more controlled and restricted, exports were less diverse, and reliance on foreign economic assistance was more extensive. Also, whereas in Eastern Europe only one alternative to the communist regime was imaginable, in the Arab world there were multiple models to emulate.[6]

In the mayhem that ensued in North Africa and the Levant in 2010 and 2011, three sets of actors made their presence felt: those wishing to reimpose the old order; those wanting to tweak but largely accommodate the system; and those seeking to overthrow it completely.[7] As it turned out, those wanting to reimpose or at most to tweak the old order so that it could be preserved came out on top in most countries. Despite pervasive demands for constitutionally guaranteed civil and political liberties, the 2010–11 uprisings did not turn into the "constitutional revolutions" that some had hoped for.[8] Only in Tunisia did a protracted process of transition get off the ground in earnest, the outcome of which is, as of this writing at least, not fully clear.

This chapter examines the political and institutional responses of Arab states to the 2011 uprisings. It begins with a broader examination of authoritarian systems and their efforts to prolong their longevity. In specific relation to the Arab world, I argue that the events of 2011 constituted a historical opportunity to craft political systems that were fundamentally different from those of the pre-uprising era. These critical junctures presented political actors with a relatively wider array of institutional choices and arrangements from which they could construct new, democratic systems of authority. For a variety of reasons, only Tunisia's political actors availed themselves of the opportunity hence presented. All others chose to rebrand, or at most to recraft, preexisting political systems, sometimes through new elections and sometimes going as far as adding new institutions. At most, however, such institutional layering amounted to nothing more than putting lipstick on a pig; the old system has persevered.

It was especially the coercive apparatuses of the state, the armed forces, that asserted—or in the case of Egypt reasserted—their political dominance. We shall see in Chapter 5 that the new states are, by and large, bereft of legitimacy, and new state actors have been unable to reestablish the hegemony of their ideological apparatuses. But they were, by and large, able to capture (or in Syria hold on to) political power through the coercive apparatuses of the state.

Why were they able to do so? The answer lies in the combination and interplay between agency and institutional dynamics. To begin with, institutions are often designed to be resistant to change—what some have called "institutional stickiness"—with institutional designers often devising rules and mechanisms that make preexisting arrangements difficult to change.[9] Moreover, "the stickiness, and therefore likely success, of any proposed institutional change is a function of that institution's status in relationship to indigenous agents in the previous time period."[10] The wider the reach and resonance of an institution among social actors, the more sticky, or durable, it is likely to be. It is hardly surprising that the Egyptian armed forces, for example, felt sufficiently confident to step in and reverse the course of the country's revolution.

Another related factor is the role of agency. Personal decisions are highly significant, especially during periods of uncertainty or in critical junctures, when the choices made can have long-term and far-reaching consequences. In the Egyptian case, President Morsi's personal lack of popularity and his seeming incompetence, coupled with General el-Sisi's ambitions and appetite for power, were clearly instrumental in shaping the direction of events. In Syria, had Bashar al-Assad met with the families of the Daraa schoolboys who were beaten by the police instead of mocking and dismissing them as agents of Zionism, most likely his continued personal popularity would have carried the day.[11] And in Tunisia, much of the credit for the crafting of an ostensibly democratic polity after Ben Ali's overthrow goes to the growing power and dominance of more moderate and far-sighted figures within the Ennahda party.

The persistence of authoritarian systems has come through various forms of institutional manipulation and at the expense of processes of economic development, or, more accurately, policy changes that may remedy economic stagnation. The flawed economic policies of the pre-uprising era remain largely in force today. Bereft of economic, and mostly political, legitimacy, the authoritarian systems of the Arab world have persisted by having been underwritten by the institution of the military. Whatever changes may have happened to the armed forces during the uprisings, the underlying logic of their relationship with civilian authorities, namely one of support for the authoritarian status quo, has remained the same. As we have seen so far, the armed forces were key to the possibilities for the eruption and then the direction of the uprisings. As such, civil–military relations continue to be central to the conduct and functions of post-uprising states. After discussing the reasons behind lingering authoritarianism and economic stagnation, the chapter moves to a survey of the causes and consequences of institutional responses to the uprisings by each of the states affected.

Authoritarian persistence and economic neglect

The 2011 uprisings may have changed political leaders, but by and large they did not alter socioeconomic conditions. In fact, there has not been any meaningful reexamination of the pre-uprising era, no critical discourse regarding the past, and no project of national reconciliation.[12] The uprisings have brought with them more continuity than change, with elites trying to reconstitute themselves.[13] As Daniel Brumberg has observed, authoritarian persistence in the Arab world has had much to do with the protection racket systems that manipulated "a wide array of ethnic, religious, and sociocultural groups by playing upon their fears of political exclusion (or worse) under majority rule and offering them *Godfather*-style 'protection' in return for political support."[14] In some countries, in fact, there has been a resurgence of authoritarianism through exclusionary and dictatorial means. After the uprisings, ruling elites in the Arab world have learned how to contain and limit the revolutionary potential of protest movements. Many Middle East states have demonstrated a capacity for authoritarian learning, therefore prolonging their durability.[15] Regimes across the Middle East have upgraded their capacities to deal with and repress street protests, uprisings, and insurgencies.[16] Over time, in fact, path dependence has undermined the political innovativeness of authoritarian survivors, reinforcing survival strategies based on increased repression.[17]

Despite their inherent susceptibility to revolutions and rebellions, authoritarian regimes often contain features within them that enhance their long-term resilience and survivability. By definition, such regimes feature limited political pluralism and are instead characterized by high levels of political apathy and demobilization.[18] More importantly, they often rely not so much on ideology but on "mentalities." Juan Linz sees these mentalities as "ways of thinking and feeling, more emotional than rational, that provide noncodified ways of reacting to different situations."[19] Authoritarian politics are often shaped by two conflicts, one revolving around the problem of authoritarian control—how to rule over the ruled—and the other the problem of authoritarian power-sharing.[20] In solving these problems, and to thwart rebellions and elicit cooperation, dictators are frequently forced into making concessions. In dictatorships, this is often done through a proliferation of institutions, which for dictators have the potential of reducing political transaction costs. As we saw in Chapter 2, one such favorite institution is that of the legislature, which is frequently used as an instrument of co-option and policy compromises.[21] Legislatures enable dictators to give limited access to select groups, avoid the potential of popular mobilization, and to engage with them in a form of controlled bargaining. Along with political parties, they ease the task of governing, since "opposition demands can be made and contained within these institutions."[22] These and other formal institutions are often reinforced and complemented by informal ones, in terms of socially shared rules that are created, communicated, and enforced outside officially sanctioned channels. Such informal institutions—which often include various forms of vote buying, organized corruption, and privatized violence—are especially central to authoritarian regimes.[23]

As we have seen so far, in Arab states, the role of leadership and the centrality of decision-making by the *hakim* (ruler)—whether the king or the president—are centrally important. Also quite significant are the secret service agencies, the military, the party, and economic cronyism. But in the immediate aftermath of the uprisings, perhaps the most important undertaking by a number of Arab states was to resort to various forms of upgraded and reinvigorated "competitive authoritarianism." Steven Levitsky and Lucian Way define such systems as those in which competition is real but unfair, and when incumbents use state resources, unfair media access, electoral manipulation, and harassment and violence to skew the playing field in their own favor.[24] In competitive authoritarian states, formal institutions are highly unstable and formal rules are weakly enforced, and the formal rules and agencies meant to constrain state actors are often manipulated, circumvented, or dismantled.[25] The Algerian, Moroccan, Egyptian (after 2013), Jordanian, and Iraqi states can all be classified as competitive authoritarian. Following the 2011 uprisings, as part of their survival strategies, such states undertook extensive reforms meant to address many of the grievances felt across the different social spectra.[26] Through these reforms, the state has sought to highlight its responsiveness to popular demands, while ensuring that its fundamentally authoritarian modus operandi remains unchanged.

Liberalized autocracies tend to be among the most resilient forms of authoritarian systems.[27] With coercion as an ever-present political factor, such systems contain inherent features meant to deflate political pressures before they reach boiling point. These features had always been part and parcel of most Arab states beginning in the 1950s and 1960s. But by the 1990s and 2000s, their sterility and stagnation had become more of a liability and a source of popular anger rather than a means to deflate tensions and deflect blame. The uprisings gave rise to hopes of a different political order, and to aspirations of keeping elected leaders in check and ensuring accountability for their actions. But old political patterns soon reemerged; the much-hoped-for "democracy" was not meant to be. Today, despite the excitement and sense of anticipation generated by the 2011 uprisings, the political systems that populate the Arab world are overwhelmingly authoritarian and autocratic.

Why did old political patterns and practices reemerge? The answer lies in the actions and initiatives of political actors and leaders. The 2011 uprisings represented nothing less than critical junctures in the lives and historical evolutions of Arab states, both those experiencing mass uprisings and those managing to hold them at bay. Critical junctures, as explained in Chapter 2, are moments of historical rupture and discontinuity in which political actors are faced with a range of choices before them, many of which were not previously available. In ordinary times, actors' choices are constrained by the institutions within which they operate. But not so during critical junctures, when temporary removals of constraint on political action increase the number of available choices. Whatever choices are made in turn set into motion path-dependent processes that become significantly more difficult to alter later on.[28]

In 2010–11, Arab political actors made a series of decisions that turned out to have significant repercussions for the institutional makeup and overall behavior of their political systems. These decisions were made for the specific purposes of reversing the intent and motives behind the uprisings, ignoring and repressing demands for wholesale political change, and reasserting authoritarian political control over society through the institutions of the state. Those states that could, regrouped and reasserted themselves—in Algeria, Morocco, Egypt, Jordan, Iraq, and Bahrain. In Libya, Syria, and Yemen the fissures were too deep for power to be easily reasserted, now reinforced by social chasms far too wide to be closed by states that were either weakened or altogether non-existent.

For their part, Arab societies also became too fragmented and too mired in the struggles of daily life to mount continued challenges to the authoritarian impulses of political actors. Instead of improvements to the daily lives of individuals, across most of the Arab world the security situation deteriorated after 2011, unemployment remained high, and the state's management of the economy has continued to be inadequate.[29] Few individuals see notable improvements in their lives today as compared to before the uprisings. In Egypt, where the excitement of the revolutionary moment was kept alive the longest by anger over the military's hijacking of the people's revolution, the popular movement eventually died down, if not by itself by the sheer repression of what became a fascist dictatorship. Elsewhere, life's impulse for normalcy slowly overshadowed popular appetite for street protests and rebellion.

The post-2011 period has been notable for its lack of economic improvements to people's daily lives. If anything, both macro- and microeconomic conditions have deteriorated drastically, hitting both the state's coffers and people's pockets. The 2014 crash in the oil and gas markets was particularly difficult for the Arab oil producers, slashing, for example, Algeria's state budget from $110 billion in 2015 to $63 billion in 2017.[30] For many of the states without oil revenues of their own, as in Morocco, Tunisia, Egypt, and Jordan, solvency meant ever-closer ties with and dependence on the oil producers of the Persian Gulf.[31] A 2016 report by the World Bank indicated that while the Maghreb region witnessed declines in extreme poverty, inequality persisted and unemployment remained especially high in Tunisia, Algeria, and Libya.[32] These economic difficulties were compounded by the state elites' inability to formulate new economic policies that would generate growth and development. State actors were unable to rethink any of the failed economic strategies of the pre-uprising era. By and large, at any rate, the composition of the ruling elite has also not changed because of the uprisings. In countries such as Morocco, Egypt, and Tunisia, the uprisings afforded the perfect opportunity to revise social policy in ways that were both congruent with popular demands and which also addressed the new, post-transition circumstances.[33] Across the board, however, policymakers "suffer from a lack of imagination in terms of economic policy options."[34]

The state's formal and informal management of the economy remains largely the same as it was before 2011. By and large, the personalization and informality that characterized the relationship between the state and the economic elite has not changed. State actors themselves have been unwilling to risk implementing comprehensive institutional transformations needed for job creation and the effective provision of essential services by the state. Neither have the negative consequences of the structural adjustment programs of the 1980s and the 1990s gone away. The earlier social policies that were meant to assist lower-income groups and to share state income with the masses, such as job-creation schemes and extensive state-provided welfare, remain in place but have proven ineffective in alleviating poverty and providing adequate safety nets. New and innovative strategies to generate economic development remain conspicuously absent.

Authoritarian resilience and continued economic neglect were, by and large, the only common denominators that the post-2011 Arab states shared in their trajectories. Across North Africa and the Levant, the three distinct patterns of state rule that were initiated during the uprisings continued once the rebellions subsided. In Libya, Syria, and Yemen, state fragility and social fragmentation ushered in civil wars. In Morocco, Algeria, Egypt, Jordan, and Iraq, the pre-2011 elites managed to hold on to power, at times barely, as was the case in Iraq, and at times after a year-long interruption, as happened in Egypt. And in Tunisia, state elites, comprised of soft-liners from the old regime and new actors emerging during and after the uprisings, set out to craft an entirely new system. Each of these cases will be analyzed in greater detail below. Before doing so, however, it is important to delve deeper into the roles that the armed forces played across the region both during and in the immediate aftermath of the uprisings. Arab militaries, after all, played central, if decidedly different, roles in the evolution of state institutions in the post-2011 period.

Civil–military relations

The uprisings and the reconfiguration of long-established political formulae presented Arab militaries with the question of how to position themselves in the post-uprising political settings. The armed forces were central to the success or failure of the uprisings, and if they splintered, as they did in Yemen and Libya, civil war was the most likely outcome. As such, the military's relationship with the institutions of political rule and its position and posture within the state have been one of the defining variables in shaping the evolution of post-uprising states. One observer of Arab armies went so far as to say in 2013 that "what is at stake is a redefinition of the role of the military in the Arab world."[35] Today, as the following pages demonstrate, there is scant evidence to suggest that any meaningful redefinition of the role of the military in Arab politics has taken place.

This section examines the nature of civil–military relations in the Arab world after 2011. It begins with an examination of the general dynamics that characterize the relationship between the military establishment and nonmilitary institutions of power in political systems similar to those in North Africa and the Levant. The section then looks at the means and consequences of efforts to prevent the occurrence of coups—what the literature has labeled as "coup-proofing"—as well as the effects on the armed forces of wars and war-making. The section ends with a discussion of typologies of Arab armies after 2011.

The 2011 uprisings put to the test the relationship between long-reigning dictators and the institution of the armed forces, many of whom—especially in places like Algeria, Egypt, and Yemen—had seen some of their enormous political power eroded as the state began relying more intimately on the police and the intelligence agencies. When nondemocratic leaders are faced with a crisis of rule, the military is likely to find itself in one of three circumstances.[36] Military elites may find that they have both the will and the capacity to rescue nondemocratic leaders; this was the case in countries such as Algeria, Jordan, Bahrain, and Oman. In a second scenario, the armed forces may have the will but not the capacity to rescue nondemocratic leaders, as witnessed in relation to Egypt and, more starkly, also Syria. As we shall see shortly, despite widespread desertions and defections, the Syrian army has remained largely loyal to Bashar al-Assad, bolstered by support from Iran and Russia. By itself, however, the military has not been able to rescue Assad's rule. Finally, military leaders may have neither the will nor the capacity to rescue nondemocratic leaders; this is precisely what transpired in Tunisia, where a politically ineffectual military had little or no appetite for rushing to Ben Ali's rescue.

Whereas direct forms of military rule are relatively rare, particularly in the twenty-first century, indirect forms of military intervention in politics—what Samuel Finer calls "quasi-civilian façade of government"—are more common.[37] Except for Egypt, where General Abdel Fattah el-Sisi, at the time chief of the armed forces and minister of defense, took over the government and overthrew an elected, civilian president, most Arab militaries have preferred to operate politically behind the scenes.[38] According to Finer, despite several built-in advantages over civilian leaders, military establishments are often reluctant to intervene directly in politics. This reluctance can be traced to the military having a defined sense of social responsibility, having internalized the principles of civilian supremacy, or structural factors such as fear of degrading its fighting abilities.[39] When the military does intervene, as it did in Egypt, it is frequently driven by a sense of manifest destiny, or by the corporate interests of the armed forces as an institution, or the interests of sections or specific individuals within it.

El-Sisi's *coup d'état* took place in June 2013, and, despite a façade of civilianization, his rule remains fundamentally anchored in the armed forces. An overwhelming majority of the country's provincial governors, for example, come from military backgrounds, as do most managers and directors of state-run and semi-public enterprises. The Egyptian military's economic empire continues to grow unabated, often with sanction and assistance from other organs of the state. Ironically, this very intimate involvement in political affairs is likely to undermine rather than enhance the efficacy and professionalism of the Egyptian military.[40] Historically, when military officers have taken over the reins of states in Arab countries, their relationship with the military establishment has not always been harmonious, having resulted in poor military performance during military conflicts.[41]

Across the Arab world, both before and after the uprisings, state leaders, even in countries like Egypt and Algeria where the military continues to be a dominant political force, have remained concerned about the possibility of military takeovers. Most authoritarian leaders, after all, lose power at the hands of regime insiders rather than to mass uprisings.[42] Autocrats tend to increase their vulnerability to coups and to other forms of opposition the more they prolong their tenure in office. At the same time, as Ben Ali and Mubarak learned the hard way, the loyalty of the officer corps and the top brass decreases the more the autocrat stays in power. Power transitions can also prove perilous for civilian leaders, especially for those whose hold on power is tenuous early in their tenure.[43] Plotters often attempt coups soon after power turnovers, as President Morsi experienced after only a year in office.

Not surprisingly, coup-proofing has been employed frequently by state leaders across the Arab world to minimize the possibility of military takeovers. Some commonly-used methods of coup-proofing have included cultivating loyalty within the armed forces based on ethnic, religious, and personal bonds (as in Syria); the recruitment of officers from among privileged minority groups (in Syria and Bahrain); the establishment of multiple security agencies that keep watch over each other; and buying off officer corps through privileges.[44] Equally widespread is resort to ideology and identity-related solidarity as coup-proofing mechanisms.[45]

Largely due to various coup-proofing measures, beginning in the 1980s, the number of coups in the Middle East dropped precipitously.[46]

Nevertheless, coup-proofing is only partially successful and does not reduce the risks faced by incumbents, especially since in autocracies coups offer one of the few means of access to power.[47] Coup-proofing may buy autocrats time but it does not always work, with timing and agency being critically important. Coup-proofing may reduce the opportunities for coups but it does not always lower the disposition toward them. Determined coup-plotters adapt to coup-proofing, and wait for the right moment to challenge weak incumbents. Morsi, for example, retired military leaders known for their loyalty to Mubarak, notably Generals Mohamed Hussein Tantawi and Sami Anan, Commander-in-Chief of the Armed Forces and Chief of the General Staff of the Armed Forces respectively, and appointed the little-known el-Sisi to command of the armed forces, only to be overthrown by him.

Perhaps no other Arab military in the post-2011 period has endured the level of stress without implosion that has been the case with the Syrian army. During the country's long and bloody civil war, the Syrian army exhibited many of the pathologies associated with coup-proofing. These pathologies have been magnified under the strains of a particularly brutal and devastating war. In many ways, the Syrian military represents the country's political hierarchy, with the Alawites over-represented in the officer corps and the rank-and-file made up largely of Sunni soldiers. As the civil war has progressed, communal and ideational differences between the officers and the rank-and-file have grown, putting the military under severe strains. In general, those military officers who are part of an underprivileged group are less likely to remain loyal.[48] This has hit the Syrian military particularly hard, with many Sunni soldiers having deserted their posts. The army's numbers shrank from approximately 295,000 soldiers in 2011 to only 120,000 in 2014.[49]

The Syrian government, in the meanwhile, has been unable to incentivize military service with continued financial and material benefits. Financial incentives from the regime and perceptions of regime strength figure in the troops' decision on whether or not to desert. Troops who receive material benefits from the regime are more likely to stay loyal, while those who do not are more likely to desert. But even the most underprivileged troops will not defect if they think that the state is strong enough to weather the crisis facing it.[50]

Civil war and desertions—often, in fact, defections to the opposition motivated by financial considerations—have significantly weakened the fighting ability of the Syrian military. Wars can have extensive structural consequences for states. They can trigger new cycles and forms of contention, legitimize or delegitimize the elite, produce new actors with new or strengthened resources, and they can change the relative power position of the different social actors. In late-developing countries, military mobilization can strengthen political institutions and the authority of political leaders.[51] In much of the Arab world, however, war-making has often exposed the fragility of the state and the weaknesses of leaders, potentially opening up opportunities for political transformation.[52] Nowhere is this fragility more apparent than in Syria, where the state is barely hanging on to power, thanks largely to the military, which is itself propped up by foreign support.

Unlike the Syrian military, in Egypt and Tunisia, and to a lesser extent in Yemen, the military was not so much pulled into politics but instead it intervened on its own in order to fill the institutional vacuum that was created because of the uprisings. As we saw in Tunisia and Egypt, the military as an institution will side with the civil resistance if it perceives that regime persistence will harm the military's financial, material, or power base. In both Egypt and Tunisia, as well as in Algeria and Jordan, the army has positioned itself as a symbol of the state, carefully cultivating an image of serving the country. This has often been complemented by the efforts of politicians whose actions have been guided more by their own interests than by the wider institutional interests of the state or the country. Iraq's former prime minister, Nouri al-Maliki, for example, tried to cultivate the cult of a strong leader, although he did not succeed. Abdel Fattah el-Sisi has employed a host of propaganda mechanisms to sing the praises of his courage and wisdom, and is trying to promote his own cult of personality.[53] His success is yet to be measured.

Some militaries saw the preservation of their corporate interests in supporting political incumbents. This is what transpired in Bahrain, Syria, and Oman, where the army repressed the uprisings. In Syria, the military elite's desire and efforts designed to defend the regime have been compromised because of desertions and the military's eroded capacity. For their part, during and because of the uprising, the military in Libya imploded, while in Yemen it became fragmented.

Except in countries where the uprisings ended in civil wars—in Libya, Syria, and Yemen—the pre-2011 trend of growth in the size of security forces has not been reversed because of the uprisings. In places where there has been no growth, there has been no reduction in the size of the security forces either. In 2011, for example, the Egyptian security sector numbered 1 million, perhaps closer to 1.5 to 1.7 million, accounting for one-fifth of state employment. In Tunisia, the police went from 49,000 in 2010 to about 98,000 in 2015, or approximately 12 percent of all state employees. In 2014, the Algerian security forces numbered about 590,000 out of a population of 40 million, representing 29 percent of all state employment and 37 percent of permanent public sector employees. In Iraq, in 2015 the security sector numbered 450,000.[54]

Neither growth in size nor the general atmosphere after the uprisings has reversed the prevalence of widespread corruption in Arab security forces. While corruption is most visible among the police, it usually extends to the other branches as well. Yezid Sayigh reports that in most Arab countries there are widespread perceptions of police and army corruption, especially in Egypt, Tunisia, and Yemen. Petty corruption, even for the most mundane of tasks such as processing identity cards, is rampant in many countries, and at the higher ranks corruption is institutionalized.[55] In several states, especially in Tunisia and Iraq, officers buy promotions to the higher ranks and posts that offer more lucrative income streams.[56] In Syria, soldiers often bribe their commanding officers in order to get home leave, only so that they can make arrangements to desert or, worse yet, to defect to opposition rebels.

Despite widespread corruption and other forms of abuse, many Arab security forces have resisted reforms, often using defense of secularism against the Islamist threat as an excuse. This resistance by the security sector to reform has been deep-seated. In places like Egypt and Syria, governing elites have used the threat of terrorism to unleash the terror of the security forces on their opponents, not only thwarting reforms but actually returning to old, bad practices. In Tunisia and Egypt, there was resistance by the security services to civilian oversight and reform. In Libya, security sector reform took the form of large-scale purges, as was done in Yemen, triggering countermobilization.[57]

In the post-uprisings era, three dynamics stand in the way of security sector reform: hyper-politicization, whereby most political decisions become the subject of zero-sum contestation; the extensive and increasing involvement of the security forces in economic activities, including corruption and criminal enterprises; and the close integration of the security forces into the social and cultural norms of society and the perceived sense of social justice. Security sector reform touches on core social values and priorities as held by divergent groups in society. By and large, the middle classes give lower priority to security sector reform and are more concerned about the elimination of crime and dissent. Given the pervasiveness of a sense of insecurity in the wake of the uprisings, public demands for security sector reforms have decreased sharply.[58]

By way of concluding the discussion on militaries in the Arab world after the uprisings, it would be useful to point to general typologies of civil–military relations as they appear to be emerging in the region. Differences in patterns of civil–military relations are rooted in several factors, including decisions and choices made by both civilian and military leaders during and soon after the uprisings; the institutional configurations and relationships that developed among the various organs of the state; and, more specifically, internal dynamics and characteristics within the military establishments themselves. The difference in the relationship between top brass and middle-rank and junior officers was one of the keys in determining whether Arab Spring militaries abandoned dictators, as in Egypt and Tunisia; stayed loyal, as in Syria; or disintegrated, as in Libya.[59] Until well after the street protests had started, for example, Egyptian army commanders stood by the Mubarak regime, abandoning the president only after assessing the costs of not doing so as too high. And as an institution, after a one-year interlude, the Egyptian military basically resurrected the same regime, this time headed by el-Sisi. By contrast, Tunisian military leaders had neither the capacity nor the desire to rescue Ben Ali. What has emerged in Tunisia is a continuation of the pre-2011 pattern of civil–military relations, namely one of civilians overseeing the military.

In the years immediately following the 2011 uprisings, three broad patterns of civil–military relations can be detected across North Africa and the Levant. Not all of these patterns are new and some predate the uprisings, especially in cases where political and systemic disruptions were minimal.[60] The first pattern is one of *intimate nexus* between the military and ostensibly civilian institutions of rule, prime examples of which can be found in Egypt and Algeria. In these regimes, military leaders control the various levers of power, especially at the highest levels of the executive and throughout the middle layers of the bureaucracy and national and provincial administrations. Even if military leaders and appointees officially resign or retire from their military positions, they still retain intimate institutional and professional ties with the armed forces and are considered a part of it. In these types of regimes, the involvement of the armed forces in politics is usually at three levels: the military as the government; the military as the security community, which ensures that the basis of the state remains secure and unchallenged; and the military as an institution, which carries out normal tasks of the military bureaucracy and, when needed, national defense.[61] Possible configurations include an apparent fusion of all three elements; security community dominance; and extraction coup by the military as an institution.[62]

A second pattern of civil–military relations in the Arab world features *civilian oversight* over the military. These include the cases of Morocco, Tunisia, Jordan, and the states of the GCC. In all these cases, the military has refrained from direct political rule of its own volition, deferring to the civilian leadership on political and administrative matters. In the monarchies, civilian dominance over the military has emerged as part and parcel of the state-building process, whereby ruling families dominated and conquered competing tribal clans, usually with foreign backing, and established their hegemony over the coercive institutions of the state early on. Today in the GCC, the higher echelons of the armed forces continue to be dominated by senior members of the ruling family. In addition to a whole array of coup-proofing measures, there is also usually a force akin to a National Guard, which is dominated by loyal tribes and whose primary function is to come to the defense of the ruler in times of need. In Tunisia, meanwhile, both Bourguiba and Ben Ali kept the military weak and small in order to curtail any appetite it might have had for political power. By all accounts, Tunisian military commanders have had no desire to take over the government either before or after the 2011 uprisings.

A third pattern, which except for Lebanon has emerged largely as a direct result of the 2011 uprisings, has been the *militia-ization* of some

Arab armed forces. In Lebanon the state has been chronically weak from the start since the country's independence in 1945. Not surprisingly, the country has had a history of having active and armed non-state actors, most notably in the form of Phalangists in the 1980s and the Hezbollah since then. The country's regular military, meanwhile, has had to contend with sectarian divisions, dwindling resources, and low morale.[63] Elsewhere in the region, in Libya, Syria, and Yemen, the 2011 uprisings led to a weakening or implosion of state institutions and opened up opportunities for non-state actors to pursue their goals through taking up arms. The same thing had occurred earlier in Iraq, when in 2003 the US invasion brought the country to the verge of disintegration and led to a proliferation of armed militias and localized forms of authority.

In all these cases, armed militias have been supported and sustained by external actors, most of them in the form of foreign patrons, and in Daesh's case in the form of recruits and volunteers also. Daesh and its affiliated groups represent anti-state militias in Iraq, Syria, and Libya. In all these cases, there are also militia groups that operate in conjunction with the official military institutions of what remains of the state. In fact, in Libya, Iraq, Syria, and Yemen, militias play important roles in counter-insurgency and counterterrorism. These militias are more flexible than the regular security forces, and they often commit violence against civilian populations with greater impunity. In Yemen, Iraq, and Syria, in the absence of central state authority, there has also been a militia-ization of policing, especially at the community level. In many instances, this militia-ization has been welcomed by local communities, which prefer militias to state-connected local sheikhs and clan leaders.[64]

Despite their prevalence and short-term utility, reliance on armed militias can prove risky for state leaders. Militias have the potential to undermine government control, especially as few are willing to give up their arms voluntarily.[65] Moreover, militias are more prone to use violence against civilians, settle scores, and ignore the rules of warfare. In the cases mentioned, the deeply-held culture of impunity by official security agencies extends to non-state actors as well, making violence a common political currency.[66] Finally, militias facilitate and deepen foreign intrusion into domestic affairs and can serve as instruments of foreign influence in war-torn and authority-deficient communities. In Libya, for example, the UAE has been supporting the renegade General Khalifa Haftar and his militia force. In addition to the Lebanese Hezbollah, Iran has been supporting the Syrian *Shabiha*, the Iraqi Popular Mobilization Forces, and the Houthis in Yemen.[67] Qatar's connections with the al-Qaʿida-affiliated group calling itself the al-Nusra Front have been well-documented, and, not to be left behind, Saudi Arabia has been funding and directing its own militias in Syria and elsewhere.[68]

Institutional adjustments

The snapshot presented here of civil–military relations represents a larger array of institutional changes and adjustments initiated by states in the aftermath of the 2011 uprisings. The impetus for each of these institutional adjustments differed from one country to the next, as did their scope and scale. Prompted by survival strategies in most instances and out of necessity in a few others, state leaders tweaked and tinkered with institutions to mollify public demands for political change and to appear responsive to the masses. Sometimes, as in Oman, Jordan, and Morocco, new elections were held and state leaders promised the dawn of a new, supposedly more democratic era, with the Moroccan monarchy going so far as to inaugurate an entirely new constitution.[69] In other instances, as in Algeria, state leaders managed to ride out the demonstrations with minimal institutional changes, capitalizing on the country's recent troubled past to emphasize the need for political continuity. In cases where the uprisings led to civil wars, in Libya, Syria, and Yemen, institutional implosion or fragmentation were the most likely outcomes. And in Tunisia, what ensued was a deliberative process of institutional engineering in order to craft an entirely new political system.

This section presents a broad survey of some of the institutional responses pursued by states in the aftermath of the 2011 uprisings. The section demonstrates that a combination of interactions between actors, institutions, and strategies constituted critical differences in transition outcomes. In all cases, the interactions of these three variables produced different results. These differences were sometimes slight as compared to the pre-2011 uprisings, and sometimes more pronounced. In all cases, context was of critical importance. For example, whereas in Tunisia the self-immolation of Mohamed Bouazizi in December 2010 was the tragedy that led to the country's mass uprising, similar, separate gestures in Algeria the following month, by two unemployed men named Mohamed Aouichia and Mohsen Bouterfif, failed to have similar consequences. Similarly, much of the credit for Tunisia's relatively peaceful transition goes to the negotiations between soft-liners from the old regime and civil society activists. In what came to be called the Tunisian Provisional Administration (TPA), preexisting state institutions continued to function. In Libya, by contrast, the National Transition Council (NTC) often struggled to reach decisions, and the institutional vacuum in which its members operated made their deliberations all the more difficult.[70]

The institutional responses to the uprisings can be divided into three broad categories. In Algeria, Morocco, and Jordan, pre-2011 states were able to ride out the uprisings with minimal or at best cosmetic institutional adjustments. As Chapter 6 will demonstrate, this was also the case with the states of the Gulf Cooperation Council. In all these cases, state strength in relation to society remained intact throughout the upheavals. Although each country witnessed protests of varying intensity, street demonstrations never reached the scale and ferocity that would threaten the state's hold on power. At the same time, in all these countries the state proactively sought to accommodate the demands of the protesters while at the same time ensuring that the institutional arrangements that supported its operations remained the same. It also appears more than coincidental that in all three countries the state's chief executive continued to retain a measure of personal popularity even as street protesters vented their anger at the state's failed policies.

In a second group of countries, state institutions fragmented or imploded, much the same as their militaries had done. The country disintegrated into civil war and a situation of "dual" or at times "multiple authority polities" emerged in which competing institutions and actors claimed to be the legitimate representatives of the state.[71] Libya, Syria, and Yemen belong to this category of states. Iraq also joined this unfortunate group, or more accurately rejoined it after having only just started to reconstitute itself in the aftermath of the 2003 US invasion and occupation.

In the third group of countries, social movements evolved into actual revolutions and resulted in the overthrow of long-ruling dictatorial regimes. These were Tunisia and Egypt. As it happened, the Egyptian revolution was hijacked by one of the institutional leftovers of the old regime, namely the military, which in turn set out to reverse most of the revolution's early gains. Thus the Tunisian and Egyptian revolutions have taken two very different trajectories, with the Tunisian revolutionaries setting out to craft a new state with new institutional arrangements, while the Egyptians have simply restored or reinvigorated the state's preexisting institutional arrangements.

Let us start with the first group of states, namely those in which the state's response was sufficient to prevent incipient social movements from turning into full-blown revolutions. This group included Algeria, Morocco, and Jordan. The domino effect of the Tunisian uprising reached Algeria in the early days of 2011. January saw frequent demonstrations in Algiers and other cities over high food prices and unemployment. There were also riots and protests in northern cities such as Constantine, Oran, and Fouka, and in the interior, in Ouargla and Béchar. The protest continued into February and March, when street marches occurred in Algiers in solidarity with the Tunisian and Egyptian revolutions. The police response was always stern, and many protests were prevented from taking place or were met with water cannons and batons once they started. But the protests eventually subsided within a few months, and their decline was due to more than the way the security forces handled them.

A number of factors explain Algeria's relatively muted participation in the Arab Spring uprisings. In addition to its police response to the protests, the state soon initiated a number of conciliatory gestures aimed at providing immediate economic relief for the protesters and meeting some of their demands. In February 2011, the country's state of emergency was lifted after nineteen years. The following month pay raises were announced for all public sector employees. President Bouteflika, by now in office more than a decade, and having earlier taken charge of pulling the country out of the morass of civil war, personally appealed to the public to join him in implementing "change at a softer pace."[72]

Perhaps even more important than the government's immediate response to the protests was the country's recent past, one that had seen a bloody and brutal civil war, or, as one of my informants called it, "war against civilians."[73] In 2011, the civil war, which had started in 1991 and lasted a decade, was still part of Algerians' living memory. Between 150,000 and 200,000 Algerians are estimated to have perished during that dark decade. After finally having achieved a semblance of political stability, few were willing to risk the eruption of further turmoil and uncertainty. In the intervening years, the government had instituted a number of highly publicized initiatives aimed at healing some of the wounds of the civil war, most notable of which included the inauguration of a new civil code in 1999; the promulgation of a National Charter for Reconciliation and Peace in 2005; monetary compensations to the families of the "disappeared;" a new amnesty law in 2006; and what appeared to be the personal commitment and determined efforts of President Bouteflika, first elected in 1999, to move the country past its dark and tragic history.[74] By 2011 there was little public appetite for going down a road that potentially might have led to a repeat of the past.

Institutional changes and adjustments undertaken by Algerian state leaders had already occurred before 2011. Apart from what amounted to marginal concessions, the state saw no need to undertake further, more fundamental changes in the aftermath of the protests. In fact, the basic institutional arrangements of the state as articulated in the 1989 constitution remain largely intact, except that the constitution keeps getting amended to allow Bouteflika to run for successive terms of office (in 2008 and 2016). In reality, the nature of "*le pouvoir*" (the power)—a term often used to describe the president, a small group of unelected civilians around him, and the military—has not changed.[75] Institutional and power arrangements remain basically the same. Although dissolved by the president in January 2016 in what appears to have been an attempt at coup-proofing, the Department of Intelligence and Security (DRS) was long considered a central pillar of the regime and was widely credited for having engineered Bouteflika's reelection campaigns in 2004, 2009, and 2014.[76]

It is not really clear whether actual power rests with Bouteflika and his entourage or with the military, or both. In 2015, Bouteflika used a terrorist attack as pretext to remove the heads of three security agencies.[77] Nevertheless, some observers believe that the president's power and influence is symbolic, with the military as the real source of power within the state.[78] The French-Algerian political scientist Lahouari Addi claims that despite being commander-in-chief of the armed forces, the Algerian president does not actually exert any authority over the country's military commanders, among whom there is often intense personal and institutional competition. It is the armed forces, in fact, that remain firmly in control of the state, and the military and its allies remain politically dominant.[79] Addi goes so far as to assert that the Algerian military is not ready to accept the emergence of a civilian power by the electorate, or to allow the president a free hand.[80]

In many ways, the Algerian state's response to the 2011 uprisings mirrored those of Morocco and Jordan. The recent history of Morocco has not been nearly as tormented as Algeria's. In fact, from 1972 to 1992 Moroccan politics was marked by what one observer has called "transitory constitutionalism," after decades in which the king and the state were one and the king completely ignored any constitutional limitations on his power.[81] A year after ascending the throne in 1999, Mohammed VI initiated a series of popular reforms, including releasing all political prisoners and instituting a number of anti-unemployment and anti-poverty measures, earning himself the nickname "the king of the poor."[82] The country was far from democratic, of course, and apart from curtailed civil liberties there were frequent reports of serious abuse and ill-treatment of political prisoners.[83] Politically, the parliament and the cabinet were widely perceived to be auxiliary institutions meant to safeguard the supreme powers and position of the monarchy. The parliament was seen as a mere rubber-stamp.[84] Not surprisingly, throughout the 2000s parliamentary elections had consistently low voter turnout, and high numbers of blank ballots were a sign of protest. The 2007 elections, for example, had a turnout of only 37 percent, and 19 percent of the ballots cast were blank.[85] And, despite the king's claims to religious legitimacy, small networks of Salafi jihadists were active throughout the 2000s.[86]

As Chapter 3 demonstrated, the response of the Moroccan monarchy to the 2011 protests, led by the demands of the February 20 Movement, have turned the state into what may be considered a "semi-constitutional monarchy."[87] Nevertheless, despite the imposition of certain constitutional constraints on the powers of the monarch and greater civil liberties since 2011, the monarchy continues to remain constitutionally and institutionally dominant.[88] Even after the reforms, the substantive powers of the king have not been lessened, and his royal decrees (*dahirs*) still carry the weight of the law. The monarch also continues to retain veto power over all major decisions.[89] As with the Algerian *le pouvoir*, the power and influence of the Moroccan *Makhzen* remains similarly unimpeded.[90] The *Makhzen* continues to have "invisible but remarkable" influence over ruling the country, and the king remains an active and high-profile ruler, as well as a major driver of the reform project.[91] In a number of instances, the Moroccan king has simply ignored or sidestepped constitutional limits on his powers. At the same time, his super-activism has made him appear as indispensable to the operations of the state.[92]

Apart from the monarch's own deft maneuverability, the halted pace of reforms in Morocco can be traced to two additional factors. First, the post-uprising difficulties of Tunisia, Libya, Egypt, and Syria make the Moroccan king's leadership seem safe to Moroccans, who see him as a source of national unity and a protector of the country's territorial integrity.[93] Though not to the same extent as in Algeria, in Morocco there is a sense of "better the devil you know than the one you don't". And Morocco's devil isn't that bad. Second, as has been the case with Jordan, since 2011 the Moroccan monarchy has drawn itself ever closer to the states of the GCC. The massive loans and financial assistance to Morocco by the Persian Gulf sheikhdoms ever since make it appear that they only support slow and incremental reforms rather than major and sudden changes.[94] A fully constitutional monarchy in a fellow Arab kingdom would not, after all, bode well for those in the Arabian Peninsula.

The response of the Jordanian state to the 2011 upheaval was different from that of the Moroccan state mostly in degree rather than in substance. Compared to what transpired in much of North Africa, the 2011 protests in Jordan were mild, and, as in Morocco, the protesters did not necessarily question the rule or legitimacy of the monarchy.[95] Jordan's protest movement, referred to as the *Hirak*, also lacked a unified political vision and remained ineffective.[96] The state responded, meanwhile, with a combination of targeted arrests and co-option. More specifically, the state's response included the establishment of an Independent Election Commission and a Constitutional Court, and also the implementation of a few constitutional amendments meant to make the political system more democratic. None of these measures amounted to any significant alterations to the state, but they did achieve their intended results. In the end, political pressure on the monarchy was not enough to prompt real and substantive changes, and the regime exploited Saudi strategy, US fears of instability, and fragmentation within the *Hirak* in order to preserve itself and the status quo.[97] By mid-2012, the momentum for change had already lost steam.

In the aftermath of the 2011 uprisings, King Abdullah replaced the prime minister and presented a reform package meant to preempt demands for fundamental political changes in the system. The reforms were top-down and were designed to reproduce the system rather than to reform it. The scope of the "reforms" in Jordan was shaped by a number of dynamics, some of which have been part of a longer-term calculus of rule in the kingdom. These dynamics included the role of and dependence on external actors, namely the United States and Saudi Arabia; territorial and demographic legacies of war; and domestic pressures for reform and the state's responses through co-option and repression.[98] The state effectively manipulated these interrelated dynamics to manage demands for reform while maintaining the political status quo as much as possible.

Given its dependence on water and oil, its demography, lack of strategic depth, and its borders with Syria, Iraq, Saudi Arabia, and Israel, the role of Jordan's leadership in statecraft is particularly important.[99] So far, the country's three kings appear to have been up to the challenge. The monarchy, in fact, remains the single most important political institution in Jordan. As compared to the case most similar to it, namely the Moroccan monarchy, the institution of monarchy in Jordan is far more powerful in relation to the country's parliament.

This pivotal centrality of the monarchy to the kingdom's politics is underwritten by the military. Both in ordinary times and in times of difficulty, as in the 2011 unrests, the Jordanian military has been one of the primary supporting pillars of the country's monarchy.[100] Jordan's security services are made up of Bedouins who are among the most loyal of the country's population. They also constitute one of the largest proportions of Bedouins of any Middle Eastern country.[101]

As a survival strategy, the Jordanian monarchy has been implementing piecemeal reforms since 1989. The regime, in fact, has long used parliamentary elections as a survival strategy.[102] Equally frequent has been the king's sacking of sitting prime ministers, with the average Jordanian cabinet lasting no more than fifteen months before being dissolved by royal decree.[103] Another centerpiece of the state's survival strategy appears to be the parliament, complete with contested elections, though in reality neither the parliament nor any of the parliamentarians hold any real power. Cabinet members do not actually come from among parliamentarians.[104] The ruling elite, in fact, often assumes that the kingdom's parliament was not expected to understand, let alone implement, the monarch's vision.[105]

Reinforcing parliamentary weakness in Jordan is the absence of organized parties and factions, prompting one prime minister to admit at a public rally that "there is no role for parliament in shaping policies."[106] That the Jordanian opposition has failed to articulate a clear political vision of its own has reinforced its weakness and the political irrelevance of the parliament.[107] As one observer has noted, "as it stands now, the parliament remains the pawn of the king, who appoints the entire upper house of the parliament as well as the cabinet, holds veto power on legislation, and retains the power to dissolve the parliament at his prerogative."[108] Others have been less kind. One commented that the Jordanian parliament has at times been "a source of comic relief."[109]

It is of little surprise that voter turnout for parliamentary elections has been consistently low. The January 2013 parliamentary elections, for example, were meant to be a key pillar of the king's reform program. But few took the elections seriously, and only 39 percent of eligible voters turned out to vote.[110] For the 2016 parliamentary elections, the state tried to increase voter participation by lowering the voting age to 18, making 17-year-olds eligible to vote if they turned 18 within 90 days of the elections.[111] In the end, only 37 percent of the country's 4.1 million eligible voters took part in the ballot. Part of the problem has been the crown's employment of a series of what it bills as "electoral reforms," all designed to maintain its hegemonic control over the parliament.[112] Across eight elections between 1989 and 2016, the Jordanian regime has employed four different types of electoral systems, with changes often being announced only shortly before the vote.[113] The result has been heavily gerrymandered electoral laws, making the parliament less representative of certain groups and parties while also undermining its effectiveness.[114] Interestingly, given the meaningful absence of political parties or ideological currents, parliamentary elections have been dominated instead by tribal dynamics.[115]

Political parties were legalized in Jordan in 1992, and one of the first parties established was the Islamic Action Front, the political wing of the country's Muslim Brotherhood. The regime's tolerance of and its modus vivendi with the Islamic Action Front constitute the main reasons for the IAF's survival so far.[116] Since its inception, the Jordanian Muslim Brotherhood itself has been more reformist than revolutionary and is relatively moderate compared to its counterparts elsewhere in the region. It has therefore had a relatively long history of operating within the system. The Jordanian Muslim Brotherhood has often been considered a loyal opposition and has been a main impetus for political liberalization.[117] The Islamic Action Front boycotted the 2010 and 2013 parliamentary elections, but did contest the September 2016 elections. Due largely to the state's manipulation of electoral laws, the party was only able to secure 15 seats out of a total of 130.[118]

In addition to the king's own deep mistrust of where a meaningful liberalization process might lead, US and Saudi influences on the kingdom, as well as Jordan's larger geostrategic predicament, also account for its halted steps toward any substantive political openings. Neither the United States nor Saudi Arabia welcome any meaningful political opening in Jordan, and both have sufficient leverage over the country to ensure that their interests are looked after. From 2013 to 2016, for example, the Obama administration provided more than $3.75 billion in loan guarantees to Jordan.[119] In 2016 alone, the United States provided no less than $1.275 billion in bilateral economic and military assistance, and a further $600 million in the form of a Counterterrorism Partnership Fund.[120] In 2016, there were approximately 2,000 US troops stationed in Jordan. Jordan has also been actively involved in the Syrian conflict, and the so-called Southern Front has used Jordanian territory as a staging ground for attacking Syrian army troops.[121] In fact, fearing a security vacuum, the Jordanian leadership was among the first to condemn Assad and also to align itself firmly with the GCC.[122]

The Jordanian response to the upheavals of 2011 may not have been as substantive as those of the Moroccan state, but were nonetheless sufficient to avert a real political crisis for the monarchy. Similar to popular perceptions in Morocco, most Jordanians appear to view developments in nearby countries with great fear and trepidation, preferring to stick with their imperfect, illiberal system than to risk descending into the abyss that is Syria or the unchecked repression of Egypt. According to a 2015 public opinion poll, 53 percent of Jordanians believe that citizens do not have a say in government decision-making on issues that matter to them, and 62 percent say that politicians are not addressing the needs of the young. Nevertheless, some 64 percent of Jordanians believe that the country is headed in the right direction.[123] Had the regional neighborhood been more peaceful, perhaps fewer Jordanians would have endorsed the country's current direction. The end result, ultimately, has been a preservation of the status quo ante. In the words of one observer of Jordanian politics, "the crux of the matter is that the King's prerogatives remain intact."[124]

Whereas the Algerian, Moroccan, and Jordanian states were able to withstand the 2011 unrests with minimal and at most superficial institutional adjustments, the states in Libya, Syria, and Yemen were not nearly as fortunate. In the former set, the comparative mildness of the protests and their demands was also central in shaping the state's response. But in Libya, Syria, and Yemen the protests soon mushroomed into mass uprisings, under the stress of which the state either fragmented or altogether imploded. The stress soon engulfed the already fragile Iraqi state as well, which was still struggling to reconstitute itself following its dismemberment by the United States in 2003. Bahrain also witnessed an uprising of its own, led by the country's disenfranchised Shia majority. It is difficult to predict which way the small kingdom's uprising would have evolved had it not been crushed by the country's security forces and by troops from Saudi Arabia and the UAE. Most likely the regime would have persevered anyway as Bahraini troops had nothing to gain from regime change but would have lost sectarian political privileges and naturalized citizenship. Military loyalty to the Al-Khalifa ruling family, key to the power maintenance for any state, is unlikely to have been reversed.[125]

For Iraq, it is also the military that has been key for the reconstitution of the Iraqi state. The process of rebuilding the Iraqi army, begun in earnest in 2005, was fraught from the start. Political sectarianism and especially quotas (*muhasasa*) weakened the army beyond repair, as they became the criteria for appointments in place of meritocracy.[126] Sectarianism soon became widespread within the military, with many of the divisions being identified with one sect or another. The spillover effects of the Syrian conflict only added potency to sectarian feelings in Iraq and across the various institutions of the state, especially the military. The army's Eighth Division, for example, is identified with the Dawa Party, the Seventh Division with the Sunni Iraqi Awakening Party, and the Fifth Division with the Shia Islamic Supreme Council.[127] Precisely because of such sectarian leanings and narrow appeals, vocal political support for the army as a national institution is conspicuously absent.

Political machinations, meanwhile, have severely undermined the military's efficacy and fighting ability. Former prime minister Nouri al-Maliki (2006–14) was concerned about the potential of a military takeover and therefore "coup-proofed the Iraqi army to death" and gutted it from above.[128] After the fall of Mosul to Daesh rebels in summer 2014, fearing a backlash, Maliki sidelined others and directly interfered in military matters, including in issues related to personnel and military equipment. Al-Maliki may have achieved his objective of neutralizing the army as a political force, but in the process he also weakened its ability to hold the country together. This only further facilitated the proliferation of local and foreign-backed militias in their efforts to exploit the political and military vacuums left by the army's absence.

In Iraq, beginning in 2003 the American invasion authorities set out systematically to dismantle the institutions of rule that had been set up by Saddam Hussein. In Libya, the task was done by the country's ruler, Moammar Qaddafi, over the course of his long reign. For all of Qaddafi's revolutionary rhetoric and his military build-up, he kept the country's military politically weak lest it launch a coup. Consistent with his vision of a stateless society, other institutions of the state were also kept underdeveloped and often suffered from lack of efficacy and insufficient penetration of society. The Libyan military was particularly politicized, lacked institutionalization, and was rife with patrimonialism.[129] What command-and-control organs existed within the military, even those of the elite units, were controlled by Qaddafi's own family members.[130]

As the uprising erupted, Libyan state institutions simply melted away. Initially, elite military units had no desire to alter the status quo.

Most units sat on the fence and were uncertain of their loyalty to Qaddafi or sympathy for the uprising.[131] The NATO intervention appears to have been the decisive factor, leading to the military's speedy disintegration.[132]

As the Qaddafi state was disintegrating, a National Transition Council (NTC) was formed to decide on the parameters of the new political order and to pave the way for new state institutions to take over. But from the very beginning the NTC proved unable to overcome the institutional dysfunction that had characterized the Qaddafi era. NTC actors came from diverse political and military backgrounds, many having very different perspectives and visions of the future. They had no history of working together, and their work was very much affected by interpersonal relations. The council also had no overall, unifying strategy, and was often unable to reach decisions. In fact, the NTC never institutionalized its decision-making process, which remained ad hoc throughout.[133]

The NTC had no baseline from which it could start, and neither did it have any constitutional—or for that matter institutional frame of reference—on which it could build a new political order. It fell short of establishing fully legitimate state institutions, and its efforts at disarming fighters and restoring stability were "disorganized and lacking a central authority or system."[134] Before long, the country was plunged into civil war, institutional dysfunctions only feeding multiple fissures along geographic lines. As in Iraq, space and opportunity was opened for foreign intrusion. The NTC was itself largely responsible for paving the way for external actors as its prioritization of external assistance came at the expense of reaching internal unity. First Qatar and later the UAE sought to capitalize on the power vacuum in Libya and to patronize militias willing to enhance their influence in the country.

Unlike Libya, in Syria the pre-2011 state has managed to survive, but just barely. Over the course of a particularly brutal civil war, sometimes the state and sometimes the collection of rebel groups fighting it have gained the upper hand. Every time one side seems to be on the verge of defeat, its foreign patrons rush to its support with additional weapons and supplies, and sometimes with actual fighters, thus prolonging the country's tragedy.

During the course of the Syrian civil war, the state has sought to position itself as a unique provider of essential services. The bureaucratic functions of the state have been consolidated into "highly defensible urban power centers" under the regime's control.[135] The regime has destroyed the alternative structures set up by Daesh in an effort to reinforce its own continuity. The brutality of Daesh, meanwhile, has reinforced the regime's narrative that it is the only source capable of providing essential services. The expansion of Daesh, extremist and brutal as it is, has benefited the Syrian state as it has undermined other, relatively moderate opposition groups and has legitimized the state's narrative. Due largely to pressure by the Syrian state, the moderate opposition has not been able to devise methods of local administration and to provide public services.[136] At the same time, the high concentration of civilians in areas under the control of the Syrian state works to its advantage as it has created disincentives for the opposition to attack. The Syrian state's ability to provide essential services even in areas outside its control is one of the key reasons for its continued ability to stay in power.

The increasing sectarianization of the conflict explains why most Syrians have stayed at home and the rebellion has not assumed the wide scale of a popular uprising.[137] In the meanwhile, war-making has compelled the Assad regime to reconfigure its social base, tighten its dependency on global authoritarian networks, adapt its mode of economic governance, and restructure its military and security apparatus. War in Syria has been a catalyst for authoritarian restructuring.[138]

This authoritarian restructuring has featured greater than ever reliance by the state on the country's armed forces, or what is left of them. Before the uprisings, the Syrian military was regarded as an instrument of political suppression and suffered from waning social prestige.[139] The military entered the uprising with little or no sectarian sentiments, despite the fact that the Alawites were overrepresented in the officer corps. But as the civil war progressed, grievances began to be articulated along sectarian lines as levels of distrust grew among soldiers and officers from the different sects.[140] With the cohesion of its military under threat, the Syrian regime started relying on counterinsurgency tactics and on irregular, pro-regime militias (*shabiha*).[141] The *shabiha* originated in smuggling and racketeering networks that operated under Bashar al-Assad's protection, and during the war they have provided some protection for Alawites and Christians.[142]

As the war dragged on and grew in scale and brutality, the regime worked to discourage desertions through promoting the sectarian narrative and increasing mistrust among the ranks. It also enhanced material incentives for military service, and turned a blind eye to corruption and self-enrichment opportunities. There have been a number of pay raises for Syrian military and security officers since the war began. Corruption within the military is rampant, with military personnel often bribing officers to get vacations—frequently in order to arrange for defections—or selling their weapons or fuel to the rebels.[143] Volunteers mostly join the Syrian army out of economic necessity, and some have experienced upward social and economic mobility as a result.

Rebel recruitment in Syria is also heavily influenced by economic factors. Desertions and defections in the regular army are primarily by the rank-and-file. Seldom are defections or desertions for ideological reasons; most soldiers simply do not want to fight.[144] Some deserters have joined the rebels for material reasons and in order to partake in the informal civil war economy that has emerged in rebel-held areas. For some defectors, joining rebel forces has proven financially lucrative.

In societies fractured along sectarian lines, as in Syria and Iraq, reliance on the militia can increase feelings of alienation and mistrust, even pushing some to join the opposition and Daesh.[145] Even if a political solution is reached by the various domestic and international actors involved in the Syrian conflict, the multiple wounds of the civil war that began in 2011—emotional, sectarian, infrastructural, institutional wounds—are far too deep to be easily healed. The mending of the Syrian state requires far more than institutional engineering. It requires the rebuilding of millions of lives.

Yemen's fate after 2011 has been equally tormented. The state that Ali Abdullah Saleh had built rested on two central and interrelated pillars, namely the military and the presidency. Saleh's presidency and the administrative apparatus over which his office presided overshadowed most other institutions of the state, except for the military, though the distinction between the two was not always clear. Among the cohort of presidents-for-life that included the likes of Qaddafi, Ben Ali, and Mubarak, Saleh was one of the wiliest, and perhaps the one to have amassed the most wealth during his long tenure in office. Saleh

(1942–2017) first became president of North Yemen in 1978, and then of the unified Yemen when North and South united in 1990. The president likened rule over Yemen to "dancing on the heads of snakes," a perilous challenge to which, he claimed, only he was equal.[146]

Much of the political system that evolved in Yemen was built around the president and his cronies, which included close family members, friends and associates, tribal elders, and a select number of top military commanders. A House of Representatives (*Majlis al-Nuwaab*) served as the country's parliament, but its functions were far more perfunctory than substantive. Even then, after the elections of 1993, 1997, and 2003, the body became dominated by Saleh's party, the General People's Conference.[147] Saleh kept himself at the apex of a system in which multiple potential centers of power—the military, the tribes, the bureaucracy—were all kept weak and dependent on him. Underwriting the whole system was the military, whose different units were commanded by the president and his close relatives.

When Saleh was finally forced out of office in February 2012, the whole system crumbled and fragmented into multiple pieces. Government services, already barely functional, mostly came to a halt. The military also fragmented, with different brigades and divisions either remaining loyal to Saleh and his relatives or counterbalancing them.[148] The restive tribes also erupted, with the Houthi insurgency spreading from its northern stronghold of Sa'ada into other parts of the country, including temporarily taking over Sanaa, the capital, in 2014–15. In his bid to recapture power, Saleh entered into a military alliance with the Houthis. But Saudi Arabia, which has always seen itself as the rightful hegemonic power in southern Arabia, saw the rise of the Shia Houthis as a sign of Iranian ascendance in its backyard. In 2015, Saudi forces invaded Yemen, plunging the country further into despair and conflict. As the alliance between the two began to falter, the Houthis turned on Saleh, killing the former president in November 2017. As of this writing, in 2018, there are no signs of peace and very few signs of functioning state institutions in Yemen.

Somewhere between the institutional continuities of Morocco, Algeria, and Jordan on the one side and the institutional collapse and fragmentations of Libya, Syria, and Yemen fall the cases of Egypt and Tunisia. In both countries, the social movements of late 2010 turned into successful revolutions in early 2011. But in one case the revolution was hijacked and reversed, while in the other it was allowed to evolve and to succeed. The deciding difference between these two cases appears to have been the interaction of agency and institutions, or, more accurately, the choices made by political leaders within the context of the institutions and institutional resources that were at their disposal. In Egypt, the institution of the military, powerful under Mubarak, remained central to the unfolding political drama. When the military saw that events were moving in a direction that was inimical to its actual and ideological interests, it took matters into its own hands and reversed the course of the revolution. In Tunisia, the military had not been that much of a political force under Ben Ali, and was in no position to dictate the course of events in the heady weeks and months after his departure. Instead it was a newly-established civilian institution, the Tunisian Provisional Authority, which was mandated to craft a new political system. The trajectories that thus ensued in the two countries could not have been more different.

In Egypt, in the final days of the Mubarak presidency, Egyptians were reintroduced to a statuary body within the government called the Supreme Council of the Armed Forces. Originally established by Nasser in 1954, the SCAF was made up of twenty-five senior military commanders and was meant to be convened in times of national crisis. Though in recent years the council had mostly existed only on paper, it previously had met during the 1956 Suez War, the Yemen conflict from 1964 to 1967, and the 1967 and 1973 wars. Only allowed to be convened by the president or the defense minister, the SCAF's last substantive meeting had been in 1981, following the assassination of President Sadat. In 2011, the council first met on 9 February, under Mubarak's chairmanship. The following day, without the president present and under the chairmanship of Defense Minister Tantawi, the council announced in a statement that "in affirmation and support for the legitimate demands of the people," it is in "continuous session to consider what procedures and measures may be taken to protect the nation." The following day, on 11 February, Mubarak resigned.

From the very beginning, the SCAF provided a powerful institutional means for the Egyptian armed forces to direct the course of events as they developed. In doing so, the SCAF faced a dilemma in how to harness or at least to cater to the demands of millions of Egyptians for change while at the same time retaining the military's own considerable political and economic interests. For several months, the SCAF was Egypt's ruling military junta, its chairman, Tantawi, issuing orders, appointing provincial governors and other state functionaries (mostly from military backgrounds), and promising new presidential and parliamentary elections. But the SCAF could not altogether ignore popular demands for change. Elections for a new parliament were held in November 2011 and January 2012. Thanks to the Muslim Brotherhood's superior grassroots organization, its candidates and parties affiliated with it won a majority of seats. Presidential elections were held the following June. Again, the Muslim Brotherhood's candidate, Mohamed Morsi, won a narrow victory. Soon thereafter, the new president saw to the retirement of a number of top military commanders, among them Defense Minister Tantawi. The Egyptian military was put on notice.

Throughout 2012 and early 2013, Morsi made a number of decisions that were highly unpopular and polarizing. Mass demonstrations continued across Egyptian cities, and a petition demanding his resignation was signed by millions of Egyptians. Galvanized by their electoral wins, Muslim Brotherhood supporters also often protested, this time in support of the president and the gains they seemed to be making. Despite apparent public support for the president, the military's July 2013 intervention was not completely bereft of popular legitimacy. The coup leader, defense minister and army commander el-Sisi, now became the ruler of Egypt, his rule legitimized through new presidential elections held in May 2014. In elections that were widely considered unfair and undemocratic, el-Sisi won nearly 97 percent of the votes cast.

Since coming to power, the el-Sisi presidency has featured the pursuit of two main political objectives. First, the new regime has sought to bring about a "general and systematic depoliticization of the Egyptian political space."[149] Revolutions release pent-up popular energies that had been brutally suppressed before, and all too frequently post-revolutionary states resort to violence and repression to force submission once again and to reestablish public order.[150] In Egypt's case, this repression has taken the form of disappearances, arbitrary arrests and detentions, unfair trials, reports of torture and ill-treatment, and clampdowns on journalists, bloggers, and activists.[151] A climate of fear reminiscent of Mubarak's *mukhabarat* days has returned to Egypt.

A second development has been the reemergence of the military as the central force in Egyptian politics. The SCAF's takeover at a decisive crossroad in Egypt's transition foretold the military's continued, central political role in whatever system would emerge after the transition. As Mubarak stepped down, the Egyptian military's assumptions about its own political significance evolved to include the belief that it should play a direct role in the country's political future.[152] Following the president's ouster, the armed forces emerged as the ultimate arbiter of the country's economic and political system.[153] This trend was reinforced in the immediate aftermath of Morsi's departure, when the military took on three interrelated roles: crisis management; political management; and the institutionalization of the military's management role.[154]

Renewed, direct control over the institutions of the state has allowed the Egyptian military to deepen its dominance and control over the country's economy. This expansive role in the economy had started long before the 2011 uprisings, but picked up pace in the months and weeks prior to Mubarak's departure. The Egyptian military prioritized not just stability but also its own parochial interests and its status in society.[155] As Mubarak's power waned, in order to secure its own economic future regardless of the direction the uprising took, the Egyptian military accelerated its efforts to enter into joint production agreements with foreign partners.[156] Since then, the military has protected the country's major strategic assets, but it has also controlled the bidding process for major government procurements. The military's break with Morsi and the Muslim Brotherhood, in fact, finally occurred when Morsi tried to sideline the military over mega-projects such as the Suez Canal development and Toshka, a massive land reclamation project.[157] Morsi's ouster and the consolidation of the military regime have only further enhanced the ability of the armed forces to channel funds to projects in which they have an interest. Today, the military has become "the primary gatekeeper for the Egyptian economy."[158]

The Egyptian military's increasing role in the economy has done little to help improve the country's economy. President el-Sisi made some administrative changes in 2014–15 meant to address some public demands, including changing governors, reshuffling cabinet ministers, and establishing councils in areas such as community services and economic development, which he headed personally.[159] In 2014, the Egyptian economy showed slight signs of improvement, with some growth in the manufacturing and services sectors. There were also small improvements in the unemployment rate.[160] But the country's macro-economy is far from healthy, and life for the average Egyptian continues to be a struggle. Data from 2013 indicate that 26 percent of Egyptians continue to live below the poverty line.[161]

Morsi's overthrow brought Egypt much closer to Saudi Arabia and the UAE, a partnership cemented through massive amounts of economic aid coming Egypt's way from the Persian Gulf. According to one estimate, between 2013 and 2015 financial assistance to Egypt from the Persian Gulf states was an estimated $20 billion, by far surpassing Washington's $1.3 billion in annual military assistance.[162] In 2015, the Gulf states pledged a support package of $12.5 billion to Egypt, resulting in some signs of improvement in the economy.[163]

Assistance from new, wealthy allies may help temporarily to alleviate economic difficulties for the Egyptian government. But the longer-term trajectory of the country's politics remains unclear. For now, the presidency and the military are politically and economically dominant. The uprisings witnessed an increasing acceptance and ascendance of liberal political ideas in Egypt. These ideas call for freedom, dignity, social justice, bread, and equality.[164] But the degree to which Egypt's liberal democrats—once praised as "the vanguard of change in the country"[165]—can play decisive roles in its immediate future is far from certain. For now, the military, in power because of a coup and ruling though a former army commander pretending to be a civilian politician, appears to be firmly in control and has shown little appetite for giving up power any time soon.

The direction taken by Tunisia's revolution appears fundamentally different, with the result so far being a functioning if imperfect democracy. Tunisian political actors have exhibited considerable "indigenous capacities for reform."[166] Here, decisions by individual actors and institutions have coalesced to produce results that are conducive to the emergence of a democratic institutional framework, underwritten by a supportive set of rules of the game. Tunisia's transition featured debate and discourse, with the Islamist Ennahda party taking center stage in debates over issues such as personal status law, basic liberties, and *sharia* being a human set of rules to be interpreted by the people's representatives as opposed to being divine and therefore immutable.[167] Ennahda's leader, Rachid Ghannouchi, has meanwhile personally played a central role in steering the country's Islamist movement in a democratic direction.[168]

The roles played by the SCAF in Egypt and the National Transition Council in Libya were fulfilled by the Tunisian Provisional Administration in Tunisia following Ben Ali's hasty departure in January 2011. What transpired in Tunis, however, was decidedly different from what occurred in either Tripoli or Cairo. TPA actors included independent activists, former government members, and members of the former opposition. They were able to develop and forge a new and constructive working relationship together.[169] Early in their deliberations TPA actors showed three characteristics: many sourced their legitimacy by being perceived as fair, non-aligned, and cooperative; despite different backgrounds and visions, all were committed to a democratic future; and both soft-liners from the former regime and the revolutionaries were willing to compromise. The TPA agreed on the importance of constitutional continuity, avoiding institutional vacuum, and preserving legal mechanisms. The group decided to operate on the basis of consensus and sought to be inclusive of as many trends and different voices as possible. It also agreed to look to historical national traditions as its guiding principles, endorsed the application of democratic values, and showed adaptability in reaching its goals.[170]

One of the primary reasons for the success of the TPA rested in the commitment of some of its key actors to making their negotiations succeed in fostering a truly new era for Tunisian politics. Soft-liners from the former regime were particularly critical in this regard.[171] Also important were the role and functions of institutions, the central significance of which the TPA was keenly aware. Special attention was paid to the security forces. Historically, the Tunisian military did not play an important political role, did not receive any special political or material privileges, and was at the bottom of Ben Ali's hierarchy of security organizations. Instead, it was the Ministry of Interior's security forces that were seen as the primary supporting institution of the state.[172] As one of its first acts, the TPA dissolved the dreaded Political Police, active under Ben Ali, and its members were absorbed into the regular police force.[173]

In Egypt, the SCAF's desire to control the pace and direction of change prompted it to hold parliamentary and presidential elections before the actual drafting of a new constitution. In Tunisia, aware of the importance of institutions and the intended and unintended consequences of institutional legacies, the TPA made provisions for the election of a National Constituent Assembly whose specific task was to draft a constitution. In December 2011 the assembly elected the human rights activist Moncef Marzouki as interim president of the republic. It took the assembly until early 2014 to draft a new constitution, one in which power is divided between the office of the president and the parliament. New parliamentary and presidential elections were held later that same year.

Both in the transition process and immediately afterward, the Tunisian military played a central role in determining the course of events as they unfolded. But this role was very different from that played by the Egyptian military. Tunisia's military is "hyper-loyalist," and its officers have strong nationalist sentiments and a "staunch sense of the state regarding the protection of national sovereignty."[174] The Tunisian armed forces clearly ascribe to the concept of civilians overseeing the military. Although they performed a number of critical internal security functions during the vacuum left by Ben Ali's departure, their return to barracks once the vacuum was filled was never in question.[175] Nevertheless, after the 2011 uprising the military no longer lives in obscurity, instead enjoying considerable prestige, more autonomy, and political clout. It also has a "modern-day national hero," General Rashid Ammar, the army's Chief of Staff, who had refused Ben Ali's orders to shoot at the protesters and who had told Ben Ali he was finished.[176]

The rosy picture of Tunisian politics painted here does not extend to the country's economy. In the three years following the Arab Spring—2011, 2012, and 2013—per capita GDP in Tunisia steadily decreased every year and investments declined substantially.[177] The major cause of the precipitous decline in the economy was a dramatic drop in investment, and pervasive feelings of political uncertainty among investors and the public alike did not help. This prompted domestic and international investors to take a wait-and-see attitude until political conditions stabilized.[178] Terrorist attacks on tourist sites, meanwhile, kept many tourists away, thus reducing a major source of foreign revenue to a mere trickle.

Tunisia naturally looked for economic assistance abroad, especially to the wealthy states of the Persian Gulf. Saudi Arabia, Kuwait, and Qatar have obliged with generous dollar sums, though not nearly to the same degree that Gulf money has poured into Morocco, Jordan, and Egypt.[179] The GCC states, it appears, prefer propping up nondemocratic allies and ensuring the continuation of the political status quo in each. Monarchies opening the door to democracy, after all, or even Egypt for that matter, could end up having deleterious consequences for the GCC authoritarians as well.

For now, Tunisia's fledgling democracy appears on track. Within a year of the uprising, the country saw the establishment of some 2,000 new civil society organizations, and the media scene was also injected with new excitement.[180] The parliament and the presidency, as well as the military and the security forces, all appear committed to making democracy work, as does, crucially, the country's Islamist movement.[181] The Arab Spring may have turned into nightmarish tragedies in most parts of North Africa and the Levant. But at least in Tunisia there are glimmers of hope. Whether this lone example can serve as a model for others to emulate is a question only time can answer.

Conclusion

For now, the Tunisian example is likely to stand out for its uniqueness. Elsewhere in North Africa and the Levant, neither democracy nor new revolutions are likely. Judging by their outcomes, other than in Tunisia, the Arab uprisings of 2010–11 appear to have amounted to no more than failed social movements. According to the sociologist John Foran, for political revolutions to become social revolutions, two conditions are necessary: "the courageous engagement of social movements and civil society organizations:" and those principles around which people mobilized must be given organizational expression.[182] Today neither condition obtains. Whereas the Iranian revolution sought to create a *homo Islamicus*, the ultimate Islamic man, the Arab Spring hoped to have paved the way for *homo pictor*, a "transgendered subject that is not devoid of choice."[183] But devoid of choice, submissive to the new political order of the day, is exactly what the political heirs of the post-2011 era expect of their peoples. Repression, so central to the domestic politics of the Arab world before 2011, has once again reemerged as an organizing political principle. Today, the prospects for another revolution anytime soon are at best dim and at worst nil.

But neither is democracy anywhere within reach. Democracy, it is worth remembering, cannot be consolidated without the commitment of the democratic elite to democratic rule, or their willingness to be obedient to democratically elected political elites.[184] Amid the euphoria that the uprisings generated, a few voices, mostly within the region, called expectations of the sudden appearance of democracy "rash and ahistorical."[185] Back in 2014, the historian David Bell also asked for a long-term historical horizon by which to judge the outcome of the Arab Spring.[186] Bell reminds us that very few revolutions have been quick successes and that they have been invariably messy, bloody, drawn-out, and often unpredictable. Victory has often come only after setbacks, and revolutions all too frequently feature abuses by all sides.[187]

Revolutions are rare historical events, and even rarer if they succeed. This rarity is largely because their necessary preconditions are so difficult to obtain. But equally important is the inherent resistance of political institutions to change, particularly those—like the armed forces in much of the Arab world—with deep and historic ties to society. This institutional stickiness can reduce the pace of change to a crawl, at most through the layering of other institutions or arrangements onto existing ones, or more likely through path dependence, whereby institutions change at their own pace and according to internal as opposed to external stimuli.

Whatever the causes, in the immediate aftermath of the 2011 uprisings, a historic opportunity to foster "positive-sum politics" was squandered. Instead, zero-sum politics have once again reemerged across the Arab world. Opponents on social media, and at times even in the traditional media, were disparaged, labeled, denounced, called names. Trust among the different actors remains minimal and there continues to be little electoral legitimacy. There is an overreliance on the judiciary to settle old scores. These challenges all remain interconnected, making their resolution even more difficult.

This is not to imply that the post-2011 states of the Arab world, especially those in North Africa and the Levant, are invulnerable. Far from it, in fact. They continue to suffer from the inherent limitations and shortcomings of all exclusionary dictatorships in terms of their fraying ties with society. Focus on the institutional mechanisms of authoritarian resilience, in fact, tends to miss the limitations of authoritarian leaders as far as information is concerned. These states are invariably poorly informed. Authoritarian leaders may have access to and control over instruments of repression, but people are angry and resentful, and, given an opportunity through an event, a spark, they may once again mobilize against their oppressors.[188]

From a longer-term historical perspective, the institutional dysfunctions that gave rise to the 2011 uprisings have not been fixed and are likely to have disruptive consequences again in the future. The competitive authoritarian systems of Algeria, Morocco, Egypt, and Jordan are likely to follow one of three trajectories: democratization; unstable authoritarianism; or stable authoritarianism. Which path they follow depends on the density of their economic, diplomatic, and political linkages to the West; on the incumbents' organizational power; or on the scope and cohesion of the state's governing structures.[189] What all of this ultimately amounts to is the impermanence of the existing systems. Sooner or later, their institutional flaws need addressing. Political systems and ideals become attractive once there is "a proper structure of incentives for the population in question."[190] Unless the current political systems found in North Africa and the Levant can deliver, their continued operations are once again likely to be challenged by the peoples they rule.

5

THE CONTESTED TERRAIN

The state does not exist in a vacuum or operate only on its own. In addition to its functions relative to other states, it also governs over society. Previous chapters focused on the odyssey of the Arab state before, during, and after the 2011 uprisings. This chapter turns the focus on the post-uprising state's relationship with society. More specifically, the chapter examines some of the most consequential ways in which state–society relations have manifested themselves in the years since the uprisings. Admittedly, there are multiple, and perhaps countless, ways in which the societal consequences of the uprisings can be organized into groups and analyzed. Here I have categorized these consequences into three broad, interrelated clusters of phenomena.

The first phenomenon revolves around notions of citizenship. The uprisings heightened the awareness of activists and protestors about their *rights* as citizens. State leaders, however, are mostly concerned about the *responsibilities* that come with citizenship. This dissonance, which actually had been one of the primary causes of the uprisings, has not been resolved. If anything, in some respects it has become even sharper and more pronounced. Citizens were presented with an opportunity in 2011 to press for their rights. In the months and years that followed, they have tried to continue doing so. But state leaders have shown little disposition to observe citizenship rights, instead continuing to emphasize citizen responsibilities to uphold law and order.

At best, the outcome has been diminished state legitimacy. At worst, it has been fodder for militancy and extremism.

Mass mobilization may have petered out and at times been forcibly put down, but the society-wide yearnings that gave rise to it have not dissipated. This touches on a second area of nexus between post-uprising states and societies, namely the phenomenon of legitimacy. With more than half a decade of governing under their belts, the post-2011 states of the Arab world seem no more, or no less, legitimate than those before the uprisings erupted. If legitimacy is broadly seen as an overall acceptance of a state's mandate to rule, based on its delivery of certain key functions and responses to societal demands, then the post-uprising states of the Arab world have by and large failed to live up to the economic, political, and social expectations of their peoples. According to polling data, explored in some detail in this chapter, since 2011, Arab states have consistently failed to attract widespread support and trust amongst their people, to rid themselves of perceptions of corruption, to create positive economic conditions, to be seen as trusted sources of information, and to reverse commonly held beliefs that they are obstacles to people's happiness, freedom, aspirations, and peace of mind. It was an absence of legitimacy that prompted mass throngs to take to the streets in 2011. But after the uprisings, the people's return to their daily routines has not necessarily repaired the state's legitimacy deficit.

One of the more dramatic consequences of this legitimacy deficit has included changes to Islam's social position and political role—a third area of state–society nexus discussed here. Survey data indicate continuously high levels of religiosity among Arabs, steady and slowly increasing tolerance for others, and, at the same time, the continued appeal and attraction of religious extremism. Salafism, popularly used in recent years to refer to ultra-conservative Islamism, seems to be neither temporary nor ephemeral. It is here to stay. Combined with deep social and cultural chasms, worsening economic disparities, and unmet expectations, this Salafism often finds a willing and complementary partner in jihadism. Salafi-jihadists are not, to state the obvious, by any means preponderant among Sunni-majority Arab societies. But they do form a small minority that has nevertheless managed to be lethal and highly disruptive of the domestic and regional orders.

Salafists and Salafi-jihadists exist in the very same societies that have given rise to what may be called "post-Islamism." Post-Islamism is as concerned with dialogue and consensus as Salafi-jihadism is uncompromising and violent. Arab societies today continue to be torn along the social, cultural, and economic lines that have long caused manifold dislocations to their peoples and polities. The latest, additional fault line—most starkly evident in the immediate aftermath of the Arab Spring, and especially the brutal civil wars of Syria and Libya—revolves around the very essence of Sunni Islam. Shiism has also been undergoing its own internal ideological and political rebellions, at one extreme advocating a modernizing "dynamic *ijtihad* [independent reasoning]" and at another extreme a missionary and uncompromisingly sectarian zeal.[1] But it is Sunnism, which predominates in the Arab world, that is the focus of analysis here.

Combined, these three areas of nexus between state and society—citizenship, legitimacy, and political Islam—tell us that the fundamental nature of state–society relations in the Arab world before and after the uprisings has not changed. If anything, hopes and expectations were raised, and new sacrifices made, only to have old patterns of state rule eventually reemerge. There has been no precipitous opening of political space, no notable improvements in the state's delivery of services, no abandonment of failed and underperforming economic policies, and no reversal of narrowing of the public sphere. Only in Tunisia is there a new political system that is more representative of social currents. But even that is struggling against unmet economic expectations and rising extremism among the youth. Arab societies, by and large, remain politically defeated and, given a chance, defiant.

Citizenship

Contestation over the meaning and essence of citizenship constitutes one of the most fundamental crises of contemporary governments in the Middle East in general and in the Arab world in particular. Citizens view themselves as members of a community that enjoys certain civil, social, and political prerogatives. But few Arab (and Middle Eastern) states share the same conceptions of and respect for the prerogatives to which citizens feel entitled. What results is a fundamentally conflictual relationship between state and society, one in which a tug of war ensues between conceptions of citizenship by social actors on the one side and by the state and its leaders on the other. Dictatorships subdue and repress those conceptions as articulated by social actors, violently if they are brutal and through co-option and bribery if they are benign. At times of weakness and vulnerability, opportunities and openings in political space enable citizenship demands to be pressed on the state, as they were during the 2011 protest movements. They were led by individuals who viewed themselves as citizens, as individuals with rights.[2]

The immediate trigger for the 2011 protests—what motivated people to go into the streets and to demonstrate—may have been economic grievances first and political freedoms second.[3] Nevertheless, throughout the uprisings, the "people," as citizens of the state, were the central reference point of the protesters. Immediately prior to the eruption of the Arab Spring, we see the emergence of a new political language, some of it direct translations of concepts in French and English, and some adaptations and adjustments. In addition to "democracy" (*dimukratiya*), "human rights" (*huquq al-insan*), and "civil society" (*mujtama 'madani*), concepts such as "rule of law" (*dawlat al-haq wa al-qanun*) and "bureaucratic state" (*dawlat al-mu'assassat*) had gained increasing currency in the intellectual discourse of the two to three decades preceding the 2011 uprisings.[4] When the revolutions did erupt, and especially both immediately before and afterward, the concept of citizenship (*muwatana*) and other concepts related to it—such as dignity (*karama*), liberty (*hurriya*), equality (*musawa*), rights (*huquq*), and social justice (*al-'adala al-ijtima'iyya*), all of which have been part of the parlance of "the people" (*al-sha'b*)—became particularly prevalent at both the mass and elite levels.[5]

The 2011 uprisings saw the resurgence of a rights-based discourse, a new language of politics, in which new notions, phrases, and expressions became popular.[6] Accordingly, several themes emerged as emblematic of the protests: citizenship and citizen (*muwatin*); respect for personal rights as guaranteed by the state; ending corruption; human rights; interest in drawing up new constitutions; renewed attention to the rights of women and minorities; new conceptions of citizenship that respect individual choice and interpretation; emphasis on the common good; and emphasis on religious virtue and personal commitment.[7] These themes, and the larger context within which they were formulated and expressed, represented manifestations of larger demands for citizenship prerogatives. Campaigns for such prerogatives have long been part and parcel of Middle Eastern and Arab histories. Historically conditioned definitions of citizenship as understood in Europe and North America, in the form of political rights, inclusion–exclusion, and loyalty–identity may not have always applied to specific cases found in Middle Eastern history. But various manifestations of citizenship have appeared in repeated political struggles in the region, from anti-colonial struggles to efforts aimed at securing property rights, fighting discriminatory laws, articulating competing nationalisms, and institutionalizing hard-won privileges.[8]

Some years before the Arab Spring, Nils Butenschøn offered a legalistic definition of citizenship for the Middle East and elsewhere, viewing it as a contractual relationship that regulates the legal status of the inhabitants of a state within its territorial boundaries. As "the organizing principle of the modern state," he argued, citizenship delineates between those who belong and those who do not, and those with certain rights and obligations as compared to those without them.[9] While not necessarily incorrect, this and other similar definitions do not take into account the fact that citizenship is innately political, and, in times of political uncertainty or instability, it is often most vividly articulated through campaigns of mass mobilization, especially if and when such campaigns lead to social movements.[10] In the case of the 2011 uprisings, extensive and multiple demands for citizenship were formulated and expressed. Some of these demands included the following:

— the state's observance of personal, human rights as compared to simply collective rights;
— ending corruption and instituting accountability, transparency, and the rule of law;
— political pluralism;
— personal autonomy and an end to a state's practice of patronage and its intervention in private matters;
— freedom of speech, the media, professional association, and civil society;
— freedom of ideology;
— civic responsibility and civic virtue; and,
— nondiscriminatory treatment of religious and ethnic minorities.[11]

Significantly, even in extreme rentier political economies, in which the state's modus operandi is to cater to the demands of its population in return for their political quiescence, demands for citizenship prerogatives are formulated and expressed. Zahra Babar has shown convincingly that conceptions of citizenship in the Arabian Peninsula's oil states may have different historical roots and decidedly different manifestations today, but they are, nonetheless, just as compelling and forceful in the Arab world as they are anywhere else. Rentierism, Babar argues, has not dulled citizenship sensibilities and demands; it has simply given them different forms and manifestations, with their own sets of demands and pressures on the state.[12] In the next chapter, I will examine the historical roots and contemporary political dynamics of state–society relations in the Arabian Peninsula, and how states in the region have responded to socially-generated demands for rights and prerogatives.

For their part, states have their own conceptions of citizenship, which in nondemocracies are centered more on the responsibilities of the governed rather than with their rights and prerogatives. As Steven Heydemann has observed, in the Middle East, as part of the state-building process, "state-centric notions of citizenship have become much more central to definitions of society than membership in some larger nation or transnational community."[13] In the corporatist populist systems that inundated the region from the mid-1950s to the mid-1970s, even processes of political mobilization became state-driven, and certain kinds of social and political identities were privileged over others. But as these excitable systems settled into run-of-the-mill authoritarianisms by the late 1970s and 1980s, state-articulated notions of citizenship had to compete with those percolating from below, within society. These rights-centered conceptions of citizenship were expressed by and through the works of intellectuals and the literati, regional movements, so-called "non-movements" (schools and political parties), formal and informal networks (trade unions, professional associations, religious institutions), and even social movements.[14]

As we saw in Chapter 4, these society-rooted conceptions of citizenship have by and large fallen victim to the vicissitudes of time, and in particular to the reassertion of authoritarianism once the dust of the uprisings was settled. Only in Tunisia does there appear to be an earnest attempt underway to codify and institutionalize some of the prerogatives espoused by the rights-centered discourse on citizenship. Elsewhere, insofar as post-revolutionary gains are concerned, society's political empowerment appears to be less emphatic though not entirely inconsequential. In Egypt, for example, in response to their demands, Egyptian workers were allowed to establish trade unions with leadership cadres that represented them and their interests. Public sector employees also got salary increases, and those on the lowest rungs were guaranteed a minimum wage.[15]

In Morocco, where youth protests never quite reached levels seen in Tunisia and Egypt, the protesters' comparatively modest demands appear to have been met halfway by the state. The protesters demanded a constitutional monarchy that rules not governs. More fundamentally, they questioned the Makhzenist culture that dominates social, political, and economic life in the country. This elitist political universe, they argued, is symbolized through an archaic set of rituals in the royal court, such as kneeling and kissing the king's hand, wearing the *shashiya*, and a royal court living in ostentatious luxury and wealth.[16] The Moroccan state's response, as we saw in the last chapter, proactive and timely as it was, appears to have succeeded in undermining the potential for a full-blown revolution. In the end, apart from cosmetic changes, the powers of the *Makhzan* have remained largely intact.[17] Similar non-changes also characterize the Algerian polity post-2011. The Algerian political system is locally referred to as *le pouvoir* (the power), and can best be described as an octopus: no one knows who its head is, but the military is a strong element, and its tentacles are everywhere.[18] While the regime's comparative openness has brought it a measure of popular legitimacy, there have been few detectable changes to the state's relationship with society, apart, of course, from those undertaken as part of the national reconciliation following the 1991–2002 civil war.[19]

A brief word needs to be said about those fractured societies in the Arab region suffering from devastating civil wars. In Libya, Yemen, and especially Syria, displacement and mass migration, both forced and voluntary, have thrown the rhythm and routine of daily life into chaos and confusion. There is no single state, or at least no single state authority, for there to be any semblance of continuity or discernible long-term patterns to state–society relations. If there is a resurgent form of authority, other than that of the Islamic State, it is that of the tribes. Especially in Syria and Yemen, it is the different tribes that have capitalized on state fragility, using the space thus created to consolidate their political and territorial autonomy. This is the case particularly in places where the state and its armed forces and civilian agencies cannot effectively penetrate.[20] In the aftermath of the 2011 uprisings, a number of Syrian tribes went so far as taking up armed self-defense, while others aligned themselves with the state's security forces. A number of tribal leaders have taken to social media to reinforce their moral authority over their followers. It appears that state fragility and political instability in the country have reinforced and reinvigorated alternative forms of authority, including that of the tribes.[21]

Not surprisingly, few post-2011 Arab states have been able to garner popular legitimacy, especially among the uprisings' primary foot soldiers, namely those whom Juan Cole has labeled "millennials." Arab millennials, born between 1977 and 2000, are urban, literate, cosmopolitan, wired, and are locally and globally connected through social networks and digital media.[22] In Egypt and Tunisia, the millennials formed the backbone of the New Left: mainly urban, middle-class students who were the generational powerbase and vanguard of the revolution. They were tech-savvy and knew how to network both in person and in cyberspace.[23] In Tunisia especially, the bulk of the protests involved diverse groups mobilized across the country, mostly through the internet, and included workers, students, and both the employed and the unemployed.[24]

Whether in Egypt and Tunisia or elsewhere, and even in cases where popular grievances did not spill over into city streets, across the Arab world, as elsewhere in the developing world, processes of social transformation affecting the youth have been underway for some time. These processes did not stop arbitrarily with the Arab Spring, and nor can they be stopped indefinitely through the force of political repression. Throughout the region, meanwhile, the youth continue to suffer from high unemployment, tend to depend financially on their parents, and are forced by lack of economic opportunities to delay leaving the family home. Those who have the opportunity, or are so inclined, express their angst however they can, as represented through the *Nayda* (on the move) art movements and other artistic festivals in Morocco.[25]

Others suffer from poverty and marginalization in silence. And a few resort to extremist acts, whether in the form of self-immolation, risky emigration to Europe, or joining Salafi-jihadists.[26]

Whatever the outlet, and whether on the young or the middle-aged, the effects of diminished state legitimacy continue to exert themselves on various manifestations of citizenship. There is an intimate connection between citizenship, its forms and functions, and state legitimacy. When states prove unable to garner popular legitimacy, at best they devise systematic preferences for subjects over citizens, and at worst they compensate through resort to repression. Legitimacy, in either case, is one of the central lynchpins of state–society relations.

Legitimacy

Despite, or perhaps because of, being one of the key concepts in political science, there is a general lack of consensus among political scientists over the precise meaning of legitimacy. Part of the debate stems from the fact that as a political phenomenon legitimacy does not easily lend itself to measurement and statistical analysis. There is, as we shall see presently, an inherently nebulous quality to legitimacy. Rather than wading through this literature, here I simply wish to highlight the centrality of legitimacy to state–society relations and operationalize the concept in relation to the post-2011 Arab world.

Some decades ago, Seymour Martin Lipset offered what has since become a generally accepted definition of legitimacy:

> Legitimacy involves the capacity of a political system to engender and maintain the belief that existing political institutions are the most appropriate or proper ones for the society. The extent to which contemporary democratic political systems are legitimate depends in large measure upon the ways in which the key issues which have historically divided the society have been resolved.[27]

Along similar lines, Peter Stillman emphasized the importance of consistencies between what he called *governmental output* and a society's *value patterns*: "a government is legitimate if and only if the results of governmental output are compatible with the value pattern of the society."[28] This emphasis on popular assumptions about the appropriateness of the political system has informed most studies of the topic, including those in the Arab world. In Michael Hudson's study of Arab politics back in 1977, he attributed "the present malaise in Arab politics, as indicated by instability, cynicism, inefficiency, corruption, and repression" to "insufficient legitimacy accorded by the people to the ruling structures, ideologies, and leaders."[29]

By and large, I endorse this received wisdom on legitimacy, and see it, in large measure, as a product of normative congruities between what social actors want and what the state has to offer. But one cannot be too sanguine about the nature of the ensuing relationship. Gramsci, after all, reminded us some time ago that the hegemony of political leadership is secured through consent, which relies on the diffusion and popularization of the worldview of the ruling class.[30] States manipulate culture, create social and political demands, and impose their worldview and maintain hegemony in all sorts of subtle and complex ways.

There is a second component to legitimacy, one that revolves around the range and quality of the services that states deliver for society. More specifically, legitimacy is generated when the performance of the state in the delivery of the services that society wants is viewed positively by a politically significant portion of the population. Political leaders make promises, both implicitly and explicitly, as to what they can or will deliver when they are in office. Depending on the broader context within which the state finds itself, there are also assumptions about its overall behavior, its policies, and its ability to meet those obligations expected of it by the people.

Whereas consistencies between the values of the population and those of political leaders are hard to measure, assumptions about the state's performance in different areas can indeed be captured through public opinion polls. Later in this section, I will present data from polling in a number of Arab countries concerning people's views on state delivery of services in a variety of areas. Before doing so, it is important to explore some of the other ways in which states in the Arab world seek to gain legitimacy.

In what is now considered a classic study of legitimacy in the Arab world, Hudson identified four dimensions of Arab authority: patriarchal, consultative, Islamic, and feudal.[31] Within these authorities, legitimacy may be derived from ideology, structures, or the power of personalities. Of these sources of legitimacy, Hudson argued, the legitimizing power of personalities has tended to dominate Arab politics. Since coherent foundations for authoritative rule are absent in the Arab world, he maintained, the role of personalities and individuals in legitimizing politics has been historically magnified.[32]

Hudson's thesis may have been valid in relation to the decades between the 1950s and 1970s, when strongmen reigned supreme from Algiers and Tripoli to Cairo, Damascus, and Baghdad. But by the mid- to late 1970s, most heroes of the Arab world had been exposed as false prophets, less interested in, or incapable of, much-promised liberations and instead preoccupied with the trappings of power and the worldly pleasures it entailed. By the 1980s and 1990s, not even the prophets of yesteryear believed in their own rhetoric. Only two were left by then. From the Libyan desert, Qaddafi's pleas for relevance were seen more as a nuisance than genuine campaigns for some illusory struggle against imperialism. His antics were tolerated because he had oil and money. His system of *Jamahiriya*, or "state of the masses", the world would later learn, was dysfunctional and rotten to the core, kept barely operational thanks to oil revenues. And in Baghdad, once Saddam's modern-day "Battle of Qadisiyyah" against the Persian enemy fizzled out, he turned on his own people, first gassing the Kurds into submission in 1985 and then turning on the country's Shia once the war with Iran ended in 1988.[33]

Qaddafi's demise, dragged from a sewer pipe and shot dead as he pleaded for mercy, symbolized the crashing end of the era of Arab strongmen. The 2011 uprisings appear to have put a definitive end to the power of heroic legitimacy in the Arab world. The era of hero-worship, of leaders-cum-liberators, has come to an end. Even Abdel Fattah el-Sisi, who sees himself and is seen by some secularist Egyptians as the country's savior from the dark clutches of the Muslim Brotherhood, will have to deliver on the promises he has made, or those ascribed to him, if he is to survive. Populism, whether emanating from Mahmoud Ahmadinejad or Donald Trump, remains a possibility in all historical settings and political systems, including those in place in the Arab world after 2011. For now, however, the days of rousing speeches in public squares, promises of liberation, of crushing enemies and rushing toward progress, seem to be over. Personal legitimacy will always remain important in politics, but not for those Arab personalities who try to become larger than life. Their days are behind us.

Personal relationships, of course, continue to remain important components of political legitimacy, especially insofar as the maintenance of neopatrimonialism is concerned. Chapter 6, on the petro-states of the Arabian Peninsula, will delve into this topic extensively. The chapter examines how the modern institutions of the state are designed to cater to and to perpetuate relations of dependence on the part of various social actors on states dominated by ruling families. Neopatrimonialism is salient especially in countries where tribes or clans remain relevant and important social forces. Across the Arabian Peninsula, and also in Jordan, for example, tribes and states have developed mutually beneficial arrangements. Not only are tribes unlikely to challenge the state so long as central authority remains intact; in some cases, they even reinforce state authority and enhance its legitimacy. Once central authority is weakened and the state suffers from declining power, however, as is the case in Syria, tribes can contribute to further instability.[34]

The example of Jordan is instructive in this respect. The country's political elite is small, and has shown remarkable continuity in its composition since as far back as the Mandatory period. It is made up of a dozen families, the most prominent being Khuraysha, Adwan, Majali, Tarawna, Shurayda, Tall, Jazi, Abu Taya, Rifa'i, Muasher, and Kawar. Since the days of King Abdullah I (r.1946–51), the Hashemite family has been operating as an honest broker among the tribes and prominent families.[35] There have also been strong alliances between the Hashemites and some of the key tribes, the Bani Sakr being chief among them. Faysal Al-Fayez, a prominent leader of the Bani Sakr tribe, has become one of the main figures within the Jordanian political establishment, having held a variety of high-profile offices, including the office of prime minister, and being one of the key allies of Abdullah II. On 13 October 2011, as the rest of the region continued to rail from the aftershocks of the uprisings, members of the Bani Sakr tribal confederacy gathered in the gardens of the king's palace in Amman to show their loyalty and support for the "reform" efforts he had initiated immediately after the revolutions in Tunisia and Egypt.[36] It is hardly accidental that compared to Morocco, its most similar counterpart in the Middle East, Jordan's post-2011 political adjustments have been much more superficial and less far reaching.

Whereas neopatrimonialism has long been used as a source of political legitimacy in the Arab world, a new source appears to be emerging, at least in Tunisia: namely, the constitution. Following Ben Ali's departure, one of the first and most consequential tasks facing Tunisians was the drafting of a new constitution, one that would lay the foundations of a new political era. The constitution-drafting process that followed was long and deliberative, taking no less than three years. What ensued was a highly consequential series of public debates, and eventually elite consensus, over such key issues as the role of religion in politics and the extent to which the state can legislate religious ethics. In the end, after much debate and discussion in society at large and within Ennahda in particular, the party was able to keep references to Islam in the constitution to a minimum. Rached Ghannouchi, Ennahda's leader, successfully argued that what was needed was not a constitutional mandate for *sharia*, but instead the creation of a larger social and political milieu within which people can freely practice their religious beliefs.[37]

It is difficult to ascertain the extent to which the norms that guided Tunisia's constitution-writing process eventually seeped into and were adopted by the country's social classes. But to dismiss the process entirely as an innately elite venture void of social resonance would be a mistake. The comparatively long and deliberative nature of what transpired in Tunisia, and the public debate that paralleled the crafting process behind closed doors, has instilled in the political system a comparatively high, and relatively unique, degree of legitimacy.

The comparisons with Egypt's constitution-drafting process are telling. In contrast to Tunisia's experience, the process of constitution-writing in Egypt was more choppy, with a document hastily prepared in 2012, in which the role of Islam was only marginally strengthened in comparison to the 1971 constitution: e.g. matters of Islamic law were to be referred to Al-Azhar for consultation (article 219), and Islamic law was defined in terms of traditional Sunni jurisprudence.[38] After el-Sisi's coup, a new constitution was written in 2014 and retained pretty much the same language and provisions on Islam as the 2012 and 1971 drafts, some minor modifications notwithstanding. While the language on personal liberties was strengthened compared to previous drafts, the overall role of religion in public and political life was retained as before.[39]

Significantly, although there was much debate and discussion surrounding the various documents, the public was kept largely outside the deliberations. The highly polarized context within which the two drafts were written in 2012 and 2014—the Muslim Brotherhood's narrow presidential victory, Morsi's contested presidency, his overthrow, and el-Sisi's proto-fascism—left little room for compromise and consensus. In many ways, regardless of how the constitution was written, or what it stipulated, the broader context of its birth doomed its social resonance from the beginning.

This is not to imply that public debate about politics was absent in Egypt and elsewhere. On the contrary, in Egypt and elsewhere the uprisings injected new life into what has always been a robust public awareness of history and politics, of the legacy of the past, especially the recent past, not just as a historical memory but as lived experience.[40] After the 2011 uprisings, as Nathan Brown's recent book demonstrates, "Arab politics has been reborn."[41] According to public opinion data from twelve Arab countries, between 2011 and 2016 levels of concern with political affairs have remained generally consistently high at about 74 percent. Those who were completely unconcerned also remained relatively consistent during the same period at 23 percent, with the remainder declining to answer.[42] Politics and political discussions have been revived, often revolving around struggles over public policy outcomes.[43]

There are two factors to consider here. First, *discussing politics* does not necessarily mean doing so in an informed manner. Second, and related, political *discussions* and *dialogue* are two different things, the former consisting of offering opinions while the latter involves discursive exchanges underlined by assumptions of a common ground. Opinion polls conducted in 2006 and 2010–11 find increasing support for democracy, as well as social tolerance, the presence of women in the workplace, diversity of ideas among politicians, and separation of religion and politics.[44] But despite consistently high levels of support, there are uneven and varied understandings of exactly what democracy is. Overall, interpersonal trust is low, political interest is low, and involvement in political organizations and civil society organizations also remains anemic.[45] In many Arab countries today, while arguments are often lively, much of the argumentation is aimed at sympathizers rather than opponents, with arguments being more in the form of preaching to the choir rather than persuading doubters. All of this takes place in a "murky fog" of blurred red lines and gray zones of what is and what is not permissible.[46] The exact freedoms and restrictions that define public debate are not clear.

The Egyptian and Tunisian experiences with drafting constitutions, different as they were, remind us once again that in themselves constitutions matter little. Whether they become living documents or collect dust on library shelves is largely up to the politicians who are supposed to abide by them. But equally important are the context and manner of their drafting, especially the insularity or resonance of the logic underpinning them.

Besides neopatrimonialism and the constitution, legitimacy comes from people's beliefs and assumptions about politics and political objects as shaped through their experiences and expectations. These assumptions and opinions can be fairly accurately measured thanks to public opinion polls on a range of topics by a variety of outlets. In what follows, I use annual polling data collected by the Doha-based Arab Center for Research and Policy Studies. Since 2011, this particular research center has gauged public opinion in a number of Arab countries. In 2016, the last year for which data are available as of this writing, the poll included a sample size of 18,310 individuals from twelve Arab countries, namely Algeria, Egypt, Iraq, Jordan, Kuwait, Lebanon, Morocco, Mauritania, Palestine, Saudi Arabia, Sudan, and Tunisia.[47] The polls paint a vivid picture of actual perceptions about the 2011 uprisings and their current conditions in a fairly large, and generally representative, sample of the Arab world.

The information gleaned from the polls can be divided into four categories: perceptions about the uprisings; the economy; democracy; and government performance. In terms of popular assumptions in Tunisia and Egypt about the uprisings which led to the 2011 rebellions, people feel generally positive about the revolts. In other countries, there is greater ambivalence (Table 5.1). Although in 2016, five years after the uprisings, there appeared to be general support for having launched the revolutions, collective enthusiasm for their outcomes appeared to be steadily declining as most of the promises that inspired them came to naught. Whereas in 2012–13, 61 percent viewed the outcomes of the protests favorably, the percentage went down to 45 percent in 2014, 34 percent in 2015, and 33 percent in 2016. In

2016, fully 50 percent of the respondents viewed the outcomes of the uprisings as negative.[48]

No doubt, much of this negative feeling about the outcome of the uprisings can be attributed to perceived declines in people's economic conditions. Table 5.2 shows overall perceptions about the economy, household income, and government policies. The proportion of those who reported their income as insufficient to meet their needs was 41 percent in 2012–13 and 29 percent in 2016, while those whose income was just sufficient to cover their needs went from 42 percent in 2011 to 49 percent in 2016.[49] Overall perceptions about the general state of the economy at home remained largely unchanged over the years from 2012–13 to 2016, with approximately 42 percent describing it as good or very good, while those describing it as bad or very bad hovered at around 57 percent. The blame for such dire economic circumstances was placed squarely on the government. Across Arab countries, economic policies remain unpopular, with only 40 percent believing that government economic policies reflect popular aspirations, while 50 percent or more believe they do not. Foreign policies remain similarly unpopular, with only 50 percent believing that their government's foreign policy reflects popular opinion.

Table 5.1: Positive or negative attitudes toward the 2011 uprisings

	Positive	Negative	Don't know / Decline to answer
Egypt	78	20	1
Tunisia	71	26	3
Kuwait	65	33	2
Iraq	57	32	12
Sudan	56	28	15
Saudi Arabia	55	36	8
Morocco	51	29	20
Palestine	48	44	7
Mauritania	43	39	19
Algeria	35	61	4
Lebanon	34	65	2
Jordan	22	75	3
Total	51	41	8

Source: Arab Center for Research and Policy Studies, *The 2016 Arab Opinion*, p. 74.

Table 5.2: Perceptions of economic conditions and government policies

	2011	2012–13	2014	2015	2016
Household income sufficient for expenditures but not savings	42	40	42	48	49
Household income insufficient for expenditures and we face difficulties	41	37	32	29	29
Economic conditions in the country are good or very good	–	42	38	43	41
Economic conditions in the country are bad or very bad	–	56	60	56	57
Government economic policies reflect popular opinion	31	39	41	43	40
Government economic policies do not reflect popular opinion	50	49	50	50	55
Government foreign policy represents popular opinion	34	42	45	50	50
Government foreign policy does not represent popular opinion	47	44	45	44	43

Source: Arab Center for Research and Policy Studies, *The 2016 Arab Opinion*, pp. 4, 6, 11, 12.

The state's poor performance is not limited to the economy and extends to a whole array of areas under its purview. In 2016, slightly more than 40 percent of Arabs viewed the security situation in their country negatively (down from 60 percent in 2012–13). In their own homes, however, a considerably larger number felt safer: 82 percent in 2016, up from 73 percent in 2012–13 (Table 5.3).

The proportion of Arabs who generally lacked confidence in their government held steady at or slightly above 50 percent between 2012–13 and 2016, with those expressing high or some confidence in the government going from 47 percent in 2011 to 57 percent in 2016 (Table 5.4). Meanwhile, as Table 5.4 also indicates, people's overall perceptions of the general political situation in their countries did not change much from 2012–13 to 2016, with 39 percent describing it as good or very good in 2012–13 and 40 percent having the same response in 2016. Those with negative attitudes toward their country's political situation remained just over 50 percent of the population in 2016, while as many as 26 percent described the political situation in their country as "very bad." Perceptions about the state's provision of essential services improved only slightly from 40 percent in 2012–13 to 48 percent in 2016. In the same years, anywhere from 22 to 24 percent of the population viewed the state's provision of services as "very poor."

Table 5.3: Perceptions of level of safety at home and in the country

	2011	2012–13	2014	2015	2016
Good safety and security across the country	–	40	46	57	59
Lack of safety and security across the country	–	47	53	46	40
Good levels of safety and security at home	–	73	72	77	82
Lack of safety and security at home	–	27	27	23	18

Source: Arab Center for Research and Policy Studies, *The 2016 Arab Opinion*, pp. 2–3.

Assumptions about corruption within the various organs of the state, meanwhile, have remained consistently widespread (Table 5.4). In 2016, 84 percent of those polled believed that corruption is somewhat or very widespread. At the same time, the percentage of those who believed that corruption was limited or altogether non-existent went from 10 percent in 2011 to 18 percent in 2016. Between 2011 and 2016, almost half of those surveyed consistently questioned the government's commitment to tackle corruption.

Such widespread assumptions about pervasive corruption translated into negative attitudes toward the various institutions of the state, especially the legislature. Lack of confidence in the legislative organ of the state ranged from 57 percent in 2011 to 54 percent in 2016 (Table 5.5). Consistently, some 47–48 percent of the population believed that their country's parliament did not reflect all social components of society and was not truly representative. The most widely-held negative attitudes toward the legislature were found among

Jordanians, only 39 percent of whom saw their parliament as working to protect their civil liberties, while the percentage of Tunisians with the same assumption stood at no less than 83 percent.[50]

Table 5.4: Government services, confidence, and corruption

	2011	2012–13	2014	2015	2016
Have confidence in the government	47	57	55	56	55
Lack confidence in the government	44	39	44	42	43
General political situation is good or very good	–	39	36	43	40
General political situation is poor or very poor	–	53	59	52	55
Government provision of essential service is good or very good	–	40	41	46	48
Government provision of essential service is poor or very poor	–	57	57	53	49
Government corruption is limited or very infrequent	10	11	13	18	18
Government corruption is widespread or very widespread	84	85	83	80	79

Source: Arab Center for Research and Policy Studies, *The 2016 Arab Opinion*, pp. 7, 9, 10, 13.

The judiciary was held in similarly low esteem in much of the Arab world (Table 5.5). Between 2011 and 2016, the percentage of those who lacked confidence in the judiciary held consistent at just under one-third, with those expressing high confidence in the institution at only 24 percent. In 2016, as in previous years, fully a quarter of the population believed that the state did not apply the rule of law in their country. When it did apply the rule of law, consistently half or more believed it did so unevenly and treated some groups or individuals preferentially over others.[51] Along similar lines, the percentage of those believing that there were no fair trials in their country held steady at just under 20 percent, with those believing in the fairness of legal procedures having gone up slightly from 13 percent in 2012–13 to 16 percent in 2016.[52]

Table 5.5: Popular confidence in legislature, judiciary, political parties, and security forces

	2011	2012–13	2014	2015	2016
Legislature is representative of different social strata	–	46	45	51	48
Legislature is not representative of different social strata	–	43	48	44	47
Lack confidence in the legislature	57	47	55	51	54
High degree of confidence in the legislature	33	48	43	46	44
Lack confidence in the judiciary	35	32	34	34	32
Have confidence in the judiciary	57	64	64	64	65
Lack confidence in political parties	60	56	65	68	65
Have confidence in political parties	23	34	29	28	31
Lack confidence in the military	16	17	18	15	12
Have confidence in the military	77	79	80	83	87
Lack confidence in the police force	40	32	31	29	27
Have confidence in the police force	55	66	67	70	72

Source: Arab Center for Research and Policy Studies, *The 2016 Arab Opinion*, pp. 15, 17, 20, 21.

Legislatures and judiciaries are not the only political institutions held in low esteem; so are political parties. Sizeable segments of Arab publics persistently lacked confidence in political parties, hovering at around 60 percent in 2011 and 65 percent in 2016 (Table 5.5). Only around 8 percent of the population showed high degrees of confidence in political parties during the same period.[53]

Significantly, while negative perceptions about ostensibly civilian political institutions—the legislature, the judiciary, and political parties—have continued to persist and predominate, the coercive organs of the state, namely the armed forces and the police, are increasingly viewed positively. Across the Arab world, as shown in Table 5.5, confidence in the military has been high and steadily rising, going from 77 percent in 2011 to 79 percent in 2012–13, 80 percent in 2014, 83 percent in 2015, and 87 percent in 2016. At 97 percent, Jordanians have the highest confidence in their country's armed forces.[54] There is also a robust and growing sense of confidence in the police force, though not quite at the same level as the armed forces. In 2011, 55 percent of the respondents expressed high or medium degrees of confidence in the police force, rising up to 66 percent in 2012–13, 67 percent in 2014, 70 percent in 2015, and 72 percent in 2016. Conversely, the proportion of those with no or limited confidence in the police force went from 40 percent in 2011 to 27 percent in 2016.

On the surface, confidence in and support for the military appears to undermine positive attitudes toward democracy. But on the contrary, across the Arab world there are broadly positive perceptions toward democracy. This is especially the case after 2012, when perceptions about democracy improved markedly as compared to the year before. Whereas in 2011, 55 percent of those surveyed saw democracy and economic development as compatible, from 2012 to 2016 on average 66 percent of respondents saw a positive relationship between the two (Table 5.6). In 2011, 54 percent of the population saw democracy as compatible with order and security, with 20 percent not knowing. From 2012 to 2016, the percentage of those who saw democracy and order and security as compatible increased to an average of 66 percent. As to whether democracy is characterized by indecision and discord, the percentage of those who disagree went from 48 percent in 2011 (and 19 percent declining to answer) to 56 percent in the years between 2012 and 2016.[55] From 2012 to 2016, the proportion of those who viewed their society as prepared for democracy held steady. As evident in Table 5.6, on average 42.75 percent see society as unprepared for democracy, while 46.75 percent believe that their society is indeed prepared for democracy.

Despite widespread assumptions about their own society's lack of preparedness for democracy, overall Arab attitudes toward the principle remain largely positive. Between 2011 and 2016, as Table 5.6 shows, the percentage of those who saw democracy as the best form of government despite its failings inched slightly upwards from 67 percent to 72 percent. At the same time, those who did not see democracy as the

Table 5.6: Overall attitudes toward democracy

	2011	2012–13	2014	2015	2016
Democracy and economic performance are compatible	55	64	65	68	68
Democracy and economic performance are not compatible	24	22	23	26	25
Democracies do well in maintaining public order and security	54	63	65	68	67
Democracies do poorly in maintaining public order and security	27	23	23	25	26
Democracies are not characterized by indecision and discord	48	53	57	59	58
Democracies are characterized by indecision and discord	33	33	35	35	34
My society is prepared for democracy	–	46	45	50	49
My society is not prepared for democracy	–	40	44	44	43
Despite its failings, democracy is better than its alternatives	67	68	72	72	72
Democracy is not better than its alternatives	15	18	17	22	22
Would like to see democracy in your own country	–	82	77	79	77
Would not like to see democracy in your own country	–	8	15	16	18
Approve of banning Islamist parties	–	28	20	21	21
Do not approve of banning Islamist parties	–	58	69	73	72
People in your country are free to criticize the government	–	63	60	57	56
People in your country are not free to criticize the government	–	27	30	38	39

Source: Arab Center for Research and Policy Studies, *The 2016 Arab Opinion*, pp. 25, 26, 27, 29, 31, 33, 35.

best form of political system went from 15 percent to 22 percent, apparently having attracted toward them more of those who were undecided, from 18 percent in 2012–13 to 6 percent in 2016.[56] The percentage of those who would like to see a democratic system in their own country—defined as a "pluralistic political system in which no political party is barred"—held steady at around 78.75 percent between 2012 and 2016. In 2012–13, 58 percent did not approve of banning Islamist parties from electoral politics. By 2016, the number had steadily risen to 72 percent. At the same time, between 2014 and 2016, public hostility toward ISIS remained stable at almost 90 percent.[57]

Although views toward democracy remain generally positive, when probed somewhat deeper, a more nuanced and mixed picture regarding democratic values emerges. Between 2012 and 2016, for example, on average 31.5 percent of those surveyed believed in the appropriateness of a political system in which electoral competition is limited only to Islamist political parties.[58] From 2011 to 2016, the proportion of people willing to accept rule by a political party which they oppose remained consistently high at about 55 percent, but the percentage of those unwilling to accept rule by a political party which they oppose also remained consistent at approximately 37 percent.[59]

In 2014, Daniel Brumberg pointed to "the existence of an expanding regional democratic ethos that no Arab government can wish away or ignore."[60] My assessment, based on the data presented here, is slightly more guarded. Democracy as a general idea may be gaining more appeal. But undemocratic views and beliefs lurk beneath the surface and remain robustly present.

Generally positive overall assumptions about democracy prevail at a time when very few people identify their country as democratic. Between 2011 and 2016, the number of respondents who viewed their country as democratic was a consistently low 5 percent.[61] From 2012 to 2016, as we saw in Table 5.6, fewer people felt free to express their opinion without fear. In 2012–13, 63 percent felt that they could express themselves freely and without fear from the government. But that proportion steadily declined to 60 percent in 2014, 57 percent in 2015, and 56 percent in 2016. Conversely, the proportion of those fearing the consequences of openly criticizing the government went from 27 percent in 2012–13 to 30 percent in 2014, 38 percent in 2015, and 39 percent in 2016.

Not surprisingly, few individuals were willing to express themselves politically through formal state institutions or the legal avenues open to them. A pretty consistent proportion of people, 85 percent, did not sign a petition or write a protest letter between 2012 and 2016.[62] Similarly, between 2012–13 and 2016, a consistent 86 percent did not take part in acts of political mobilization regarding an issue of public concern.[63] Across the Arab world, between 2012 and 2016, membership in political parties remained low at about 11 percent, while more than half of those polled, 54 percent, were neither party members nor did they feel that existing parties adequately expressed their views.[64]

Finally, when asked about the personal and public aspects of religion, Arab publics appear to hold complex, and at times contradictory, views. To begin with, from 2011 to 2016 levels of religiosity stayed pretty much the same, with 22 percent identifying themselves as very religious, 65 percent as religious, 9 percent as not religious, and 4 percent declining to answer (Table 5.7). Religious tolerance—in terms of respecting the rights of co-religionists who adhere to different interpretations—appeared to be inching upwards: 69 percent in 2012–13, 73 percent in 2014, 75 percent in 2015, and 77 percent in 2016. At the same time, the percentage of those professing intolerance remained fairly steady at 18 percent from 2012–13 to 2016. Along similar lines, tolerance for people with other religions increased incrementally: a total of 67 percent in 2012–13, 70 percent in 2014, 72 percent in 2015, and 73 percent in 2016. At the same time, the percentage of people at the opposite end of the spectrum, namely those expressing intolerance for people with a different religion, held steady at 21 percent.

Views about whether religion should remain a personal or a public matter also held pretty steady from 2011 to 2016, with a slim majority, 53 percent, believing that "religious practice is a personal concern and should be separated from public life," while 38 percent believe that the two should not be separated. There appears to be seemingly robust and growing support for religious individuals to fill influential positions in the state, starting at 39 percent in 2011 and rising to 43 percent in 2012–13, 44 percent in 2014, and 50 percent in both 2015 and 2016. Interestingly, while the overall percentage of those who do not think that influential political positions should be held by religious individuals was steady at 47 percent between 2011 and 2016, the percentage of those who did not know or declined to state an opinion on the matter went down from 16 percent in 2011 to 6 percent in 2016.

The percentage of those who think that religion and politics should be separated also went up: a total of 43 percent in 2011, 46 percent in 2012–13, 51 percent in 2014, 52 percent in 2015, and 53 percent in 2016 (Table 5.7). This steady if slow growth appears to be due to the fact that in every subsequent poll more people were willing to answer instead of opting for the "do not know" option. Nevertheless, the percentage of those who think that religion and politics should not be separated has consistently remained at a robust 41 percent. Between 2012–13 and 2016, approximately 70 percent of the population believed that the clergy should not influence government decisions, although on average 24 percent thought that clerical influence in government decision-making is permissible. In the same period, the percentage of those who believed that religious clerics should not influence voter choices during elections held steady at around 78 percent, as did the percentage of those who believed that the clergy should influence voter choices, at 16.5 percent.[65]

Similar breakdowns appear concerning the use of religion to win popular support by states or by candidates for political office. As the data in Table 5.7 show, between 2012–13 and 2016, the percentage of those who believed that the state has no right to use religion to win popular support for its policies held constant at approximately 73 percent, with another 20 percent believing that the state should be allowed to use religion as a tool for justifying its identity. Similarly, during the same period, 23 percent of those polled believed that candidates for public office should have the right to use religion to win votes, 70.5 percent believing that they should not, and the rest not knowing or declining to answer.[66]

Collectively, several important conclusions can be drawn from the information gathered through the polling data presented here. To begin with, Arab populations largely view the uprisings positively and are generally glad that they occurred. Their outcomes, however, are viewed increasingly negatively. Not only have the uprisings failed to deliver on their promises, with time, they have actually led to a deterioration of the overall quality of life and of political circumstances. In particular, most Arabs perceive their economic situation extremely negatively and

Table 5.7: Attitudes toward religion

		2011	2012–13	2014	2015	2016
Levels of religiosity	Self-identification as very religious	19	21	24	24	20
	Self-identification as religious	66	67	64	63	65
	Self-identification as not religious	11	8	8	9	11
	Don't know or declined to answer	4	4	4	4	3
Co-religionists who believe in a different interpretation are not infidels	Strongly agree	—	27	32	30	30
	Agree	—	42	41	45	47
	Disagree	—	14	12	14	13
	Strongly disagree	—	5	5	6	5
	Don't know or declined to answer	—	11	9	5	5
Those who believe in a different religion are not infidels	Strongly agree	—	27	30	30	27
	Agree	—	40	40	42	46
	Disagree	—	15	14	16	15
	Strongly disagree	—	6	6	7	7
	Don't know or declined to answer	—	12	10	5	5
Religious practices are a personal concern and should be separated from public life	Strongly agree	26	20	24	22	22
	Agree	21	32	30	35	34
	Disagree	18	27	26	27	26
	Strongly disagree	20	10	12	12	13
	Don't know or declined to answer	15	11	8	4	5

Religious individuals should fill influential positions within the state					
Strongly agree	14	12	13	14	15
Agree	25	31	31	36	35
Disagree	24	33	33	30	29
Strongly disagree	21	12	15	15	15
Don't know or declined to answer	16	11	8	5	6
Religion and politics should be separated					
Strongly agree	26	19	24	22	23
Agree	17	27	27	30	30
Disagree	16	27	25	27	25
Strongly disagree	26	14	15	16	16
Don't know or declined to answer	16	13	9	5	6
Clerics should not influence government decisions					
Strongly agree	30	25	29	26	25
Agree	29	43	41	44	44
Disagree	17	19	19	21	21
Strongly disagree	8	3	4	5	6
Don't know or declined to answer	16	10	7	4	4
The government should not use religion to secure support for its policies					
Strongly agree	—	29	33	33	29
Agree	—	41	40	44	45
Disagree	—	16	14	15	16
Strongly disagree	—	4	5	5	6
Don't know or declined to answer	—	11	8	4	4

Source: Arab Center for Research and Policy Studies, *The 2016 Arab Opinion*, pp. 48, 50–51, 54–6, 60.

with little prospect for improvement. The blame for the prevailing, negative economic circumstances is seen to rest with the government.

Another important conclusion has to do with assumptions about democracy. There are broadly positive sentiments toward democracy across the Arab world, although very few see their own country as democratic. Nevertheless, just under a quarter of the population, 22 percent, do not see democracy as the best form of government. Similarly striking is the relatively high percentage of people, 31 percent, who do not mind political competition being limited only to Islamist parties. Other ostensibly anti-democratic values are also prevalent, with sizeable segments of the population unwilling to accept rule by a party which they oppose.

Similar divisions appear to mark popular views toward religion. There appears to be increasing tolerance for others with different religions and views. Slightly more than half of the population in Arab countries (53 percent) believe that religion should be treated as a private matter, but an almost equal number believe that religious individuals should be allowed to fill influential state positions. Religious tolerance is on the rise and is substantial, at around 75 percent, but intolerance is also persistent and robust, at approximately 20 percent.

Lastly, states in general and government agencies in particular are generally seen as inefficient, unresponsive, corrupt, and bereft of legitimacy. The state is largely seen as incapable of or unwilling to perform some of its basic functions, especially in enforcing laws and in providing physical or economic security. It is also seen almost universally as corrupt. Similarly, there is little freedom, and nearly 40 percent of people fear expressing political views. Existing outlets for political sentiments are viewed with general cynicism. The state legislature is at best elitist and at worst irrelevant. There is only confidence that the military and police forces can effectively perform their tasks.

Even when massive state intervention designed to improve the lives of citizens works, political cynicism may still remain and people are likely to retain a cynical and unhappy attitude with the general state of politics. "Political legitimacy," as Hudson rightly observed some time ago, "basically cannot be bought."[67] Legitimacy, it is important to remember, is a matter of degree.[68] So it would be inaccurate to maintain that Arab states are altogether illegitimate before their publics. But legitimacy is compromised in those cases in which society's values are "bifurcated, too chaotic, or too contradictory."[69] As the polling data presented here amply demonstrate, Arab societies tend to remain deeply divided when it comes to some basic assumptions about politics. What consensus there is revolves around negatives: the economy is bad; the state is corrupt; and state institutions do not work. The state, by and large, lacks legitimacy. But especially when it comes to the ideal type of polity, in terms of the role of religion in politics and the essence and practice of democracy, there are deep divisions.

Political Islam

The deep divisions that characterize attitudes toward religion have led to different forms of engagement between Islam and politics. This engagement, of course, is nothing new, and has been a regular feature of the religion since its inception and through the ages. Today, in the post-2011 Arab and Muslim worlds, we find four broad, loosely interconnected types of political Islam. These different types include, at one extreme, what in recent years has been called post-Islamism, followed by Islam of the kind adhered to by the likes of the Muslim Brotherhood organization, then by Salafism, and lastly, at the extreme end of the spectrum, by Salafi-jihadism. Islam has been and continues to be a powerful mobilizing ideology. But, more importantly, it is both a subject of political contestation and its object.[70] None of the four varieties of political Islam discussed here is necessarily new or was born out of the 2011 uprisings. All, in fact, predate the Arab Spring. But it was during the uprisings that they came into sharp contrast with one another and made their presence most acutely felt. There are, needless to say, intense and multidimensional struggles within Islam itself over the religion's very soul and direction. In this section, I examine each of these different manifestations of political Islam not in terms of theology or jurisprudence but in relation to the state.

In recent years, a number of scholars have observed that younger Arabs, especially those under the age of thirty-five, tend to be religiously less observant than those older than thirty-five.[71] Salafists and jihadists get a lot of press, but those ideologically on the left or in the center are more numerous, especially among the young. These millennials may not be strictly secular, but they are far more likely to be religiously less observant. Opinion polls indicate that, at least in Egypt, millennials tend to identify with national identity first and then with religion, a reversal of how earlier generations identified themselves in 2001 and 2007.[72] There also appears to be an emerging consensus among younger Arabs that religious officials should not seek to influence the behavior of ordinary citizens.[73] Although such observations are difficult to substantiate through empirical research, manifestations of apparent declines in religiosity among Arab youths are hard to refute. I would not go so far as maintaining that the 2011 uprisings meant "the end of political Islam as we have known it."[74] But at least for sizeable numbers of Middle Easterners and Arabs, especially the youth, we are in fact witnessing a process of "'autonomization' of politics from religion and of religion from politics."[75] In other words, for many in the Muslim world, the two spheres of politics and religion are becoming, or are trying to become, increasingly autonomous of one another.

Asef Bayat describes this phenomenon as "post-Islamism," which he defines as follows:

> Neither anti-Islamic nor secular, but spearheaded by pious Muslims, post-Islamism attempts to undo Islamism as a political project by fusing faith and freedom, a secular democratic state and a religious society. It wants to marry Islam with individual choice and liberties, with democracy and modernity, to generate what some have called an "alternative modernity."[76]

Upon coming to power in Iran, Bayat argues, Islamism exhausted itself of appeal, energy, and legitimacy. It was eventually forced by its internal contradictions to abandon its underlying principles and to reinvent itself in pragmatic, practical ways. The outcome is neither anti-Islamic nor un-Islamic but is rather an amalgam of "religiosity and rights, faith and freedom, Islam and liberty."[77] In Iran, this post-Islamism has proven its social and political resilience despite trenchant opposition from more "principalist" strands of post-revolutionary currents.[78] In another non-Arab country in the region, Turkey, we see a similar phenomenon, but with different roots. Here a fragile balance emerged between two political value systems, Islam and secular nationalism. Lacking universal popular support, neither value system could altogether eradicate the other, and therefore decided to compete in the political arena.[79] Albeit at times rocky, the result has been a marriage of political Islam and democracy.

In only three countries of the Middle East, two of them non-Arab, has post-Islamism been able to reach political power. In each of the three countries—Iran, Turkey, and Tunisia—the path to this political ascent has been different. Whereas in Iran post-Islamism was a product of the evolution of the 1978–79 revolution, in Turkey it was a result of the institutional context in which two competing political and ideological currents found themselves: one secular nationalist and the other Islamist. In Tunisia, a political system based on post-Islamism is being deliberately crafted by the heirs of the 2011 uprisings. Elsewhere in the Arab world, post-Islamism remains a largely social and cultural phenomenon, albeit one with a strong political impulse. And, as a social phenomenon, it appears to be most pervasive among the youth.

Much older than post-Islamism is a socially and culturally more conservative variant that traces its roots back to Hassan al-Banna and the Muslim Brotherhood organization he founded in Alexandria back in 1928. From its Egyptian birthplace, the organization grew and expanded into different Arab countries as its ideals and premises were adopted by Islamists across the region. With each expansion, this conservative Islamism adapted to local contexts and circumstances and tweaked its goals and objectives accordingly. Nevertheless, both in Egypt and elsewhere the Muslim Brotherhood sought "to expand the scope of religion in the public sphere and foster an organic link between the Islamization of society and political participation."[80] Despite much perseverance, in the long run few Islamists were able to succeed in their objectives. They were often a victim to the inflexibility of their own ideology and worldview. More commonly, Islamists were viewed with suspicion and skepticism by political elites who continued to bar them from taking part in the narrow political space that was allowed. The same suspicion extended to secular intellectuals, who often viewed Islamists with disdain and as relics of a bygone era.[81]

This all changed with the Arab Spring, which opened up political space, at least temporarily, and brought new actors to the fore. In the immediate aftermath of the uprisings, Islamists were particularly energized thanks to their history of grassroots organization; they reconnected with their constituents, and were able to win parliamentary majorities in both Tunisia and Egypt. But only in Tunisia have they had political staying power now that the dust of the uprisings has mostly settled. To begin with, in places where they were allowed to contest in parliamentary elections, the Islamists' electoral strength did not exceed 25 percent of the electorate.[82] More importantly, the same suspicions and restrictions that inhibited the Islamists' political ascent before the uprisings continued to linger afterwards. Except in Tunisia, where the Ennahda is itself changing along with the new political space it is helping to craft, Islamists elsewhere have done little to adapt to new demographic, cultural, and political realities.

Demographically, the support base of Islamists lies not in the youth but among older generations. They remain largely out of touch with the youth, for whom they offer neither real solutions to pressing economic concerns (such as employment), nor nuanced cultural cues about how to navigate the pressures of modern society. The electoral victories of the Muslim Brotherhood after 2011, underwhelming as they were, were mostly due to the efforts of older activists rather than those of the young. The religious right is not unimportant among Arab millennials. But its core strength lies among the older generation, the forty-somethings and above, rather than among the twenty-somethings and younger.[83]

Although Islamist parties came to the fore during the Arab Spring uprisings, and although these parties are not known for their adherence to and promotion of democracy, the uprisings did set off a process of democratization in the societies in which they occurred.[84] Like all other social movements, Islamism is the product of particular social and historical circumstances, whose efficacy is likely to recede once its goals have been achieved. Before the uprisings, Islamist movements used religious credentials as a source of popular legitimacy. The degree to which they can continue doing so in the post-uprising period is questionable; a political party will ultimately be judged by its performance in office, not its founding principles.[85]

Most Islamists have also been unable to adapt their worldview to the new political realities of the post-2011 era. What adjustments they have made have so far failed to garner substantial popular support beyond their core, preexisting support-base. In the immediate aftermath of the 2011 uprisings, the Egyptian Muslim Brotherhood adopted "justice" and "freedom" as two of its chief objectives. It had always believed in justice, but its adoption of freedom as a goal was new. The draft program of the Freedom and Justice Party included the promotion of freedoms for political parties and civil society organizations, and the recognition of the *umma* as the source of governmental power.[86] The *sharia* continued to be upheld as the fundamental system of rule, along with liberal ideals of separation of powers, democracy, civic freedoms for all citizens, and respect for the wishes of the majority.[87] But both the constitutional debates that followed Mubarak's ouster and the brief tenure of the Morsi administration revealed few substantive changes to the Brotherhood's overall social and political agendas.[88] In the end, the Muslim Brotherhood's political failures have been as much a product of its own doing as that of the el-Sisi autocracy.

Despite the apparent failure of political Islam of the kind advocated by the Muslim Brotherhood, or more likely because of it, literalist interpretations of the religion have gained increasing hold among a growing number of Arabs. Most Salafists tend to be politically quietist and eschew political activism, seeking instead to emulate the lifestyle of the Prophet and the earliest Muslims. In Egypt and Kuwait, Salafists have, largely unsuccessfully, sought to take part in mainstream politics through parliamentary elections. The reasons for their lack of political success, both at the formal institutional level and at the popular level of the masses, are not that different from the obstacles faced by conservative Islamists. Similar to Muslim Brotherhood Islamists, Salafists face a political space that has certain multidimensional constraints. These constraints tend to be demographic; are shaped by a political culture influenced by political Islam's checkered past and uneven successes; are influenced by the political consequences of social change, including processes of individualization; and are influenced by the appearance and attraction of post-Islamism.[89] Not surprisingly, as we shall see shortly, the very constraining environment within which Salafists find themselves makes many of them susceptible to radical jihadism.

Precisely how many Muslims are attracted to Salafism is difficult to ascertain. In some of the more conservative quarters of society across the Arab world, there is a new norm emerging at the heart of Arab identity that is anchored in "unapologetic Islam" and is "vaguely Salafi." Secular voices are even afraid of challenging it for fear of backlash and of being accused of undermining Arab authenticity and Islam itself.[90] If there are voices of dissent, they are often cast as courageous and out of the ordinary at best and un-Islamic and anti-religious at worst.[91]

Salafi literalism and its hold on the more marginal elements of society lends itself to radical jihadism. Although frequently quietist, Salafi activism all too often manifests itself in extremist forms, with jihad interpreted in its most literalist meaning, as in holy war. We have long known that the effects of religiosity on collective political action are highly context dependent.[92] Civil wars and sectarianisms (more on this in the next chapter) have only polarized preexisting sentiments and aggravated feelings of isolation and victimization. Besides joining Salafi-jihadists, many North African youths engage in other extremist and risky acts in desperate hope of giving meaning to their poverty-stricken and marginalized lives.[93]

Pervasive and cruel violence, and anarchy in Libya, Syria, Iraq, and Yemen, have become additional sources of polarization for otherwise nonviolent believers.[94] There are, for example, Tunisian terrorists who carry Libyan passports, and close to 1.5 million displaced Libyans are estimated to be living in Tunisia. In the aftermath of the 2011 uprisings, Tunisian Islamists assumed that Salafist radicals could be co-opted into the political mainstream. The Salafists were euphoric and proliferated by taking advantage of the permissive environment, amassing weapons and moving freely between Tunisia, Libya, Turkey, and elsewhere.[95] In 2014 alone, 7,000 Tunisians were prevented by the authorities from leaving the country to pursue jihad in Syria. That same year, the authorities estimated that some 4,000 Tunisians were already fighting for ISIS.[96]

Salafi-jihadism constitutes a fourth manifestation of political Islam in the post-2011 Arab world. Salafi-jihadism has become a "traveling and expanding ideology," fed by "raging sectarian fires in Iraq and Syria and the clash of identities that is ravaging Arab countries."[97] Again, this is not a new phenomenon. The most notable of Salafi-jihadist organizations, Daesh, is an even more violent and more extremist offshoot of al-Qaʿida, its source of ideological and practical inspiration.[98] Similar to the Muslim Brotherhood, Daesh has other franchises that affiliate with it only loosely and more through ideological and tactical affinities rather than tangible institutional linkages. Before announcing its dissolution in May 2017, for example, Daesh's affiliate in North Africa was called the Ansar al-Sharia.[99] Here I will focus on Daesh, for now the biggest and most organized of such groups.[100]

Daesh's appearance and rise, and its transformation from an organization into a state, have been documented and analyzed in a number of excellent studies.[101] Here I will highlight the composition of Daesh's leadership and its rank and file, reasons for its seemingly unrestrained resort to violence as a political tactic, and its efforts at establishing an alternative state, a caliphate, in territories under its control.

Within the broader context of global jihadism, the social origins of the Islamic State of Iraq and Sham (ISIS, or Daesh in Arabic) lie in the Iraqi and Syrian civil wars. Iraqi Prime Minister Al-Maliki's growing authoritarianism, especially after 2010, combined with the increasing petty bickering of the elite and the general paralysis of the political system, only helped fuel growing disillusionment with traditional politics and deepened the appeal of ISIS.[102] The 2010–11 uprisings, the ability of the precursor to ISIS, the Islamic State of Iraq (ISI), to connect with rural youths, and Al-Maliki's inability to reintegrate Sunni tribal chiefs into the political process all combined to give ISI a new lease on life and increased its popularity and power.

The organization was originally set up by Abu Bakr Al-Baghdadi, *nom de guerre* for Ibrahim Awad Ibrahim al-Badri (b.1971). Like hundreds of other Iraqis, Al-Baghdadi's experience in the American-run Bucca prison near Baghdad, dubbed Camp Bucca, was a watershed in his transformation into a Salafi-jihadist and his determination to avenge Iraq's occupation by the Americans and the Shia-dominated government in Baghdad.[103] Al-Baghdadi has proven himself to be a shrewd and calculating military strategist, and he appears to inspire as much respect among his followers as Osama bin Laden did a generation ago.[104] Al-Baghdadi has always paid attention to organization and institution building, having over time created various Salafi-jihadist organizations meant to instigate and direct armed activities. His military exploits and his ability to evade capture, coupled with his rare public appearances, have created a mystique and account for much of his popularity.[105]

Former Ba'athists from Saddam Hussein's regime comprise the bulk of Daesh's top leadership and its chief strategists. Al-Baghdadi's two top lieutenants are both former military commanders in Saddam's army, one having attained the rank of major general and the other lieutenant colonel.[106] While Daesh's leadership is solidly middle class, its rank and file is largely poor, rural, agrarian, and "lacking in both theological and intellectual accomplishment."[107] Most of the earlier local and foreign recruits to Daesh were radicalized by the 2003 US invasion of Iraq.[108] Later on, Daesh's ranks grew as Prime Minister Al-Maliki's overt sectarianism drove many Sunnis to the insurgency. Daesh and violence appear to have had a symbiotic relationship together. The US withdrawal of its forces from Iraq in December 2013 saw the country descend further into the abyss, with the number of deaths rising from more than 4,500 in 2012 to 8,000 in 2013.[109]

From the very start, almost unrestrained violence became one of the central hallmarks of Daesh's modus operandi. This pervasiveness of violence is a product of several developments. Before Daesh was born, its predecessor, al-Qaʿida in Iraq, was led by Abu Musab al-Zarqawi. Zarqawi, who was particularly brutal and indiscriminate in his use of violence, shifted al-Qaʿida's focus to identity and communal politics. There was also an Iraqization of Daesh through instrumental use of Baʿathist tools of repression. A simultaneous ruralization of Daesh's rank and file occurred, along with a stream of foreign fighters entering both Iraq and Syria.[110] Lacking any personal or emotional ties to their new surroundings, foreign fighters have basically, within certain limits, been acting as they please. Daesh has thrived through the ingress of these foreign fighters, and so has its employment of violence.[111]

This use of violence has found doctrinal justifications in a number of Salafi-jihadist tracts. There are three particularly influential Salafi-jihadist manifestos that outline and justify the use of violence: *The Management of Savagery*, by Abu Bakr al-Najji; *Introduction to Jurisprudence of Jihad*, by Abu Abdullah al-Muhajjer; and *The Essentials of Making Ready [for Jihad]*, by Sayyid Imam al-Sharif.[112] Zarqawi and other jihadists are believed to have been especially influenced by *The Management of Savagery*, which sees violence as an essential ingredient of processes of state- and nation-building prior to the establishment of an Islamic State.[113] According to all three manifestos, uncompromising viciousness is the key to military success and victory, and the end of establishing the Islamic State justifies the violent means. The manifestos advocate offensive jihad and all-out war.[114] All three books convey a message of how to instill fear in the hearts of enemies through beheadings and burnings. The deliberate employment of savagery, they argue, strikes fear in the heart of the enemy and attracts new recruits.[115]

Through social media, Daesh has done its best to give maximum exposure to its acts of violence and savagery. Most of the group's commanders and recruits are tech-savvy and maintain active profiles on social media. Digital psychological warfare, in fact, has emerged as one of Daesh's most effective tools.[116]

On 29 June 2014, Al-Baghdadi declared the establishment of a caliphate. The proclamation represented Daesh's deep-rootedness in Islamic law, one that is at the same time highly apocalyptic.[117] Although as a political entity the Caliphate represents Daesh's blueprint for political and administrative organization, it is identity politics, and more specifically "a reaffirmation of its 'Sunni Islamic' identity and its redefinition of true Islam," that lie at the core of the enterprise.[118] Not surprisingly, the proclamation struck a deep chord among Sunni militants worldwide, who then flooded its ranks.[119]

In his "Proclamation of the Caliphate," Al-Baghdadi showed great care and concern about the foundations of the state he was proclaiming. For Al-Baghdadi and others within Daesh, the Caliphate signaled the end of the Sykes–Picot agreement and the reemergence of an organic, natural regional order.[120] Al-Baghdadi told his followers that the conditions for establishing a Caliphate were right, and that other leaders were unjust and had no authority to lead the faithful. He declared that the name of the entity would no longer have Iraq or Syria in it and would just be the Islamic State. With the Caliphate being the only true *umma*, or global Muslim nation, he exhorted his followers, it would need to be proactively defended from the inevitable attacks of infidels.[121]

Once the Caliphate was declared, IS moved quickly to establish institutions and other trappings of a state, including its own currency, banks, car license plates, freshly painted police cars, and police uniforms.[122] Deeply concerned with institutional set-ups and organizational dynamics, Al-Baghdadi wasted no time in efforts to solidify the new entity's administrative apparatus. The declaration of the Caliphate was followed by spectacular attacks on two Iraqi prisons—Abu Ghraib and Taji— from which some 500 al-Qaʻida fighters and commanders were released, boosting IS's cadre of fighters and administrators.[123] Soon, an elaborate institutional set-up was established, with Caliph Ibrahim

(Al-Baghdadi) at the top, followed immediately by two lieutenants, a cabinet, and no fewer than seven councils: security and intelligence; economics; education; Islamic services; provincial council; council for public and provincial concerns; and the *sharia* council, to deal with all religious and judicial matters and supervise a *sharia* police.[124]

All states need money to finance their budgets, and the Islamic State is no exception. It so happened that the territory the Caliphate had captured is rich in oil. It is difficult to determine the Caliphate's revenue flows and expenditures accurately, but, in 2015, IS was estimated to extract 50,000 barrels of oil per day in Syria and another 30,000 bpd in Iraq, earning an estimated $3 to $5 million per day.[125] Supplementing its income has been money earned through kidnappings, mainly of Western journalists and aid workers. In 2014 alone, ransoms from kidnappers brought IS an estimated $20 million.[126] At some point, IS was thought to be "the richest terrorist group in history."[127]

Regardless of its precise revenues, in areas under its control the Islamic State has been generally able to deliver basic services, administer justice, and establish law and order, therefore gaining a modicum of support among the population.[128] By encouraging the inflow of immigrants with various skills, Al-Baghdadi seemed to be trying to create an entirely new nation.[129] Dissent, of course, is not allowed in any form, and public morality—in extreme forms such as a ban on music and smoking, strict observance of the *hijab*, and obligatory closure of businesses during prayer times—is strictly enforced. Daesh's worldview has always been totalitarian and millenarian, with no room for social mobilization, political organization, competition, pluralism, or diversity of thought.[130]

Olivier Roy, the French scholar of Islam, maintains that Daesh's Caliphate is a contradiction in terms, rendered impossible by its innate nihilism. "The caliphate is a fantasy," he writes:

> It is the myth of an ideological entity constantly expanding its territory. Its strategic impossibility explains why those who identify with it, instead of devoting themselves to the interests of local Muslims, have chosen to enter a death pact. There is no political perspective, no bright future, not even a place to pray in peace. But while the concept of the caliphate is indeed part of the Muslim religious imagination, the same cannot be said for the pursuit of death.[131]

I agree with the general premise of Roy's argument. No political system based on such extreme forms of control can last indefinitely, at least not in its present form. But neither will it collapse on its own. Often dismissed and derided as archaic and barbarian, the Islamic Caliphate is engaged in a serious process of state- and nation-building, one that cannot be simply ignored or dismissed. Much of its success hinges on its military hold on the shrinking territories it has captured. If it can indeed hold on to its territorial gains, which admittedly remains doubtful, there is little reason to believe that its project will not succeed.

Conclusion

As all uprisings go, the Arab Spring gave Arabs hope and a sense of the possible. Revolutions are by definition hopeful endeavors. People mobilize, shout, and sacrifice because they believe a better future is possible. They feel empowered. They sense the possible. But only in Tunisia has the future turned better, if not economically at least politically. Elsewhere, autocracy has been reestablished and reinvigorated, or worse yet, neighbors and clans have turned against each other and plunged their societies and countries into seemingly endless civil wars.

As if the mixture were not already lethal enough, external actors continue to pursue their own agendas regardless of the costs to those whose lives are ruined in the process. The US invasion of Iraq in 2003 started a chain reaction that led to the declaration of the Caliphate by Abu Bakr Al-Baghdadi on 29 June 2014. Today, the world in general and the Middle East in particular is still grappling with the consequences of George W. Bush's war in the Middle East. Not to be outdone, the Qataris, Saudis, Iranians, Emiratis, and even the Russians joined the fray. The Arab world's post-2011 quagmire is no longer strictly Arab.

Once again, Arab politics has come to be defined less by the legitimacy of the state than by the nature of the state's power relationships over and with society. Arab societies have always shown remarkable creativity, vibrancy, and resilience in finding avenues for contemplation, expression, discussion, and debate even under the most repressive of political circumstances. The 2011 uprisings brought those forms of expression to the surface, out on the streets, and in public squares. But before long old power relations reemerged, coercive apparatuses reasserted their political dominance, and creativity and free expression were pushed into the shadows. Censorship in all forms reigns supreme.

Within Arab societies themselves, few signs of hope for a better political future are present. Violence, sectarianism, jihadism, the rule of the military, and technocracy have all combined to end the public debate over demands for citizenship and legitimacy. States instead seek a forcible imposition of unity and conformity. Legitimacy has been redefined and reduced to forcible acquiescence. Citizenship is now seldom seen in terms of the common good, but is assumed to revolve around parochial, specific demands for the rights of the sect, the tribe, the clan, and the family.[132] And dialogue, when it is allowed to take place, tends to emerge out of strategic alliances and accommodations against mutual enemies, rather than agreements over rules of the game and respecting opponents.[133]

Despite Daesh's brutal excesses, therefore, there are few indications that extremist impulses are likely to recede any time soon. Should Daesh be defeated, as it appears to be as of this writing, there is always another like-minded militant group that is likely to emerge to fill the power vacuum in the region. Regardless of what happens to the Islamic Caliphate, the ideology of Salafi-jihadism is here to stay and is likely to gain new converts.[134] Given the brutality of military regimes in Egypt, Algeria, Syria, and Yemen, and the discourse of stability by the West, "the question is not why ISIS has emerged out of this merciless blood bath, but why ISIS has not yet grown stronger."[135]

What Michael Hudson wrote in the 1970s continues, tragically, to hold true to this day:

> When I look across the Arab world today, I can only conclude that the basic problems of identity, authority, and equality remain unresolved. Because they are unresolved, Arab politics appears to be going neither forward nor backward: the radical future seems unreachable and the traditional past unrecoverable. Politics thus is largely the art of manipulating appealing ideological symbols and trying to generate personal popularity.[136]

For Arab societies, today as in the years past, states remain by far the biggest impediment to realizing their own full potential.

6

ADAPTIVE POLITICS IN THE ARABIAN PENINSULA

Unlike the states of the Levant and North Africa, those in the Arabian Peninsula did not experience significant political upheavals in the final weeks of 2010 and early 2011, with Bahrain being a notable exception. Oman also witnessed a few scattered demonstrations, though not nearly to the same extent and scale as the ones that occurred in, for example, Algeria, Morocco, and Jordan. This chapter examines the institutional responses of the petro-states of the Gulf Cooperation Council to the 2011 uprisings and the 2014 collapse in oil prices.[1]

In June 2017, a dispute erupted among four GCC member states when Saudi Arabia, the UAE, and Bahrain accused Qatar of sponsoring terrorism, severed all ties with Doha, and imposed a comprehensive land and air blockade on the country. Despite earnest negotiating efforts by Kuwait, the dispute, even if and when resolved, has put into question the long-term viability of the GCC as a collective regional trade and security organization. Nevertheless, even if the GCC has lost its viability, the underlying historical, political, and economic similarities of its six member states warrant their analysis as a separate category.

This classification of the GCC states into a category of their own is based not on the ways in which the uprisings transpired there—or, more accurately, did not transpire—but because of differences in patterns of state-building and institutional evolution that separate states in the Arabian Peninsula from those elsewhere in the Arab world. Historically rooted patterns of state-building and institutional evolution, reinforced along the way with considerable material and financial resources since the discovery of oil, have given the states of the GCC enhanced capacity and adaptability, enabling them to better absorb and cope with potential pressures from below. Rentierism has not made political contestation moot altogether. But it has reinforced the state's ability, along with other built-in characteristics the state already had, to better cope with domestic political opposition.

The chapter starts with an examination of the institutional composition of the six petro-states before, and their evolution after, oil. It traces these states' sources of built-in adaptability and enhanced capacity, which have in turn bestowed on them greater resilience over time. These petro-states may be suffering from the institutional consequences of the resource curse,[2] but whatever "development" their institutions may have had so far has been sufficient to allow them to ride out, or altogether fend off, crises of the kind that engulfed many of the other Arab states in 2011.

The chapter argues that one of the key differences between the political systems of the Arabian Peninsula and those in North Africa and the Levant is state capacity. In terms of geography and demography, the countries of the Peninsula are among the smallest in the Middle East. Yet despite their small size, oil revenues have given these states considerable capacity to bring about rapid and far-reaching transformations of their societies, build highly modern infrastructures, and, somewhat uniquely in the Arab world, to place themselves at the crosscurrents of global commerce, investments, and transport networks.

Reinforcing the economic dimensions of state capacity have been a number of additional, historically rooted social and cultural linkages that have tied the state to social actors. At the center of these linkages is the most basic unit of society, the family. The states of the Arabian Peninsula, in fact, have historically pretty much behaved like oversized family enterprises, with those at the center of the ruling circle tied to the rest of society through a succession of marital and commercial bonds. These multiple, overlapping linkages blur the distinctions between "state" and "society" even more than is generally the case. More importantly, they give the state a measure of capacity and a level of political resilience that other states, especially those in North Africa and the Levant, can only dream of.

State capacity has generally enabled the monarchies of the Arabian Peninsula to ride out challenges to political rule, including those of 2011. In fact, as this chapter demonstrates, with the exception of Bahrain, the 2011 uprisings for the most part skipped the Arabian Peninsula. But when the very same state capacity was threatened in 2014 as oil prices suddenly collapsed and incoming revenues dipped, then state survival strategies kicked in and corrective measures were taken. Long before political power arrangements were threatened, and before historically rooted patterns of state–society relations were disrupted so as to prompt social actors to agitate against the state, political leaders undertook institutional adjustments needed to remedy declining state capacity. Regime survival strategies have fostered political adaptability, while at the same time keeping the state and the underlying premises of its relations with society unchanged.

It goes without saying, of course, that the six petro-states are not all the same and are separated by notable differences among them. Although many Persian Gulf states share similar macro-economic characteristics, they also feature considerable variations in terms of demography, extent of hydrocarbon-driven wealth, patterns of state-building and institutional evolution, levels of social cohesion, political traditions, and the relationship between the ruling family and other tribal clans. Nevertheless, as the following pages demonstrate, their historic, cultural, economic, and political and institutional similarities by far outweigh their differences.

Legitimacy, Clientelism, and Rentierism

Prior to the large-scale discovery of oil between the 1930s and the 1950s, the states of the Arabian Peninsula had experienced different historical processes in their state-building efforts as compared to the rest of the Arab world and the Middle East. These differences became even more pronounced and were further deepened in the 1950s and the 1960s, when much of North Africa and the Levant underwent significant and profound political changes. Not only did the emerging states of the Arabian Peninsula escape many of these changes, often through their own deliberate efforts, in fact they were able to employ their growing oil revenues to strengthen preexisting, and what were becoming increasingly comparatively "traditional," patterns of rule. Starting in the 1950s, in fact, we see two very divergent paths in processes of state-building in the Arab world. Ostensibly republican states, typified by Nasserist Egypt, set out to create what they defined as modern and progressive political and economic systems. In doing so, they deliberately and often coercively dismantled those aspects of tradition that impeded their supposed march toward modernity. In the Arabian Peninsula, however, state leaders, who had always resorted to the past as one of the central pillars of their continued legitimacy, were helped in building a counter-narrative through newly found wealth. Oil money helped consolidate traditional patterns of rule, giving them institutional form and, in the process, resilience.

State structures in the Arabian Peninsula owed their genesis to the growth and expansion of tribal formations and alliances, at the center of which often were located one of the larger and more dominant family clans. Clans and families clustered into tribes, and tribal alliances grew into and formed tribal confederations. Political power traveled not only vertically, from the top to the rest of the tribe, but also horizontally, cemented by an implicit modus vivendi, a division of labor that accounted for the provision of protection and rule by the tribe's leader and his family, supported financially by merchants, and, when needed, militarily by the rest of the tribe.[3] The emerging states of the region were, and in many ways still continue to be, "natural" in the sense that ruling families are part and parcel of the social fabric of the country, tying the "state" and "society" together at countless levels and in multiple dimensions. Granted international recognition by the British Colonial Agents, tribal leaders steadily emerged as state rulers. Their domestic legitimacy, meanwhile, was enhanced through the increasing array of services they were able to offer their flock and by the accouterments and symbols of the state that grew around them.

Not surprisingly, the states that emerged were organized around the centrality of the ruling family and the person of the ruler. Subsequent developments, and especially the discovery of oil, only served to reinforce political patterns that had been set earlier. Long before the discovery of oil in the 1930s to the 1950s, sheikhly and patrimonial patterns of rule, under the auspices of the institution of the ruling family, had already been established across the Peninsula. It was only then that the flow of oil revenues into the coffers of the state kicked in, and by doing so consolidated existing patterns of patrimonial rule. With the discovery of oil, the state began controlling oil revenues, stayed out of the activities of the merchants, provided for the welfare of the populations, and thus consolidated itself. Across the region, the family was, and remains, by far the most important source of support, as well as constraint and threat, to the monarch. To this day, constraints come not in the form of constitutions and other institutional mechanisms, but in the form of dynastic rules, with monarchs often having to place relatives in lucrative, and at times even influential, positions. Across the GCC today, the state is neopatrimonial, and the regime is organized around individuals. The flow of oil revenues and the rentier political economies that emerged did not create new patterns of rule from scratch. They merely reified and reinforced existing ones.

As we have seen so far, there are multiple ways in which oil has shaped the formation and evolution of the Arab petro-states. Oil, to state the obvious, did not create institutional formations and practices but merely reinforced and strengthened them. This reification occurred through the convergence of three mutually reinforcing phenomena, namely legitimacy, clientelism, and rentierism.

While analytically and conceptually distinct, in actual practice in the Persian Gulf region these three phenomena are part of the same continuum and are often so intertwined as to be indistinguishable. Legitimacy, in the sense employed here, revolves around the acceptability of sources of authority of power-holders by a majority of members of the community. Clientelism refers to relationships of patronage between people in the higher rungs of the socioeconomic ladder who use their status to facilitate access to goods and services by those below them. And rentierism denotes the state's ability to draw on revenues accrued through the sale of resources, or the provision of services, whose profits are disproportionately larger than the efforts needed to secure them.[4] Across the Arabian Peninsula, state leaders have solidified the authority of their office (legitimacy) through a proliferation of networks of patronage and dependence (clientelism), using the inordinate revenues coming their way through the sale of oil (rentierism).

The legitimacy of the states of the Arabian Peninsula is derived from a combination of historical, cultural, and economic forces that have given these states multiple means of nexus with various actors and groups in their societies. To start, there is the legitimacy inherent in the position of rulership itself, be it the Emir (literally, commander) or the king or sultan. Rulers portray obedience to the system as a religious and cultural obligation.[5] Central to the legitimation of the system is the notion of the ruler as the paramount sheikh, *Sheikh al-Mashayikh*. Not surprisingly, the state pursues a delicate balance of feverish economic modernity, thanks to oil revenues, while remaining committed to preserving cultural heritage and tradition. In places such as Manama, Doha, Abu Dhabi, and Dubai, high modernity coexists side by side with tradition. Museums and "cultural villages" form robust and expansive heritage industries that hold up an imagined past, anchored in the heroics of the ruling family, as supposed tangible connections with the present and the future. The same visionary determination that made these pearling villages and desert oases into what they are today will guide them to a better tomorrow.[6] The past, as represented even in the national dress, and the larger invention and reinvention of culture, assume important political roles.[7]

This notional legitimacy is reinforced through a series of direct and indirect relationships between the ruler and his subjects. The growth of the modern state has in many ways further facilitated both the symbolic and the actual links between rulers and their subjects. Using the new mechanisms of the state, rulers can now appeal more directly to tribesmen as fellow countrymen and without the mediating figures of tribal leaders.[8] Across the region, moreover, political bonds between those at the highest echelons of the state and successive layers below them are frequently cemented through marriage and commercial relations, making the ruling family in general and the state in particular part and parcel of the fabric of society.[9] While the "state" and "society" remain conceptually and practically distinct and separate, they are also intimately intertwined at multiple points of contact and intersection. This is particularly the case in Saudi Arabia and the smaller emirates of Qatar and the UAE, where members of the ruling family are also prominent and influential social actors. In Bahrain, the Al-Khalifa family has a similar relationship with the rest of the country's Sunni population.

To maintain, therefore, that rentierism is the overwhelming or even the primary source of legitimacy of the Arabian Peninsula's petro-states is to miss the societal, cultural, familial, and commercial connections that bind ruling families—which are the core, constituent elements of the states—to the rest of society. These bonds had already secured the position of the ruling families on top of the power hierarchy for at least a century before oil revenues started flowing into the coffers of the state. Rentier political economy goes a long way in deepening pre-existing, complementary sources of legitimacy rooted in history and sociocultural networks.

One way to conceptualize legitimacy in the Arab petro-state is in terms of a social contract between the state and a broad spectrum of social actors. Despite differences, in all Arabian Peninsula states, emergent social contracts have come to govern state–society relations. Across the region, these social contracts—in terms of informal understanding of the mutual responsibilities of political leaders and social actors to each other—have not been static and have changed and adjusted over time. Given the relative absence of major demands for radical political change, and the prevalence of comparatively benign forms of authoritarianism in much of the Peninsula, we have seen that social contracts are inherently adaptable and changeable. Many of these changes have come about as a result of the access by different groups to sources of wealth. For example, when the pearl trade dominated the economies of the southern Persian Gulf up until the 1930s, the wealthy merchants supported and patronized ruling families, which on their own were generally not wealthy. But in the independence era, by which time ruling families were firmly in control as oil revenues flowed into the coffers of the state, the relationship changed to one of the state's patronage of merchants (through the awarding of contracts) and of other social classes (through entitlements). As we shall see later in the chapter, now that oil prices are declining, the social contract is being revised again.

State patronage networks, in the form of clientelistic bonds, have multiplied in recent decades because of massive flows of oil revenues into the state. In his study of Saudi Arabia, Steffen Hertog observed a "heterogeneous system of formal and informal, rent-based clientelism in which vertical links dominate."[10] This observation applies to other states of the Arabian Peninsula as well. Thanks to oil, the state, and along with it, the ruling family, has become the primary source of patronage to a whole host of social actors ranging from the merchant classes, on whom the ruling family used to rely for financial support, to medium-and small-scale entrepreneurs and public sector employees. This patronage occurs through a variety of ways, the most commonplace forms of which are direct entitlements to ordinary citizens and the awarding of contracts to entrepreneurs. Engaged in infrastructural growth at breakneck speeds, the Arab petro-states have become the chief awarders of contracts to the entrepreneurial classes for the import and construction of everything that goes into the cities being built into the sea and into the sky.

Similarly, in all six petro-states, the state and its sundry of agencies have become one of the main investors in many commercial enterprises, especially banks and real estate companies, therefore underwriting their solvency and success even in times of economic downturn. Through contracts, licenses, and investments, the state solidifies its ties to society with merchants, who are generally the second stratum of power holders. In all instances and regardless of the overall nature of the state, the links between state and the entrepreneurial classes can be as important and consequential as the state's institutional structures.[11] In petro-states, links with the state are especially important, and business interests, firms, and individuals do what they can to maintain links of patronage with the state in order to get maximum benefits from trade regulations, state-awarded contracts, cheap imports, and high tariff barriers.[12] State–business relations are especially consequential means through which the state maintains bonds of patronage and clientelism with an important and influential group in society. In times of economic downturn, when opportunities for international business ventures are fewer, these merchants tend to look more toward the state for receiving contracts and maintaining cash flows, thus strengthening clientelistic bonds and the state's primacy as a source of patronage. Given the ways in which the regional political economies have evolved, therefore, oil busts (in 2008 and after 2014) do not confront the state with crises but in fact increase the dependence of the entrepreneurial classes on it.

It is not only entrepreneurs who benefit from state largesse and patronage. Oil revenues enable the state to proliferate the public sector, at times even creating multiple agencies that perform parallel functions. As with the rest of the Arab world, and other developing countries for that matter, public sector employment in the petro-states forms an important aspect of the state's clientelistic efforts. To maintain that the public sector is inefficient and even ineffective is hardly revelatory. What is interesting is that in the Arab petro-states, patterns of development have been such that there are occasional, and in some instances frequent, "islands of efficiency" in otherwise notoriously inefficient seas of bureaucracy.[13] In Qatar, for example, in the late 1990s and the early 2000s, Sheikh Hamad created new, highly efficient institutions meant to operate as a parallel bureaucracy, usually under the name "Supreme Council," and empowered them to carry on his modernist vision for the country. At the same time, the highly bloated and inefficient bureaucracy was kept going as a source of employment for the country's high school and university graduates, and as a place for senior, and often older, members of the elite to hang their hats.

In resource-dependent Arab countries, public sector employment is particularly pervasive, driven by considerations of the redistributive political economy on which the state relies.[14] Rents have in fact resulted in badly distorted labor markets in which public sector employment pays more than market wages and the private sector relies on cheap labor.[15] Although public sector bureaucracies were said to have reached a saturation point some time ago and could no longer continue to absorb new graduates in search of employment,[16] their growth in recent years has been unimpeded. This growth has been particularly pronounced in the three wealthier states of the Arabian Peninsula, namely Kuwait, Qatar, and the UAE, where the bulk of the labor force is employed by the state and the private sector is comparatively small. In these countries, most citizens who want jobs in the public sector can get them, while the capitalist classes can rely on cheap imported labor. In the three other comparatively less wealthy countries—Saudi Arabia, Bahrain, and Oman—the state cannot provide civil service jobs for all citizens, and therefore the private sector is more robust.[17] Saudi Arabia and Oman have responded to citizen demands by aggressive labor nationalization policies. Bahrain, for its part, has sought to strengthen Sunni capitalists as a main source of support for the ruling family.[18]

There are a number of drawbacks to excessive reliance on clientelism as a favored mechanism of rule. To begin with, clientelism tends to have a self-perpetuating momentum that makes it difficult for states to break out of. Once in place, clientelistic relations become difficult to abandon, both for the state's clients and for the state itself. State autonomy is not constant and shifts over time. Early on in the state-building process, before clientelistic networks are firmly established, sate autonomy in relation to potential clients tends to be comparatively high. With time, however, new patterns of patron–client relations get firmly established and become difficult to alter.[19] Albeit differently, the state becomes as beholden to its clients as clients are dependent on the state. Although the state can break or switch its patronage from one client to another, it risks alienating clients with whom it has had long-standing, mutually beneficial relations. Senior Kuwaiti cabinet ministers, for example, including the prime minister, often complain that the country's bureaucracy is too bloated and ineffective. But they are unable to carry out many of the needed structural reforms for fear of alienating clients.[20] Moreover, in all of the six countries, the ruling families are themselves important capitalist classes, and public policy reflects their economic interests as well as the interests of their clients. Long-term national development often takes a back seat to short-run, more immediate economic interests.

In the Arab petro-states, the resource curse has resulted in highly skewed labor markets in which public sector employment is both guaranteed and well-paid and in which private sector labor, imported from abroad, is cheap.[21] As we shall see later, in the aftermath of the Arab Spring the petro-states opened up their public sectors even further to make room for more of their graduates. But how much wider the public sector doors can become is open to question. By 2021, in the GCC and Algeria the labor force is expected to grow by an estimated 3.8 million entrants, which the public sector cannot possibly absorb.[22] This is at a time when lower oil prices are likely to continue pushing up unemployment. And, even if possible, public sector expansion by itself is no guarantee of public employees' political complacency. The Arab Spring, in fact, was a sobering reminder to Persian Gulf rulers that public sector employment cannot be ignored or taken for granted in favor of their own wealth and real estate investments.[23] Especially in bigger polities like Saudi Arabia and Oman, despite the growth and expansion of the bureaucracy, society remains pretty much detached from it.[24]

The relationship between clientelism and rentierism is both direct and complex. Rentierism facilitates and deepens clientelistic networks and tendencies within the political system. It also helps mask many of the negative economic side effects of clientelism, at least so long as revenue flows remain relatively uninterrupted. As we have seen, given the evolution of clientelistic ties between the state and its clients in the petro-states, in instances when rent revenues have declined, the clients' dependence on the state has deepened. This is when clients need both direct and indirect state assistance the most. In fact, it is only in relatively less wealthy rentier states—those found in Iran, Iraq, Algeria, and Libya, where the best the state can do is to simply pay salaries to middle-class public sector employees—that economic downturns can have problematic political consequences for the state. In the Arab petro-states, where the state remains in charge of awarding contracts to the private sector and has pockets deep enough to give raises to the public sector (as it did in 2011), declines in state rent revenues do not directly manifest in trouble for the state.

Across the Persian Gulf, there are gradations of rentier political economies, from the wealthiest to the less wealthy. The spectrum of rentier political economies can be mapped out as a continuum, stretching from Qatar, Kuwait, and the UAE at one end of the spectrum, and then Bahrain, Saudi Arabia, Oman, and finally Iran and Iraq (as well as Algeria) at the other end. Michael Herb uses the categories of "extreme rentiers" (Kuwait, Qatar, and the UAE), "middling rentiers" (Saudi Arabia, Bahrain, and Oman), and "poor rentiers" (Algeria and Iran) to distinguish between the three types of rentier states.[25] In many instances, the difference is one of degree and extent rather than type. The petro-states of the Arabian Peninsula belong only to the first and the second categories, and, as such, they all share a number of common political economy features and characteristics. To one extent or another, all employ a number of direct and indirect means to distribute rents into the wider economy. These include domestic public investment; land purchases; public transfer payments and pensions; subsidies on housing, utilities, foodstuffs, and other essential commodities; public sector employment; facilitating foreign investment; public transfers to the business sector; and state investments abroad.[26]

In extreme rentiers, the overall political economy is geared toward private wealth accumulation by the very top elite and wealth distribution to the rest of the population. Doha, Abu Dhabi, and Dubai often feel as if they are geared toward satisfying high-income foreigners who are there to manage the real estate assets of the ruling family. Kuwait, with its history of parliamentary politics, is by contrast a city geared toward satisfying its middle-class citizens.[27] In the three cases of Qatar, the UAE, and Kuwait, the overwhelming majority of wage-earning citizens work in the public sector, therefore becoming dependent on the state for their earnings. These states provide extensive and generous employment opportunities for their citizens in the public sector. Not everyone gets a job, however, as some women with low skills and education may be unwilling to work in jobs that are available, or there are simply no positions for them. Citizens, meanwhile, make up a very small minority of the private sector.[28]

The distorted labor market produces two classes: capitalists and public sector employees. The relative size of the two classes is not always clear, and neither are they always easily distinguishable from each other because of frequent and multiple overlaps between them. Only capitalists have a strong incentive in the success of the private sector. In both the extreme and in the middling rentier states, meanwhile, the segmented labor market is inefficient and extremely expensive.

In the middling rentier states of Saudi Arabia, Oman, and Bahrain, the state's wealth does not always allow for direct transfers or even expansive public sector employment. The state, therefore, often aggressively pursues labor nationalization policies and pressures the private sector to hire nationals. For its part, the private sector continues to have a preference for foreign labor, which is much cheaper, is more easily disposable, and is far less mobile. Whereas in Qatar and the UAE most citizens are employed in the public sector, in Bahrain, Saudi Arabia, and Oman it is the private sector that employs most citizens.[29] In fact, Bahrainis with public sector jobs make up a privileged group in society.

In examining rentierism, it is important not to reduce the population to "bribed loyal subjects and their leaders as benevolent, paternalistic patriarchs."[30] Even in wealthier rentier states, as in Kuwait and even more commonly in Saudi Arabia, there can be a fair amount of political tension and contestation. The assumption that citizens in rentier states are always bought off does not apply to every circumstance and in every case, or even to every social group. The middle classes are not always bought off. In fact, in the extreme rentiers, when there has been oppositional activism outside of the ruling family, it has come from among the middle classes (more on which below). The entrepreneurs, dependence on the state makes them less prone to oppositional activism, but even among them there is a fair amount of diversity and autonomy. Oil exporters, as mentioned earlier, are not necessarily prone to regime breakdown or even instability during periods of economic downturn. What matters is how leaders respond. In times of economic downturn, the "cushion effect" works only if the leadership responds effectively.[31] The precise nature of this response varies from case to case and depends on specific circumstances. But, as we shall see below, in the Arab petro-states a carrot-and-stick combination of arrests and clampdowns on the one hand and sweetened state patronage on the other appears to have been quite successful in fending off widespread troubles for the state in the aftermath of the unrests elsewhere in the Arab world in 2011.

These responses were part of a broader, two-pronged approach that the petro-states adopted following the events of 2011, one ideational and the other institutional. Ideationally, almost all, with the exception of Oman, played the sectarian card, framing Bahrain's largely Shia uprising in February 2011 as the work of Iran-directed Shia zealots. Significantly, the extent to which public and state-sanctioned discourse was sectarianized differed from case to case and depended on the state's overall political agendas and its level of security in relation to its citizens. The same factors also largely accounted for differences in the ways states responded institutionally. Ultimately, the petro-states' more consequential responses occurred not in reaction to the 2011 uprisings, which remained mostly superficial and cosmetic, but to the continued declines in oil and gas prices beginning in 2014. The drop in prices—from around $110 per barrel of OPEC oil in 2012 to $49 in 2015—has so far shown no signs of recovery to pre-2014 levels.[32] The petro-states have therefore had to adjust to the "new-normal."

The State and Identity Politics

The type of politics found in rentier states is shaped largely by the broader political economy within which social actors articulate and express their demands, and by the responses of state actors to those demands. In the less wealthy rentier states of Algeria, Iran, and Iraq, and even in Saudi Arabia, political demands reflect the varied and complex nature of society. Such demands may be expressed by or on behalf of the lower and the middle classes and reflect their preferences and biases, or revolve around issues of political accountability, social and economic equity, or political corruption and arbitrary rule. In other words, political demands reflect those issues with which the average citizen has to contend on a daily basis.

This is not, however, necessarily the case in the extreme rentier countries—in Qatar and the UAE, and to a lesser extent in Kuwait— in which the issues that animate public discussion and discourse revolve less around politics *per se* and are more concerned with culture. In the extreme rentiers, in fact, all too frequently culture becomes political. Because of pervasive ties of patronage and clientelism, expressions of political concern in countries like Qatar and the UAE do not necessarily revolve around demands for political accountability, representation, freedom of expression, or transparency. Instead, when they do exist, political concerns frequently manifest themselves in the form of cultural and identity politics. Most of the issues that animate public discussion revolve around questions such as the preponderance of foreign cultural content in society, the prevalence and use of English as the *lingua franca* as compared to Arabic, especially among the young, and the availability and consumption of alcohol.

In extreme rentier states, under certain conditions, since the population does not have large-scale economic grievances around which political demands can be articulated, it is often moral and cultural issues, not economic ones, that form the basis of challenge to the state. As Hootan Shambayati argued some time ago, "in rentier states claims against the state are based on noneconomic grounds."[33] Further, Shambayati notes:

> Unable to legitimize themselves on their performance, rentier states try to legitimize their rule on moral and cultural grounds. By appealing to golden age myths, rentier states try to create a semblance of legitimacy. The unintended consequence of this move is that culture and ideology become the main arenas of conflict between the state and civil society.[34]

This politicization of cultural issues is reinforced by two developments. One has to do with the overall sources of legitimacy on which these states rely. As we saw earlier, reliance on tribal and religious symbols continues to form the basis of the Arab petro-states. Tribalism and Islam, in the version adopted by the state, provide important cultural and institutional support for the state. By limiting the public space to tribal and Islamic values, it is natural that political opposition also coalesces around cultural issues related to identity, family and tribal dynamics, the mosque, and religious schools.[35]

A second development has to do with the overall institutional makeup of these systems, which more often resemble large, family-run corporations rather than complex and variegated states.[36] The state remains fundamentally personalist. One of the defining features of such systems is their decided lack of ideological goals for society. Instead, as important instruments of rule they rely on the institution of the family and on other preexisting, privileged social groups.[37] These regimes, especially personalist ones, often rely not so much on ideology but on what Juan Linz sees as mentalities.[38] Combined with clientelism, patronage, and rentierism, such polities often push politics away from demands for accountability and representation and instead in the direction of cultural and social issues.

Culture and identity are particularly salient political issues in the Arab petro-states, especially because of sizeable populations of non-locals. The proportion of foreigners to citizens has grown exponentially across the region in recent years as these states have experienced massive growth and infrastructural development, therefore creating demand for throngs of imported labor at all levels of skill. Today, foreign labor in the GCC, both skilled and unskilled, comes from an estimated 150 countries.[39] The proportion of non-citizens to citizens ranges from approximately 88 percent in Qatar and the UAE to nearly 44 percent in Oman (table 6.1). Such glaring demographic imbalances only exacerbate cultural and identity issues and reinforce their prominence in public and political discourse. The Qatari author Faisal Al-Marzouqi, for example, complained bitterly in a newspaper article that foreign workers not only take jobs away from locals but earn higher wages. "Management positions should be held only by Qataris," he argued. "It is unreasonable to give foreigners more power than the king."[40]

Table 6.1: National and non-national populations in the GCC

Country	Total population	Percentage nationals	Percentage non-nationals
Bahrain	1,377,000 (2015)	48.9	51.1
Kuwait	3,892,000 (2015)	31.2	68.8
Oman	4,491,000 (2015)	56.3	43.7
Qatar	2,597,453 (2016)	11.5	88.5
Saudi Arabia	31,540,000 (2015)	67.3	32.7
UAE	9,157,000 (2015)	14.8	85.2
Total	49,551,653	51.5	48.5

Note: Data ranges between years 2014 and 2015.
Source: Data collected from United Nations, http://esa.un.org/unpd/wpp/Download/Standard/Population/; Gulf Labor Markets and Migration, Gulf Research Center, http://gulfmigration.eu/gcc-total-population-and-percentage-of-nationals-and-non-nationals-in-gcc-countries-latest-national-statistics-2010–2014/; and Qatar Ministry of Development Planning and Statistics, www.mdps.gov.qa/en/statistics1/StatisticsSite/Pages/Population.aspx.

One of the biggest fears arising from migrant workers is the erosion of national identity as represented by increasingly infrequent use of Arabic as the local *lingua franca*. According to the Bahraini scholar Baqir al-Najjar, there is a widespread fear of the emergence of "a new set of hybrid identities."[41] Another author, the Qatari Mohamed Azwain, has written of the need for a country like his to maintain its Arab identity and to encourage the use and spread of Arabic as the country's medium of communication.[42]

Language isn't the only side effect of hosting so many foreigners. They bring their own habits and customs, and before long their cultural values could take over local ones. The ubiquitous displays of the "Christmas spirit" in late December in countries like Qatar and the UAE has emerged as something of a point of contention. Many nationals see Christmas trees and celebrating Christmas as another manifestation of erosion of local identity. "Are we really in a Muslim country or one that has been taken over by non-Muslim foreigners?" asks the Qatari writer Abdullah Ghanem Albinali Almohannadi sarcastically. "By celebrating Christmas in our streets, we feel like we're in a Christian European country."[43]

To imply that the Arab petro-states are gripped with "existential questions of identity," as Sean Foley does, is perhaps an exaggeration.[44] But there are local intellectuals, such as the Emirati Mishaal Al Gergawi, who write plaintively of a sense of "melancholy" at a loss of national identity they see around them.[45] Another Emirati intellectual admits that "[we] fear that we may lose everything that we have built... This feeling comes from the fact that we are a small minority in a city that's full of foreigners. We are very scared."[46] This fear of being overwhelmed in your own country is particularly pervasive in Qatar and in Dubai and Abu Dhabi, where the foreign population by far outnumbers locals at about 80 to 90 percent. In press interviews, op-ed pieces, and other forums, many Qatari and Emirati intellectuals express fear and discomfort about the demographic imbalance in their society, often "concerned about the possibility of what amounts to national dispossession."[47] Frequently, at least in private, they blame the ruling family, or specific individuals within it, for what they perceive as the erosion of national culture around them.

There is a "profound feeling of vulnerability among an important segment of GCC Arabs in the twenty-first century."[48] On rare occasions, even state officials and officially sanctioned columnists have expressed anxiety over perceived erosion of identity.[49] Foley's observations in this regard are worth quoting at length:

> Gulf Arabs worry that international institutions, the prevalence of the English language, European conceptions of gender, and marriage to expatriates are so influential that they will compel everyone to conform to Western social norms and to abandon the traditions and social practices that define Gulf life. Despite their wealth and their distance from military conflicts in the Middle East, Gulf Arabs often view themselves as unable to combat forces that are altering life in their societies.[50]

The case of Dubai is especially emblematic of this phenomenon, where the preponderance of expatriates in the city has led to the geographic marginalization of Emiratis as they move out of the center and into the suburbs. This has reinforced Dubaians' cultural marginalization, in turn prompting the government to take deliberate steps to strengthen Emirati national identity.[51]

In dealing with "the labor issue," one of the options pursued by the regional states has been to segregate blue-collar laborers from the rest of the population as much as possible, often under the auspices of protecting "families" from "bachelors," shorthand used by locals to describe low-income migrant workers. In the 1970s and the 1980s, Arab labor was far more influential in shaping local attitudes and identities. But as their numbers have dramatically dwindled in recent years, states have increasingly viewed the ensuing demographic imbalance through security lenses. Not only has the shift in preference for migrant workers from South and Southeast Asia over those from other Arab countries picked up pace in recent years—the former more easily separable, generally cheaper, and with far fewer political inclinations—there has also been far less tolerance of instances of nonconformity or demands of any sort. Local governments have responded harshly to strikes by foreign workers. At the same time, the various ethnic communities of Iranian, Pakistani, Indian, Filipino, and Nepali workers are presented with few opportunities for integration into host societies. Foreign workers find little opportunity to integrate with workers from other nationalities and instead socialize mostly with those who share their nationality or sect. This perpetuates a certain "social ghettoization" of the different migrant communities.[52]

Migration to the Arab petro-states is not recent, with many migrants, both from Asia and from the rest of the Middle East, having set up long-term roots in their host countries.[53] And, despite pervasive ghettoization and identity differences within the host countries, many second-generation immigrants have identities that are closely tied to the host societies. In fact, even if they are classified as non-locals, many second-generation immigrants view themselves as part of the host society, culturally, socially, and economically.[54] Importantly, while paths to integration and even citizenship may be restricted in the petro-states as compared to elsewhere in the Arab world or the broader global south, they do nonetheless exist. Given their long history of relying on migrant workers, especially after the discovery of oil, and given the extremely large number of migrants in Gulf countries, there are increasing numbers of foreigners, especially those with greater means, who have found their way into local citizenship.[55]

Religion is another arena that animates the public imaginary and discourse. The relationship between state and religion in the Arabian Peninsula is historic, complex, multifaceted, and beyond the scope of the task at hand.[56] Briefly, across the Arabian Peninsula, state-building has required the taming of religious institutions. Once the supremacy of secular authorities was secured, rulers incorporated Islamic institutions into the agencies of the state. The last several decades have seen a steady bureaucratization of the religious establishment across the Arabian Peninsula (and in other parts of the Middle East for that matter), with most *ulama* being employees of the state as judges, preachers, teachers, or scholars.[57] Through such efforts, the state has largely succeeded in tying the corporate interests of the religious establishment with its own interests. By doing so, state authorities have for the most part "tamed" Islam as a politically oppositional force.[58]

This political taming of Islam has been far from complete. In fact, in some ways, especially in countries like Saudi Arabia and to a lesser extent Kuwait and Bahrain, the state's instrumentalist use of religion has inadvertently empowered political Islam as a medium of popular expression for non-state, and at times even anti-state, sentiments and activities. Perhaps nowhere is this more apparent than in Saudi Arabia, where both al-Qa'ida and Daesh claim to be the true, legitimate standard-bearers of Wahhabism. Apart from the obvious terrorist threat, the biggest challenge to the Saudi state from groups such as Daesh are their claims to be the only legitimate guardians of the Wahhabi tradition.[59] For the authorities, such claims cannot be ignored or easily dismissed. According to one report, Daesh retains considerable popularity and support among the estimated 4,000 Salafi-jihadists serving prison terms in Saudi Arabia and also among the kingdom's clerical class.[60] The fact that in their war effort in Yemen the Saudi authorities are employing Salafis to fight the Houthis is only likely to add to the former's popular appeal and their social status at home in the long run.[61]

The often conflictual relationship between state authorities and religious extremists in Saudi Arabia is not necessarily replicated elsewhere in the Arabian Peninsula. In the Arab petro-states, Islamist groups, and more commonly individuals with Islamist leanings, frequently take part in various aspects of mainstream politics. More specifically, such groups tend to channel their political involvement in three different arenas. First, in cases where elections are allowed, either at the national level (in Bahrain and Kuwait) or the municipal level, they tend to compete in electoral campaigns. More often, their activities take place through religious associations and charity organizations, as in Qatar, Saudi Arabia, and the UAE, with their focus on social issues rather than on politics. By far, the most common form of political participation by Islamists is through positions in the various government ministries and agencies, especially those related to education, *awqaf* (religious trusts), culture, judicial affairs, and the like.[62] Significantly, Salafists tend to become more pragmatic than ideological when they get involved in politics.

Since 2011, thanks largely to state efforts in Bahrain and Saudi Arabia, religious sensibilities in the Arabian Peninsula have become tainted with steadily darkened hues of sectarianism. What started in Bahrain in 2011 as an anti-authoritarian movement was quickly framed by the country's monarchy as a sectarian ploy by the Iranian theocracy to spread Shia orthodoxy beyond the Islamic Republic. That the Bahraini movement was spearheaded by the kingdom's Shia majority only lent credence to the state's sectarian framing. Instrumentalist sectarianism was soon adopted by the Saudi state, now even more vocally, as one of the tools to combat and indeed to reverse the tide of the Arab Spring from the shores of the Persian Gulf. Before long, Saudi Arabia and its allies were inflaming sectarian tensions across the region as a way to defeat uprisings elsewhere and to deflect domestic attention from themselves.[63] The Bahraini state went one step further, setting in place demographic policies designed to increase the number of foreigners, especially Sunnis, in the kingdom in order to strengthen the position of the ruling family. Between 2000 and 2010, the number of foreigners in Bahrain nearly doubled from 630,000 to 1.2 million.[64] Sources sympathetic to the Bahraini Shia claim that between 2011 and 2014, another 95,000 foreigners were given Bahraini citizenship.[65] By 2017, following pressure from Sunni quarters due to increasing unemployment and rising housing prices, the practice is said to have been stopped.

To ascribe the rapid spread of sectarianism to its instrumentalist use by the state is to underestimate its resonance among the average population in the Arabian Peninsula and in the larger Middle East. For state-articulated sectarianism to have become so compelling so quickly it needed to have already had salience among the people. The petro-states, in fact, did not construct sectarianism; they simply tapped into it. As Madawi Al-Rasheed has observed, sectarianism does more than reinforce communal identity in fractured societies such as those found in Lebanon, Syria, and Bahrain. It can also mask internal differences and provide for a semblance of unity against supposedly hostile outsiders.[66] Not surprisingly, the sectarian framing initially adopted by the Saudi and Bahraini states was soon also embraced by their neighbors, albeit with varying degrees of intensity. More significantly, sectarianism quickly became one of the dominant frames of reference for social actors across the region. Before long, Friday sermons in mosques, talk shows on local and satellite television channels, newspaper columns and opinion pieces, individual and group expressions on social media, and even conversation topics in the *majalis* and *diwaniyat* revolved around supposedly deep, historic chasms separating Sunnis from the Shia.

Institutional Adjustments

Sectarian framings were complemented by a series of institutional adjustments that the petro-states undertook in the wake of the 2011 uprisings. These adjustments paled in comparison to those initiated after steady declines in oil prices beginning in 2014. The Arab petro-states did in fact respond to the events of 2011. But by and large these responses were not institutional in nature; they did not involve fundamental changes to the composition of various state institutions, their functions or personnel, or their overall position in relation to the other institutions of the state. Instead, the petro-states pumped more money into the economy by increasing state salaries and subsidies on basic goods, hired more nationals, and deepened and reinvigorated patronage bonds with those groups already within their orbit. There were, of course, arrests, including those of a famous television personality in Kuwait, and cyber-laws were inaugurated to regulate and contain potential anti-state sentiments on social media by "rogue citizens."[67] In order to anticipate and preempt potential criticism, the state also embarked on the prosecution of several high-profile corruption cases, especially in the energy and contracting sectors.[68] By and large, however, the preference of states across the GCC was to buy their way out of trouble rather than to confront it head-on.

Perhaps the petro-states were merely delaying the inevitability of reforms to the untenable rentier arrangements they were creating. In

2011, at any rate, there seemed to be no end to the steady rise in oil prices. According to one estimate, after falling by more than $30 a barrel from 2008 to 2009, OPEC oil prices steadily increased until 2013: $61.86 in 2009; $77.38 in 2010; $107.46 in 2011; $109.45 in 2012; and $105.87 in 2013.[69] The state could afford to solidify its rentier arrangements, and it did so in dramatic fashion, as I outline below. It was only when the good times came to a crashing halt beginning in 2014—with oil prices slipping down to $96.29 in 2014, $49.49 in 2015; and $40.68 in 2016—that the state had no alternative but to embark on an earnest rewriting of the social contract.[70] Institutional adjustments could no longer be delayed, or masked over with rent money.

Why was it that the petro-states responded decisively to the 2014 oil slump but not to the 2011 uprisings? The central factor appears to have been state capacity. Whereas the consequences of the 2011 events on the capacity of the petro-states were minimal or even non-existent, the 2014 price declines had the potential of severely eroding their capacity. Faced with the very real possibility of eroded and diminishing state capacity, the petro-states sprang into action by taking a two-track approach. On the one hand, they repeatedly assured their publics that there was no crisis and that they had enough financial and natural resource endowments, and the astute leadership needed, to navigate their way out of the on-going financial downturn. On the other hand, they began to slowly trim the fat they had accumulated in happier years. Large, state-owned enterprises began undergoing restructuring campaigns that led to the layoff of thousands of well-paid, skilled migrants. Many infrastructural projects were delayed or cancelled altogether, and costly or inefficient institutions with similar or parallel functions were merged into each other. Subsidies for domestic oil consumption were rolled back. Once unheard of, the idea of taxes were floated in the media, and a value added tax (VAT) was set to be introduced across the GCC in 2018.[71] The rentier social contract was slowly being rewritten.

This rentier social contract has bestowed the petro-states with comparatively enviable levels of state capacity. Especially in relation to the other countries of the Arab world, the petro-states of the Arabian Peninsula enjoy much greater levels of state capacity. There are various definitions of state capacity and, accordingly, yardsticks for measuring it. One of the more common definitions, in the social science literature produced in the US at least, revolves around a state's ability to levy and extract taxes from the population.[72] Given the types of political systems that predominate in the Middle East, however, which have comparatively low levels of taxation, it is difficult to measure state capacity in the Arab world with any degree of precision. Not unlike legitimacy, in fact, in most nondemocratic political systems state capacity is nebulous and unquantifiable.

In its broadest sense, state capacity may simply be viewed as the state's ability to achieve the goals it sets for itself and to act autonomously from social forces and groups. From this perspective, a "strong" state resembles a rational and unitary actor, and has extensive control over civil society, where power and resources are highly concentrated in the executive. In this sense, state capacity may be defined as "the sum total of a state's material ability to control, extract, and allocate resources as well as its symbolic or political ability to create, implement, and enforce collective decisions."[73] More specific examinations of the concept have focused on combining various dimensions of the state's capacity, especially its extractive, coercive, and administrative apparatuses, as well as the quality and coherence of its political institutions.[74]

Some of these criteria, interestingly, have been adopted by scholars not necessarily because they adequately capture the essence and scope of the phenomenon of state capacity but largely because they are measurable.[75] My operationalization of the concept may not necessarily lend itself to qualitative analysis, but I believe it more thoroughly captures the different dimensions of the phenomenon. State capacity may be viewed along five, interrelated dimensions: functions, institutions, legitimacy, identity, and agenda setting. Insofar as state *functions* are concerned, the greater the state's capacity the more it can guarantee domestic and international security and provide other services for the population. State *institutions*, of which the bureaucracy is a prime example, become operationalized in relation to society, particularly in terms of their quality, efficacy, and depth of their connections to social actors. A related dimension of state capacity revolves around the state's *legitimacy*, especially in terms of the degree to which it has to force itself on society as opposed to being accepted by social actors without resort to violence or the threat of coercion.

The last two dimensions of state capacity, namely identity and agenda setting, are somewhat unique to the states of the Arabian Peninsula. The *identity* dimension revolves around the success of the state's efforts to build on, and in turn to shape and influence, "national" identity in the country. All states engage in identity construction, some more blatantly than others. Given their relative youth, in the states of the Arabian Peninsula the process of constructing national identity, especially those that are distinct from the one next door, is not just an ongoing process. It is one of the main projects of the state and receives much state attention and resources. Similarly, the small demographic size and the comparatively inordinate wealth of the state derived from hydrocarbons give state leaders wide latitude to shape, or at least influence, public discourse and thinking. This type and level of *agenda setting* for the nation is, again, the envy of the other Arab states.

The state's ability to extract taxes is often cited in the literature as one of the defining features of state capacity. In the Arab petro-states, taxes, fees, and fines have so far constituted a low percentage of total state revenues compared to elsewhere in the Middle East, and, especially, compared to the countries of The Organisation for Economic Co-operation and Development (OECD).[76] But the paucity of taxation in the GCC does not automatically translate into the state's detachment from, or the fragility of its links to, society. In fact, given the patterns in which the institutions of rule historically evolved in these countries—from dominant clans within large tribes and tribal confederacies to contemporary ruling families—and the pervasiveness of patronage and clientelistic networks between state and social actors, state–society linkages tend to be quite robust and multifaceted. In the absence of such links, taxes may play a bonding role between state and society, enabling the state to penetrate and extract from society the resources it needs, and in turn giving society a vested interest in how the state operates. But in the Arabian Peninsula, the evolution of state–society relations has rendered unnecessary the need for such bonds through taxation. As we shall shortly see, in the post-2014 period, when oil prices fell drastically, there has been talk of introducing various forms of taxation in the GCC. If this were indeed to happen, as explained below, the state's capacity is likely to be even further enhanced.

In her otherwise perceptive study of the effects of the resource curse, Terry Lynn Karl claims that contrary to appearances, petro-states have limited capacity.[77] That may well be the case for the likes of Angola and Venezuela, or Iran and Algeria, which suffer from institutional deficiencies far beyond those inflected on them because of the curse of oil. But the effective, multi-dimensional means of nexus that the Arab petro-states have been able to establish with their societies has given them considerable "embeddedness" and has enhanced their state capacity. Embeddedness "implies a concrete set of connections that link the state intimately and aggressively to particular social groups with whom the state shares a joint project of transformation."[78] A completely autonomous state lacks sources of information and intelligence. Incomplete or impaired links with society hamper state capacity. Only when embeddedness and autonomy are joined does the state have the capacity to fully implement its goals and agendas.[79] Autonomous and yet embedded in their societies, resource-rich and able to effect change, small and centralized and agile and yet largely seen by their populations as politically legitimate, the petro-states of the Arabian Peninsula have comparatively high levels of state capacity.

A couple of the Arab petro-states, Qatar and the UAE, may actually have so much state capacity as to be classified as developmental. Capacity and internal coherence are defining characteristics of developmental states. In addition to autonomy, the state needs dense ties with social actors who share its transformational goals. Effective and efficient state organizations, along with dense public–private ties, enable states to become developmental.[80] At times, when the transformation of the bureaucracy is not feasible, political leaders try to create "pockets of efficiency" that would modernize the state bureaucracy by addition rather than transformation.[81] States that have the capacity to be transformative are also more intimately involved in the international system and have deeper international connections. These are all features found in Qatar and the UAE: state autonomy; dense ties with social actors who largely share the state's transformational vision; pockets of efficient state organizations; and deep international connections. Significantly, both the developmental trajectory of these two states and the manner of their institutional evolutions have turned out to be quite beneficial for their ruling families. Their societies, the combination of absolutism and extreme rentierism have enabled the ruling families of the UAE and Qatar, as leading capitalists in their societies, to pursue their own economic interests.[82]

Among the Arabian Peninsula's petro-states, the reactions to the oil price collapse differed not so much in kind as in degree. The poor rentiers have political economies in which largely indirect rent distributions frequently take the form of government jobs. Civil service salaries tend to be most directly affected by drops in oil prices, therefore negatively impacting the economic well-being of the middle classes and increasing their potential for oppositional activism. Poor rentiers, therefore, often respond most forcefully to perceived or actual challenges to, and cracks in, the ruling bargains on which they rely. What we have seen ensue in places like Algeria and Iran, and previously in Iraq, is the state's employment of a carrot-and-stick approach. The state responds to potential strikes or other demonstrations of popular anger to rising prices through greater repression (closing down newspapers, jailing journalists and union organizers) and other similar acts meant to frighten and silence citizens. The carrot is usually in the form of opening up more positions in the government and hiring more public sector employees.

In the middling rentiers of Saudi Arabia, Oman, and Bahrain, the state's response is largely the same. Here, however, the state is wealthier compared to the poor rentiers because of access to more rent revenues and also because of its smaller demographic base—therefore fewer mouths to feed, children to educate, and graduates to employ. The same carrot-and-stick approach is used here, with the carrot including hefty raises in public salaries. In the extreme rentiers—Kuwait, the UAE, and Qatar—the state is extremely wealthy, populations are very small, and rent distributions most direct, in the form of entitlements and extensive subsidies. The need for the stick has been minimal despite the fact that the state has purposefully set out to roll back some subsidies, as in cuts in fuel and water and power charges for nationals in the UAE and Kuwait.

Not surprisingly, the extreme rentiers—especially the Qatari and Emirati states and to a lesser extent the Kuwaiti and even the Saudi states as well—have used the current slump in the oil markets to trim some of the fat they had accumulated during the boom years. They have streamlined state budgets, laid off thousands of expatriate workers from their workforce, folded some parallel state agencies into one another and abolished others altogether, and emphasized the need for pursuing "balanced development" and combatting the "culture of consumption" almost every chance they get.[83]

The oil price falls have been occurring at a time when the petrostates are embarking on a number of costly endeavors, such as massive weapons purchases, the war in Yemen, and propping up cash-strapped regimes in Pakistan, Jordan, Sudan, Egypt, and Morocco. The Saudi state in particular has faced significant additional costs during the Yemen war ($22.2 billion in the first twenty months of the conflict), and other mounting expenses as the war of attrition continues.[84] So far, the average Saudi citizen appears to have been shielded from the consequences of the war, which the Saudi state has portrayed to its population as a localized conflict. But how long the state can keep up this façade is an open question. The oil revenue slowdown has also hit Bahrain very hard. Between 2008 and 2016, public spending (on public sector wages, transfers, subsidies, and interest payments) doubled. Although capital spending fell by 12 percent, the government had a fiscal deficit of 13 percent in 2015 and 16 percent in 2016.[85]

Apart from efforts to make state agencies leaner and more efficient by laying off foreigners and scaling back on their spending on megaprojects, the petro-states have started to gingerly roll back some state subsidies, most notably on gasoline and utilities. But the extent of the drop in revenues has been such that for the first time, there is open talk of taxation. As one Emirati commentator has noted, taxation, in forms more direct than is currently the case, may result in a rewriting of the petro-states' social contracts.[86] He goes on to say that Gulf citizens may be willing to accept taxation if it means safety, but it is not clear how they may react, and foreign investors may also be scared away. Ultimately, the consequences of taxation are unpredictable, and may even lead to "the dreaded further expansion of democratic participation among the citizenry."[87]

For now, the only form of taxation formally proposed is the new GCC-wide value added tax (VAT), which would exclude food products, education, and health services.[88] The VAT is seen as a preferred option since it does not curb employment or investment. Other, more direct forms of taxation would clearly be a paradigm shift for the GCC. Preliminary public opinion polling indicates that, at least in Qatar, citizens are willing to accept taxation if it means the continued provision of free state services such as education and healthcare and guaranteed government jobs.[89] Qataris are more concerned about loss of government subsidies and free services than taxation. For them, some government subsidies are considered highly essential, including free education, free healthcare, free water and electricity, and access to public sector employment. However, free housing and land allotment, social allowances, and marriage allowance are generally seen as less important.[90]

Clearly, state responses to ongoing oil price adjustments have varied, and will continue to vary, based on the specific domestic and regional contexts within which the state finds itself. In what follows, I trace the institutional responses of the states grouped according to the classification introduced earlier, beginning with the extreme rentiers of Kuwait, the UAE and Qatar, followed by those of the middling rentiers, namely Saudi Arabia, Bahrain, and Oman.

Of the six Arab petro-states, the wealthiest, and perhaps also the most politically stable, is Qatar. Qatar began experiencing a remarkable transformation process starting in the mid-1990s, after Sheikh Hamad bin Khalifa Al-Thani took over power following a palace coup against his father. Immediately upon assuming power, Hamad engaged in an aggressive campaign of infrastructural development, institution-building, and branding for his country, in the process consolidating power within his immediate family by steadily pushing potential rivals out of the political inner circle. An ambitious plan for the country's grand transformation was outlined in a document entitled 'Vision 2030', meant to help guide the country to a post-oil era by fostering a knowledge-based economy and sustainable development.[91]

Hamad sought to ensure that the implementation of his high modernist vision caused as little disruption as possible to established bureaucrats and old guard left overs. He therefore established a series of alternative, parallel state agencies, alongside the traditional bureaucracy, which he entrusted with carrying out his vision. These included, among others, agencies tasked with carrying out routine bureaucratic functions—such as the Supreme Councils of Health and Education, and the Qatar National Food Security Program (which was later amalgamated into the Ministry of Finance)—and state-funded foundations charged with helping achieve a knowledge-based economy. This expensive and inefficient allocation of state administrative resources, with essentially two parallel bureaucracies whose functions greatly overlapped, was affordable at a time when oil and gas prices were at their height and as Qatar secured its place as the world's largest supplier of liquefied natural gas (LNG). Qataris, meanwhile, continued to benefit from generous state largesse through direct entitlements, an expansive job market, lucrative state contracts, and Doha's seemingly endless construction boom. Doha became a serious competitor to Dubai and Abu Dhabi as rapid expansion took all three cities in the direction of the desert, the sea, and the sky.

Hamad retired in June 2013, at a time when his popularity appeared at an all-time high. The retirement itself was a radical departure from the norm in a region in which few presidents, never mind monarchs, relinquish power voluntarily. He was succeeded by his son Tamim, soon after which the 2014 oil slump occurred. Earlier, in 2011, whereas most regional states had seen the Arab Spring as somewhat of a threat, Qatar had viewed it as an opportunity to capitalize on the turmoil to expand its influence and to enhance its reputation. The Qatari state's domestic response to the 2011 uprisings, what little of it there was, included giving substantial raises to those in government employment and in the military. This was not necessarily meant to buy off state employees but to bring their salaries in line with those of the rest of the GCC states, where deepened state patronage had resulted in major raises for those in the military and the civil service. There was no Arab Spring in Qatar, not even a murmur. The state had no reason to respond one way or another.

This absence of social activism of any kind in Qatar in the wake of the 2011 uprisings was due largely to the state's successful co-option of those social actors who could potentially challenge its narrative of the country's politics, economics, or future direction. This "soft state co-optation" was pursued with particular success in relation to both the Salafis and the Brotherhood.[92] In 1999, the Qatari branch of the

Muslim Brotherhood dissolved itself because, it claimed, the state was carrying out its religious duties and the need for the organization had dissipated. Since then, because there are no elections or other formal institutional means for Qataris sympathetic to the Muslim Brotherhood to pursue their objectives, they have instead opted for pursuit of social policy and charity activities.[93] Similar to the UAE, since in Qatar formal means of participation for organized Islamist groups is not an option, they have opted to work through social organizations, charities, schools, and businesses.[94] At least in the case of Qatar, such individuals do not seem to harbor ambitions beyond intellectual and spiritual pursuits, and they can therefore coexist with the state. Many, in fact, often work within state institutions, without tensions or conflicts. Qatar's Salafis appear especially more dominant in the Ministry of Awqaf and Islamic Affairs, all the while ensuring that mosque sermons are not too incendiary.[95]

There has, nevertheless, been a steady conservative social trend in Qatar since Tamim's assumption of power in 2013. Some of this social conservatism can actually be traced back to before 2011, when some restrictions were placed on alcohol consumption in places frequented by Qataris, public statues deemed socially offensive were covered up, and Western expats were encouraged to dress more modestly in public spaces. These moves, however, appear to have less to do with the efforts of Qatari Islamists *per se* than with developments within the Al-Thani ruling elite.[96] The ruling family appears to embody two tendencies. One wing of the family—represented by the former emir Sheikh Hamad, his wife Sheikha Moza, their son Sheikh Mohammed and their daughters Sheikha Al-Mayassa and Sheikha Hind—appears to be less traditional and more willing to move between and within both traditional Qatari and Western cultural spheres.[97] Another wing of the family—represented chiefly by Tamim, his older brother Jassim and younger sibling Abdullah—appears less eager to embrace Westernism wholeheartedly and has shown greater attentiveness to more traditional and local social and cultural sensibilities. The more conservative wing of the family has been in ascendance since 2013.

In addition to greater attentiveness to culturally conservative sensibilities, Tamim's rule brought with it greater attention to administrative professionalism and efficiency, bureaucratic streamlining, and

Qatarization of the workforce. Many of the newer, parallel institutions that Sheikh Hamad had set up earlier were steadily disempowered and sidelined or were merged into older institutions. State-owned enterprises, including the national oil company, Qatar Petroleum, experienced massive layoffs and underwent major reorganizations in order to become more efficient. Cabinet ministers deemed underperforming were removed, including the emir's brother-in-law, and those retained or promoted were generally seen as efficient and hardworking. New appointments appear to be made based on merits.[98]

If motivated by a desire to reinforce his domestic popularity early on in his reign, Tamim's very slight but still discernible tilt toward social conservatism appears to have had its intended consequences. Although opinion surveys on the issue are not available, by all accounts the young emir retains high levels of popularity among Qataris.[99] What public opinion data is available indicates overall Qatari satisfaction with the state's performance. In a 2016 survey, for example, most Qataris expressed high levels of satisfaction with government services such as the provision of free water and electricity, cultural activities, healthcare services, and government administration (on all issues a score of 7.5 on a scale of 1 to 10). Only K-12 education (6.2) and infrastructure (6.5) scored somewhat lower.[100]

Whereas the Qatari state has pursued a policy of co-option in relation to the country's Islamists, the UAE authorities have instead opted for crackdown, a strategy greatly intensified in the wake of the 2011 uprisings.[101] This crackdown was reinforced by the Emirati state's fears, well-grounded in this case, that its own citizens, and not its resident population from other Arab countries, were attracted to Islamist groups, especially to the country's branch of the Muslim Brotherhood known as the Islah Society. The state's reaction to Islah was swift and decisive. In fact, displeased that Qatar seemingly harbored Muslim Brotherhood activists and gave them financial and other forms of support during the uprisings, the UAE, along with Saudi Arabia and Bahrain, recalled its ambassador from Doha from March to November 2014 and again in June 2017.

Unlike the Qatari Brotherhood, the Islah Society itself initially pressed for political reforms and representation, joining secular forces after 2011. Far from trying to co-opt the Islah, in December 2011 the

Emirati state proactively decided to prosecute it, first stripping citizenship from seven Islah members who had signed a petition for reforms and then sentencing them to prison terms.[102] Those arrested included academics, social activists, and even a member of the ruling family of Ras al-Khaimah.[103] Nevertheless, the state has been willing to tolerate some Islamic charities, including those with supposed Salafi leanings, such as the Dar al-Birr Society, and it also patronizes some Salafi preachers, such as the Egyptian Sheikh Mohammed Hassan.[104]

While difficult to substantiate empirically, much of this Islamist opposition seems traceable to anxiety over the incredible pace and Western-oriented direction of the country's development over the last several decades. This development has been most vividly symbolized by the so-called "Dubai model," about which a good many Emirati citizens appear to have deep apprehensions.[105] If there has been a casualty of the Dubai model it is Emirati identity, therefore opening up space for Islamism as a compelling means of reasserting national identity.[106] Especially in the emirates of Dubai and Abu Dhabi, the state makes little effort, especially compared to the Qatari state, to balance out its modernist vision and efforts with sufficient attention to matters involving Emirati culture and national identity.[107]

The UAE's development path in general and that prescribed by the Dubai model in particular resemble that of a developmental state, with a strong vision and clearly articulated developmental goals, along with state involvement in the economy.[108] In specific relation to Dubai, there are several key "parameters" that characterize the emirate's developmental state. They include state-led development (or ruler-led development); quick and agile decision making in order to facilitate fast-track growth; a flexible and affordable labor force; bypassing industrialization and creating a service economy; internationalization of service provisions; creation of investment opportunities; supply-generated demand; branding; and development in cooperation with international partners.[109] The model is premised largely on optimism and vision, and the authorities are always keen to contain pessimism.[110]

Given the apparent economic success of the Dubai model over the last decade and a half or so, and its seeming resilience in the face of global economic shocks in 2008 and again in 2014, the model has become increasingly attractive to the rulers of the other emirates within the UAE and even to others in the region. This allure rests primarily in two areas. First, as a regional hub for many service industries, Dubai offers a viable model of economic development without overwhelming reliance on oil. Although the model had its own drawbacks—chiefly, vulnerability to global slowdowns and the need to rely on Abu Dhabi to be bailed out if needed—it has at least saved Dubai from many of the negative consequences of the resource curse. Second, meaningful and large-scale diversification away from oil has opened up countless opportunities for investments, partnerships, licensing agreements, and other potential revenue sources for citizens and rulers alike. As capitalists and investors themselves, rulers in all seven of the UAE's emirates have greatly benefited from the country's rapid growth and infrastructural development, and, in the process, many have become major real estate developers themselves.[111]

Centralized decision making, as mentioned earlier, is one of the reasons that Qatar's comparatively agile leadership has been able to capitalize on opportunities as they develop and, in fact, to create opportunities for the country. The same holds true for the UAE, again especially for the emirates of Abu Dhabi and Dubai, but within a somewhat different context. The UAE is a collection of seven absolutist monarchies, by far the biggest and wealthiest of which is Abu Dhabi, followed in second place by Dubai. Michael Herb's observations about the nature of the emerging state in the UAE are spot on:

> Today a UAE state exists, in the sense that the UAE is a well-governed territory, but that state, compared especially to the Kuwaiti state, is the creature of the ruling families, molded around their arrangements for sharing power, presiding over a population consisting mostly of foreigners, and oriented toward the interests of the ruling families.[112]

The state does have something of a parliamentary body, the forty-member Federal National Council, but its functions are far more cosmetic than substantive. Not surprisingly, elections to the body have consistently attracted low voter turnout, with 28 percent in 2011 and 35.2 percent in 2015.[113]

Up until 2008, Dubai's commercially minded rulers, especially Sheikh Mohammed Bin Rashid Al Maktoum (r. 2006–), often showed an independent-mindedness that was not always appreciated by Abu Dhabi. In the mid-to the late 1970s, in fact, there were considerable tensions among the various emirates over the degree and type of autonomy they would have within the confederation. Since 2008, when Abu Dhabi was rumored to have given billions of dollars to Dubai to weather the global financial meltdown, Dubai's penchant for greater autonomy within the UAE has been kept in check. Since then, the country's emirates have all been in greater sync with one another in toeing Abu Dhabi's line.

Apart from clamping down on the Islah, the Emirati authorities did little in the form of responding to the 2011 uprisings. The state did steadily and perceptibly change its conduct internationally and regionally, assuming a far more assertive and militaristic posture in its foreign and security policies. But that was more a response to Qatar's growing inward focus after 2013, coupled with the United States' less hostile attitude toward Iran in the final year of the Obama administration. The first development provided the necessary space for the UAE to make its presence felt on regional matters, and the second development prompted its leaders to show greater independence in pursuit of their national interests. It was within this context that the UAE joined the Saudi-led attack on Yemen in March 2015. In slightly more than a year after the Yemen military campaign started, the UAE was reported to have lost a total of 100 soldiers in battle. As the Yemen conflict dragged on, and as Emirati casualties increased, voices of discomfort and even dissent were heard. In response, and in order to project a sense of shared sacrifice, many younger UAE royals signed up for duty in the Yemen theater.[114] Similar to the Saudi state, the UAE has sought to shield the larger population from the unpleasantness of the Yemen conflict. Depending on the course of the war, however, it is unlikely to be able to do so indefinitely.

The other extreme rentier state, Kuwait, did experience some disquiet in the aftermath of the 2011 uprisings, largely a product of its unique institutional set-up among the Arab petro-states and a tradition of political activism by its population. Soon after the uprisings broke out in North Africa and the Levant, public discontent manifested itself in Kuwait in the form of parliamentary opposition. In subsequent months, especially in 2012–2013, more visible public unrest broke out across the country. Beginning in late January 2011, there were a few signs of popular anger, mostly through speeches and moves to question cabinet members and to press on issues of corruption, leading to the resignation of the prime minister the following November.[115] The ensuing public unrests were animated mainly by the perceived privileges of members of the ruling family.

The state's response was two-pronged, on the one hand showing little tolerance for any dissent while also massively increasing public spending and state subsidies. Beginning in 2012–2013, there were imprisonments and citizenship revocations for "insulting the Amir" on social media.[116] This was codified through the enactment of a tough cybercrime law in July 2015. A number of naturalized citizens also had their citizenships revoked and became stateless.[117] Although the state significantly expanded its capital spending and launched a number of megaprojects, scattered protests and acts of opposition continued throughout the 2010s.[118]

Within the context of the GCC, Kuwait is exceptional for its parliamentary politics and its tradition of political activism and contestation. This exceptionalism grew as a result of the confluence of two factors: the initiatives of the country's emir at independence, Abdullah Salim (r. 1950–1965), and the existential threat posed by Iraq. After a decade of absolutist rule, Abdullah Salim, known more for his pro-Arab rather then pro-British sentiments, decided to push through a relatively liberal constitution in response to the Iraqi threat.[119] The resulting establishment of a parliament was seen as a guarantee of the country's independence and sovereignty against threats emanating from Baghdad. Once the National Assembly was established and acquired a life of its own, the state found it all but impossible to dismantle it. Since its establishment, on several occasions the country's emirs have dissolved the parliament when it has challenged the government too aggressively. The state has also enacted various election laws designed to limit participation of opposition members in parliamentary elections.[120] But the institution has persevered, having become an important forum for political input and, especially, economic policymaking.

Kuwait's parliament has today turned into a viable institution through which the country's middle class could press its political demands and engage with the country's ruling elite on a range of policy issues. Not surprisingly, the work of the National Assembly has resulted in a series of political and economic outcomes that differ from those in the other regional petro-states, none of which have a similarly positioned parliament.[121] In Kuwait, the middle classes have a majority in the parliament and therefore some kind of a political voice, while the country's capitalists do not. In the UAE, by contrast, the middle classes have little political voice while the capitalists are politically strong.[122] And in Qatar, one can make a credible argument that what local middle class stratum there is has been absorbed into the orbit of the state through direct government handouts and entitlements and the expansive civil service.

In Kuwait, economic policy is shaped by the parliament. This is quite a contrast with the cases of Qatar and the UAE, where a handful of wealthy capitalists who happen to also be members of the ruling family make state policies regarding economic and infrastructural development. One of the most noticeable outcomes of policies pursued by the Kuwaiti parliament has been the country's relative economic and infrastructural underdevelopment, given its wealth, as compared to the other two extreme rentiers. Within the context of an oil-based welfare state, the Kuwaiti middle classes, through the parliament, have preferred a steady expansion of public services, various forms of direct and indirect state subsidies, and the flow of state and foreign investments that enhance rather than in any way potentially threaten middle-class interests. The end result has been political paralysis and frequent clashes between the parliament and the country's wealthy merchants, including the ruling family. There has also been a conspicuous absence of official efforts to reduce dependence on oil. Since the average citizen is assumed not to benefit from diversification, state policies have not encouraged the growth of non-oil sectors.

Free education, healthcare, and social security may have resulted in a relatively egalitarian economy and rising standards of living in Kuwait, but they have also led to major economic distortions.[123] Some of the economy's structural difficulties include the public sector's inability to absorb large numbers of Kuwaitis entering the labor force, misallocation and inefficient allocation of resources; and an uncompetitive and deteriorating business environment that stifles private and foreign investment.[124] There also appear to be no efforts to direct social benefits to the poor. Social benefits and transfers, in fact, distribute income but do not redistribute it.[125] At the same time, many

Kuwaiti capitalists see their country's investment environment as "hopelessly hostile" and prefer investing abroad.[126] But this displeasure has not been limited to the country's wealthy. Kuwait has also had a tradition of middle-class and worker activism. Throughout 2011 and into early 2012, the country saw repeated protests by members of the country's bidoon (stateless) community and by opposition activists demanding greater political freedoms. The protests finally died down thanks to a combination of police action and political and economic concessions by the monarchy. In 2014, workers in the Kuwait Petroleum Company threatened to strike because of poor work conditions, and in April 2016 they actually conducted a three-day strike over the right to organize and join a union.[127]

Similar to the other countries in the region, religious extremism has been somewhat troublesome for the Kuwaiti regime. The state has endeavored to prevent Islamist and secularist cooperation, a task at which it has not always succeeded because of the nature of parliamentary politics. The country's Salafi movement, meanwhile, aims to reform the system rather than to work within it or to bolster it.[128] In fact, by mid-2016 an estimated 100 Kuwaitis, both citizens and bidoons, were thought to have joined Daesh.[129] Inside Kuwait, the country's strategic sites as well as its Shia population have also been targeted for attacks by Daesh.[130] There are also reports of "highly organized" efforts by several well-known and wealthy Kuwaiti individuals to donate funds to extremist groups in Syria, including the al-Nusra Front, known for its affiliation with al-Qaʿida. In 2014, a leading al-Nusra donor, Nayef al-Ajmi, was appointed as Minister of Justice and Minister of Awqaf.[131]

Islamist sentiments, and political activism in general, are products of Kuwait's historical and political evolution. The country has a more robust middle class, one for which political sensibilities have often been heightened either by state leaders or by members of the parliament, or because of existential threats posed by Iraq, or by the generally volatile nature of regional politics. The economy has in the meanwhile experienced relative stagnation thanks largely to efforts by the parliament to protect entitlements and middle-class privileges at the expense of investments and diversification. The relationship between the emir and the parliament is far from smooth at all times, and the parliament tends to be more proactive than docile. But the very existence of parliamentary activism, coupled with significant wealth from oil, tend to give the Kuwaiti state long-term stability and, in fact, considerable capacity.

Whereas the three extreme rentier petro-states were able to deal with the fallout from the Arab uprisings with relative ease, the middling rentiers had a much harder time. As we saw in chapter 3, the uprising was particularly troubling for the Bahraini monarchy, which was rocked by a fast-spreading uprising that was quickly beginning to consume the entire island. The scope of the demonstrations and the intensity of the protests appear to have caught the Bahraini authorities off-guard. They seem to have been convinced of their rhetoric that the system as it existed was perfectly fine and that whatever trouble there was in the country was due to Iranian intrigue and interference. When Sheikh Hamad bin Issa came to power in 1999, he promised the inauguration of a new, open and democratic era. This was enshrined in a new constitution that was approved in a popular referendum in 2001 and inaugurated the following year. But structural inequities have remained, with the county's Shia majority continuing to feel disenfranchised, and there being little democracy of any form.[132]

Domestic security remains the state's top priority, and many otherwise mundane aspects of daily life are securitized.[133] There is a bicameral parliament, but it has no real power to effect significant policy or changes. In fact, the Council of Representatives (Majlis al-Nuwab), which is meant as a popular assembly, is often packed with Sunni supporters of the monarchy. Even then, largely in response to pressure from Saudi Arabia, the Bahraini monarchy has manipulated electoral rules in order to limit the participation of Islamist groups in parliamentary politics.[134]

Bahrain has witnessed a steady reinvigoration of authoritarianism since 2011, with those commonly perceived as hardliners inside the country in increasing ascendancy. One report went so far as to conclude that given the hardliners' ascendance, for the foreseeable future, "the prospects for less confrontational politics are bleak."[135] In what is largely a marriage of convenience, regime hardliners have found allies among the country's Islamists. For example, since the Muslim Brotherhood is not considered a threat to the state's monopoly of power but is, in fact, anti-Shia in orientation, it is allowed to contest parliamentary elections and is given some freedom of activity.[136] Another organization called Al-Asalah, known for its Salafist orientation, is also pro-government and enjoys close relations with Saudi Arabia as well.[137]

Within the state itself, there are three distinctive but interrelated power centers. The first group is a comparatively moderate faction, headed by King Hamad and his son, Crown Prince Salman, who are moderate only compared to the other factions. Te second center of power coalesces around Prince Khalifa bin Salman Al Khalifa, the prime minister, and has a pragmatic but conservative approach to politics. Prince Khalifa is powerful and popular within the bureaucracy, and has very close connections to the Saudi ruling family. The third power center revolves around two brothers: Khalid bin Ahmed bin Salman Al Khalifa, the minister of the royal court, and Field Marshal Khalifa bin Ahmad Al Khalifa, the Commander-in-Chief of the Bahrain Defense Forces. This third group is known as uncompromising, and by some accounts have "a visceral hatred" for the Shia. Their main source of support lies within the security forces.[138] The whole system, from the royal court down, is underwritten by the military. As one observer has noted, "Bahrain's army is the army of the royal family and is not a *national* army."[139]

Oman is the other middling rentier in which there were protests in 2011, though not nearly to the extent and ferocity of what transpired in Bahrain and elsewhere. Despite the gathering of several hundred protestors in February 2011 in Muscat and Salalah, the protestors did not call for the Sultan to step down. Instead, their main demands revolved around the need for improved economic conditions and especially employment opportunities. The state's response was both swift and largely effective. In addition to pouring money into the economy, Sultan Qaboos made a series of minor institutional tweaks designed to enhance the state's apparent representativeness and its transparency. In March 2011, the powers of the legislature were expanded so that deputies could question ministers, draft legislation, and select their own leadership. This was followed in October by amendments to the 1996 constitution meant to make the system more open.

Despite these well-publicized changes, the various participatory institutions and practices of the Omani state have remained anemic. In fact, the Sultan continues to remain the central fount of power in the country. Ever since his takeover of power in a palace coup in 1970, Sultan Qaboos has preferred measured and very slow institutional layering as a favored method of gradually opening up political space. Nevertheless, today the Omani legislature's powers remain quite limited, and the Sultan rules with hardly any institutional restraints. Throughout his reign, Sultan Qaboos has formally held the positions of prime minister, defense minister, foreign minister, finance minister, and governor of the Central Bank. Other officials hold the position of "minister of state" for each of these portfolios and perform as *de facto* ministers. As early as 2000, observers of Oman were pointing to the state's need, and awareness, that its centralized hold on power is untenable in the long run.[140] Despite the institutional need for one, Sultan Qaboos has refused to establish the office of the prime minister.[141] And, not wanting to risk the potential of being overthrown by an heir apparent, the Sultan has deliberately not chosen a successor, at the same time keeping the pool of potential candidates very small.[142]

Cosmetic though Oman's institutional openings of 2011 were, they did have their desired results, and political life in the country soon returned to its previous state of benign authoritarianism. Several factors explain the brevity of Omani protests. First, unlike Bahrain, sectarian and regional relations in Oman are relatively harmonious, especially after the end of the Dhofar Rebellion in 1975. Second, despite his near complete hold on power, Sultan Qaboos remains personally popular with the Omani population both in the cities and in the countryside. The Sultan has also historically maintained very close and cordial relations with the country's tribal and commercial elites.[143] Last but not least is the pervasiveness of patronage and clientelism as one of the primary links, perhaps the primary link, between the state and social actors. In the face of the country's fragmented labor force, any anti-state sentiments would most likely be from among the middle and lower classes, most of whom are public sector employees and are reluctant to jeopardize their state jobs or their social benefits. During ordinary times, these developments have combined to give Omani politics considerable political stability.

The relative stability of Oman's benign authoritarianism is something that the authorities in Saudi Arabia can only dream of. In Saudi

Arabia, formal trust toward the state is low, and society retains a largely skeptical, often adversarial, relationship with the state and its organs. The relationship between the Saudi state on the one side and Saudi society on the other is often complicated, complex, multifaceted, and over time changeable. By and large, the Al Saud ruling family continues to have broad legitimacy within the kingdom. Even rare calls for the removal of a sitting ruler, as represented in an open letter calling for the removal of King Salman in 2015 by one of the royal princes, are anchored in the legitimacy of the Al Saud as the kingdom's ruling family.[144] Nevertheless, the large size of the ruling family—the total number of Al-Saud family members is estimated at around 7,000 to 8,000 princes and princesses—the relationship between the state and Islam,[145] the dependence of the economy on oil revenues, and the country's developmental trajectory all combine to pose unique and at times very difficult challenges for the state.

Within the Saudi state itself, it is not necessarily nepotism or corruption that prevent coherent policymaking. It is the pattern of evolution of state agencies that makes the system unresponsive and slow in policymaking and policy-implementation, with multiple "veto players" situated across the state bureaucracy.[146] Bureaucrats often find themselves structurally handicapped from performing their functions. Oil revenues and promises of guaranteed employment have resulted in the continued expansion of the state's bureaucracy. By late 2014, approximately 50 percent of the government's total budget went toward state salaries, wages, and expenditures, making the need for reforms necessary and urgent.[147] When King Salman ascended to the throne in January 2015, one of his first initiatives was to devise and launch an ambitious development plan called 'Vision 2030', which largely follows the structural adjustments recommended by the IMF.[148] In June 2016, the government launched a National Transformation Plan, meant to complement 'Vision 2030'. While its details are sketchy, the new plan makes provisions to raise state revenues through new levies, fees, and charges.[149] In 2015, taxes accounted for approximately 6 percent of government revenues, but the state is very careful not to arouse popular anger with excessive talk of taxation if there are no significant political changes to accompany them.[150]

The behavior of the Saudi state, and the underlying logic of many of the policies it undertakes, cannot be fully understood without attention to the innate fear that has long characterized the state's leaders. Saudi rulers have long felt a deep sense of vulnerability to forces emanating from within the kingdom and especially from outside its borders. This vulnerability stems from the combined effects of the kingdom's rapid development over the last several decades, the volatility of regional politics, chronic infighting within the ruling family, dependence on oil export for continued sustainability and development, and the pursuit of regional and international ambitions outsized by human and other natural resource limitations.

Initially, in 2011, Saudi leaders feared that the tide of the Arab Spring would carry the uprisings into their own borders, and therefore quickly crushed it in Bahrain (and in the Eastern Province) and did what they could to reverse its tide elsewhere.[151] Once the dust of the uprisings settled, or at least the intensity of the rebellions had died down, Saudi leaders began fearing the consequences of other developments. Four of these developments stand out in Saudi calculations: the regional ambitions of Iran and its soft power among regional Shias; the regional and especially domestic influence of the Muslim Brotherhood; the extremism and appeal of Daesh and other Saudi Jihadis coming back from Syria; and the country's liberal intellectuals and human rights activists.[152] Despite a pervasive sense of worry and fear by the royal family, none of these four perceived threats poses an actual existential threat to the kingdom. Yet they continue to form the prism through which Saudi policymakers view the world around them. Among other things, given the self-perception of Saudi leaders as highly vulnerable, the kingdom's foreign policy has been designed to overcome its supposed strategic weaknesses without overreliance on the United States.[153]

This sense of vulnerability was heightened in 2011 when Saudi leaders discovered that oil revenues do not necessarily make them immune to protest movements.[154] Typical of those of the other petro-states, the response of the state to shows of public disquiet combined state crackdown with heightened patronage. The state toughened anti-terrorism laws, closed several independent media outlets, arrested a number of activists, and sponsored major media and public relations campaigns. Some young Saudis had earlier resorted to social media, in particular YouTube, for purposes of entertainment and information, at times having more than one million subscribers to their channels. To make a point and to scare off others, the state arrested many of those responsible and sentenced them to long prison terms.[155] But the positive inducements by far outweighed the punishments the state meted out. King Abdullah (r. 2005–2015) gave a speech praising his subjects' restraint from pouring into the streets. The government also launched a major campaign to create jobs and build affordable housing, and significantly increased the salaries of state employees. The $137 billion that the government allocated in 2011 to patronage efforts was greater than the country's total budget in 2007.[156] The state created 60,000 new jobs through the Ministry of Interior alone. It also established an anti-corruption institution called Nazaha, and directed an estimated $500 million in financial support to various religious institutions.[157]

Such largesse was more easily affordable in 2011–2012, before the crash in global oil prices in 2014. It was not until the dramatic decline in oil prices that the kingdom's new rulers decided to embark on drastic reforms. While it is not quite clear how much Saudi Arabia has in oil reserves, or at what rate Saudi oil fields are being depleted, they nevertheless remain substantial.[158] Nonetheless, the sharp decline in oil prices and therefore in state revenues resulted in severe government cutbacks beginning in 2015. The Saudi government stopped awarding many previously scheduled contracts to the private sector, and the need for efficiency and self-help have become the government's new mantra.[159] Once unheard of, the threat of bankruptcy became a reality for a growing number of Saudis.[160]

There has been a reinvigoration of political debate in Saudi Arabia in recent years. This heightened interest in political matters stems in large part from the confluence of a number of politically charged developments, not the least of which were the 2011 uprisings, where the kingdom played significant and at times decisive roles. Within Saudi Arabia, opinion seems divided between those with a "deep and abiding confidence in the kingdom" and those who are apprehensive about its culture, the institutions, and future direction.[161] In recent years, economic difficulties have only added fuel to both latent and overt displays of political discontent. Much of this opposition comes from those with strong Islamist tendencies, most recently in the form of sympathy and support for Daesh. Although difficult to state with certainty, there is apparently extensive support for Daesh's ideology inside Saudi Arabia and many Saudis appear to also support Daesh financially.[162]

In the 1990s, a small opposition movement named *Sahwa* (Awakening), was launched by a group of Saudi students and religious dissidents. In response, the state sought to enhance its religious credentials and drew itself closer to the *ulama*.[163] With the state having thus dominated the mainstream space of political Islam, within the Saudi context that is, Islamist opposition has tended to take extremist forms. Saudi authorities have therefore taken several steps designed to curb public support for Daesh and other terrorist organizations, including imposing jail sentences on individuals wanting to travel to Syria to fight. By 2016, officials in the kingdom had arrested over 1,600 Daesh supporters.[164]

For its part, Daesh has mocked state-backed Saudi clerics who have denounced the group, labeling them as "palace scholars" unequal to the task of interpreting Islam.[165] Of all the GCC states, Daesh poses perhaps the biggest threat to the Saudi state. The group's leader Abu Bakr Al-Baghdadi has directly challenged the credentials of Saudi leaders and their ability to defend Islamic and Salafi Sunni principles. The ongoing war in Yemen, meanwhile, appears to have only strengthened al-Qaʻida in the Arabian Peninsula (AQAP), bringing the threat of religious extremism ever closer to Saudi borders.

Saudi Arabia's new leaders, meanwhile, appear to have started the Yemen war as a result of their pursuit of more assertive foreign and security policies. The official reason Saudi authorities gave for starting the war was to curb supposed Iranian influence among the rebellious Houthis of Yemen. But "the evidence to date tends to confirm there has been periodic but limited Iranian involvement" with the Houthi rebellion.[166] Whatever the actual reasons for its start, in every sense the Yemen war has been an extremely costly undertaking by the Saudi state.[167] Apart from the inordinate sums the kingdom has spent on hardware and personnel, the human costs of the war have been incalculable. The devastation wrought on Yemen has been indiscriminate. According to the United Nations, by January 2017, some 10,000 s had been killed as a result of the war, another 40,000 injured, and close to 10 million are in need of "urgent assistance."[168] As one report has noted, "the war, and particularly the inept and even vicious way it is being carried out, is turning nearly all Yemenis from contempt for Saudis to outright hatred."[169]

The war's toll on the kingdom itself has not been nearly as costly, but is still much heavier than its leaders anticipated. From the start of the war in March 2015 until November 2016, at least 86 Saudi servicemen had lost their lives in the conflict, with close to 90 percent of the casualties occurring inside Saudi territory and only 9 percent inside Yemen itself.[170] In late 2016, one credible report put the financial cost of the war for Saudi Arabia at around $66.5 million a day.[171] Rather than being an expression of strength, as it was partially meant to be, the war has arguably made the kingdom look weaker.[172] Whatever its outcome, the long-term consequences of the Yemen war do not bode well for Saudi Arabia.

For Saudi Arabia, much like its smaller neighbors in the GCC, institutional adjustments were made necessary not so much in response to the 2011 uprisings but as a result of the slump in the oil markets starting in 2014. The kingdom's new crop of rulers, in power since 2015, soon embarked on two seemingly contradictory campaigns. They rolled out ambitious plans to curb government expenditure, to encourage the private sector to hire more nationals, and to make state enterprises, including the hallowed national oil company Aramco, even more efficient and profitable. On the other hand, they launched a very expensive, and ill-conceived, attack against Yemen. The war's human and material costs are difficult to calculate. Ironically, the most serious threats to Saudi leadership so far do not appear to emanate from the structural factors it has feared—i.e. Iranian-inspired Shia rebellions, Daesh terrorism, Saudi liberals and human rights activists, or non-state religious activism. The biggest threat so far has been from the leadership's own missteps, most notably walking hurriedly into the minefield that is Yemen. How and under what circumstances the Saudi state extricates itself from the Yemeni quagmire, and deals with the human catastrophe it has exacerbated there, will be the true test of its capacity, its developmental trajectory, and its domestic popularity.

Conclusion

A mere few decades ago, the young and small countries of the Arabian Peninsula were dismissed as improbable states bound to collapse at the first indication of regional tension or domestic uprising. That certainly must have been the assumption that prompted Saddam Hussein's invasion of Kuwait in 1990. A country that small and ruled over by a gaggle of archaic cousins must necessarily be fragile and easily overwhelmed. At least insofar as the limitations of size and demography are concerned, Saddam wasn't far off the mark. Keenly aware of such vulnerabilities themselves, the six states of the GCC have sought to guarantee their safety through collective security arrangements and the eager embrace of the US security umbrella. Such survival strategies have been far from limited to the field of foreign policy. Much of the petrostates' domestic politics, in fact, has also been driven by survival strategies of one kind or another.

Such domestic survival strategies have differed from time to time according to the domestic and regional contexts within which the petro-states have found themselves. In the immediate aftermath of the 2011 Arab uprisings, specific national variations notwithstanding, survival strategies mostly featured three interrelated initiatives. Most immediately, the states responded with crackdowns and demonstrations of intolerance toward any kind of dissent. Second, just as the costs of dissent were raised, so were the rewards of conformity. Preexisting patronage networks were reinforced and new ones were forged, civil service and military salaries were raised, and new jobs for nationals were created. Finally, beginning with Bahrain and Saudi Arabia, the state aggressively promoted a sectarian narrative of us versus them, Sunni versus Shia, in which the primordial bonds of the nation to rulers, those living descendants of tribal and religious guardians, were reinforced. To abort any possibility of revolution, states spread the most reactionary and atavistic of sentiments among their peoples.

It was under these circumstances that the petro-states of the Arabian Peninsula faced the 2014 crash in global oil prices. When huge revenues from hydrocarbons flowed into the coffers of the state, it was easy to mask the negative consequences of natural resource dependence. But after 2014 problems could no longer be solved by simply throwing money at them. Slowly but steadily, the effects of the resource curse began to reveal themselves to local economies: the underdevelopment of other economic sectors because of the oil sector's preferential treatment by policymakers; the inability of the workforce or the larger economy to diversify; overt dependence on the state to bail out private enterprises in tough times; and overdependence on largely unpredictable international markets. It was at this point that institutional adjustments could no longer be delayed.

State capacity, this chapter argued, was sufficient to carry the six petro-states of the Arabian Peninsula through the 2011 uprisings with minimal need for adjustments. Whether or not the same holds for the consequences of oil price decline in the post-2014 period, in the era of a "new normal" for oil, is too early to tell at this point. By themselves, natural resource endowments are a blessing and not a curse. What turns these blessings into a curse is the ways in which they are managed, or, more accurately, mismanaged. For some time, policymakers have known what the remedies for dealing with the resource curse are: minimizing the risks of uneven growth among economic sectors and overreliance on oil; instituting policies that enhance growth in short to medium terms; promoting good governance and reducing corruption; preparing for the depletion of oil resource income; and regularly assessing the appropriate policy mix.[173] Long-term savings plans, in the form of investments by sovereign wealth funds, can also help alleviate some of the pitfalls of dependence on and depletion of natural recourses.[174] Of these policy options, the GCC states have already made good use of their sovereign wealth funds, and with varying degrees of conviction and success, they have begun to slowly diversify their economies. But on most other scores, including also economic diversification, the political will and the capacity to make difficult decisions seem to be conspicuously absent.

By itself, wealth does not buy state capacity. The capacity that the petro-states have enjoyed so far is rooted in other, complementary phenomena, such as state evolutionary patterns and state–society linkages. But whether on their own, without the additional element of oil-driven patronage, these are sufficient to enable the GCC states to operate as they have been in the past, without substantial changes to their very institutional set-up, is an open question. Within the region, state leaders and opinion-makers frequently talk of the need to be prepared for the inevitable arrival one day of the post-oil era. Little of this talk has so far been translated into actual reality, with, of course, the notable exception of Dubai. How readily the rest of the region can adapt and adopt the Dubai model, and whether by doing so this will impede or expedite the need for other, political changes, is a question that only time can answer.

7

CONCLUSION

Power and politics in the Arab world have always featured contention and contestation. For the foreseeable future, there are few signs that the fundamental nature of power and politics in the region, and more specifically the ways in which Arab states and societies relate to and interact with one another, are headed for any meaningful change. Just as it has been, Arab politics is likely to remain ridden with conflict and discord.

Several important conclusions can be drawn from the analysis of Arab politics offered here. In these concluding pages, I highlight some of the more salient ones, beginning with an insight we have known for some time, namely that authoritarian regimes are often adaptable and therefore durable. Whether it is through co-option and partial opening, or rigged elections and other safety valves, authoritarian systems exhibit far greater durability than is often expected of them. Autocrats may be isolated and prone to making rash and counterproductive decisions. But the larger coercive and ideological apparatuses on which they rely give the authoritarian enterprise a measure of staying power beyond the person of the leader. In the Arab world, even outside the Arabian Peninsula but especially there, the political salience of social and cultural dynamics gives authoritarian states additional scaffolds on which they can hoist their legitimacy and erect ideological apparatuses.

Another conclusion has to do with the nature of social movements, more specifically the conditions under which they might take different directions. Social movements emerge out of collective pursuits by social actors regarding specific goals to which the state has been inattentive. Once a social movement gets underway, it may follow several different paths. If the state steps in and proactively addresses its demands, thereby deflating the primary purpose for which the social movement originally came about, then the movement is likely to fizzle and peter out. This occurred in Morocco and to a lesser extent in Jordan. If, however, the state dismisses or ridicules the very rallying cry around which people feel strongly enough to mobilize, as happened in Syria and Bahrain, then the social movement is only likely to grow in strength and intensity.

At this point, the cohesion of the state elite is key. If state elites face internal desertions and are abandoned by key allies, as Ben Ali and Mubarak were, then their continued hold on power is questionable. But if elites remain united in the face of mounting societal opposition, or are in fact strengthened because of external support, then they can hang on to power nearly indefinitely (as in Syria) or even altogether crush the people's revolt (as in Bahrain).

A related conclusion revolves around state strength and capacity. State capacity greatly influences the shape and direction of social movements, and, in fact, can determine whether they even emerge at all. More importantly, state capacity enables political leaders to retain a level of autonomy from social actors, implement and carry forward developmental agendas, and enhance their own legitimacy. This is closely tied to another insight, namely that popular perceptions matter. Popular perceptions play key roles in the start of social movements, and more broadly in the people's impulse to obey their leaders or rebel against them. How people view the state—strong, weak, invincible, vulnerable, corrupt, efficient, repressive, etc.—determines their individual and collective willingness to avail themselves of the political opportunities presented to them.

Perceptions and memory are closely related, the political significance of memory being another insight worth repeating. It was living memory, of a dark historical episode not that long ago, that served as a natural brake to Algeria's non-rebellion in 2011. Few Algerians today have forgotten the brutality of the civil war that ravaged their country in the 1990s. The lessons of Algeria are bound to have far-reaching consequences for future developments in Libya, Syria, and Yemen. However, even if the nightmares of these civil war-ravaged countries end, regardless of the type of incoming systems, the hellish memory of what has transpired for the past several years is bound to keep future regimes intact for some time. In these instances, as in Algeria, popular memory may serve as a source of stability irrespective of future power arrangements.

Integral to popular perceptions are assumptions about one's own identity and the identity of the larger society to which the individual belongs. One of the outcomes of the 2011 uprisings has been the spread of sectarian identities in the Arabian Peninsula and in other heterogeneous Arab societies. Largely as a result of political leaders framing the mass-based uprisings as the work of disgruntled and marginalized groups, sectarianism quickly found receptive ears among populations feeling besieged and under threat. The monarchies of Bahrain and Saudi Arabia from one end of the Arab world, and the regime of Bashar al-Assad from another, were arsonists pretending to be firemen, rallying the support of their own, narrow sectarian followers but oblivious to the broader consequences of their actions for the wider region. How this sectarianism evolves from this point on, and whether or for how long it may have staying power, is anyone's guess.

Finally, by way of conclusion, I come back to one of the central and recurring themes of this book, namely that in looking at state–society relations, political analysis requires attention to institutions, actors, and processes. Institutions may change on their own or be immobile and static, be strong or fragile, or have manifold other features that influence their political nature and significance. Actors have agency, their choices often shaped through the institutional arrangements within which they find themselves. At times, during critical junctures, actors' decisions can even shape institutions. The agency of political actors, especially at times when these actors have greater freedom to shape institutions and processes, make political outcomes difficult to predict. Ennahda's lead role in crafting a democratic polity in post-uprising Tunisia, thanks largely to the efforts of its leader Rachid Ghannouchi, is a case in point. And the outcomes of other evolving circumstances—in Yemen, Syria, and Libya—are similarly impossible to predict.

Given all that the region has been through, conjectures about future power arrangements and state–society relations may be dismissed as altogether misplaced. The Islamic State, after all, has turned on its head our assumptions about power, sovereignty, state capacity, citizenship, and the like. The very question of how much of a state the Islamic State really is, or was, remains in many ways unanswerable. For the time being, we see both *de jure* and *de facto* power-holders in the Arab world, and finding a way to stabilize the relationship between them might be the best we can hope for.[1] In fact, it is quite possible, as Ahram and Lust have speculated, that in the coming years we see a scenario in which sovereign and non-sovereign entities coexist in a patchwork of diluted sovereignty.[2]

That may well be. I am convinced, nevertheless, that states, both as sovereign territories with well-defined borders and as collections of institutions with power over society, are not about to dissipate altogether any time soon, whether in the Arab world or elsewhere. And, in those Arab countries where the powers and institutions of the state remain intact, there are few signs that the fundamental nature of state–society relations are about to change anytime soon. Power and politics in the Arab world, in other words, are likely to remain the contested terrains that they have been.

APPENDIX 1

SURVEY METHODOLOGY FOR *THE ARAB OPINION INDEX*

The Arab Opinion Index provides information on public attitudes in the Arab countries surveyed, as well as the Arab region as a whole. Within individual countries, sampling follows a randomized, stratified, multi-stage, self-weighted clustered approach, where sampling at all stages is probability proportional to size (PPS) of population, giving an overall margin of error between +/- 2 and 33 percent for the individual country, taking into account that the size of the sample is at least 1,200 respondents in each country sampled. The use of PPS at all stages is meant to guarantee fairness in the representation of various population segments. Using this sampling method ensures that each and every adult citizen has a fair chance of inclusion within the surveyed sample. Applying the use of random selection methods as well as the PPS at every stage of sampling means that the relative populations of highest-level administrative regions ("governorates," also known as provinces or states) and the rural–urban divide are adequately accounted for in the final sample, and also that other demographic variables such as gender, education, age, and income groups are well represented, as per the last available census.

The number of respondents assigned to a given governorate is based on that governorate's share of the overall country population, as per the last available census. Inside individual governorates, the number of respondents drawn from within urban centers or from rural communities is determined based on the distribution of population within that governorate, as per the latest available census. The same method is repeated to select random clusters of primary sampling units (PSUs) in each administrative unit. At the level of cluster, a well-defined algorithm specifies exactly which households are approached to ensure eight randomly selected households from each cluster. Fieldworkers are given technical training in opinion surveys and in ethical standards employed by the surveying body. They are instructed to complete the questionnaire with one member of the selected household before moving on to the next household, the choice of which follows the same principles to ensure that there is no bias in the selection of households.

In 2016, all interviews were conducted face to face, with the Arab Center for Research and Policy Studies contracting local partners in each country to conduct the interviews. The size of samples in individual countries ranged from 2,399 (Egypt) to 1,119 (Mauritania). This meant that the margin of error for all countries included in *The Arab Opinion Index* is between 2 and 33 percent. When the results are aggregated for an overall sample of the Arab world, the findings from individual Arab countries are all given the same weight. This is to ensure that in the final output of an "Arab public opinion," opinions in larger countries do not unintentionally drown out the opinions of individuals in less populous countries. In specific clusters, a number of households interviewed are chosen for a return visit on the day following the survey to ensure the completeness and integrity of the data.

This information was kindly provided by Mohammad Almasri of the Arab Center for Research and Policy Studies.

NOTES

1. STUDYING ARAB POLITICS

1. Steven A. Cook, *False Dawn: Protest, Democracy, and Violence in the New Middle East* (New York: Oxford University Press, 2017).
2. Bülent Aras and Richard Falk, "Authoritarian 'geopolitics' of survival in the Arab Spring," *Third World Quarterly*, Vol. 36, No. 2 (2015), p. 323.
3. Ibid., p. 324.
4. On this point, see Peter Evans, "The Eclipse of the State? Reflections on Stateness in an Era of Globalization," *World Politics*, Vol. 50, No. 1 (October 1997), pp. 62–87; and Peter Evans, "The State as Problem and Solution: Predation, Embedded Autonomy, and Structural Change," in *The Politics of Economic Development*, Stephan Haggard and Robert R. Kaufman, eds. (Princeton, NJ: Princeton University, Press, 1992), pp. 139–82.
5. Louis Althusser, "Ideology and Ideological State Apparatuses," in *Literary Theory: An Anthology*, 2nd edn, Julie Rivkin and Michael Ryan, eds. (Maiden, MA: Blackwell, 2004), pp. 693–702.
6. As discussed in the next chapter and as Joseph Sassoon reminds us, the eight Arab republics have more in common in their modus operandi than is maybe assumed, especially in their systems of repression. In all of them, leadership was centralized and decision-making concentrated in few hands. Economic management varied widely, but the leaders ensured that their systems of cronies and economic dependents remained in place. See also Joseph Sassoon, *Anatomy of Authoritarianism in the Arab Republics* (Cambridge: Cambridge University Press, 2016), p. 7.
7. Margaret Levi, "Theories of Historical and Institutional Change," *PS: Political Science & Politics*, Vol. 20, No. 3 (1987), p. 684.
8. Avner Greif, "Historical and Comparative Institutional Analysis," *American Economic Review*, Vol. 88, No. 2 (1998), pp. 80–84. Original emphasis.

9. Elinor Ostrom, *Understanding Institutional Diversity* (Princeton, NJ: Princeton University Press, 2005), p. 3.

10. Gretchen Helmke and Steven Levitsky, "Introduction," in *Informal Institutions and Democracy: Lessons from Latin America*, Gretchen Helmke and Steven Levitsky, eds (Baltimore, MD: Johns Hopkins University Press, 2006), p. 5.

11. Douglass North, *Institutions, Institutional Change and Economic Performance* (Cambridge: Cambridge University Press, 1990), pp. 4–5.

12. This definition is in line with the one offered by Levi: "All institutions are embodiments of rule," she writes, "all have a legalistic aspect, and all possess enforcement mechanisms. They are considered political institutions when the state enforces the rules, social institutions when enforcement is through mechanisms such as approval and shunning, and economic institutions when enforcement is by means of profits and loss." Margaret Levi, "A Model, a Method, and a Map: Rational Choice in Comparative and Historical Analysis," in *Comparative Politics: Rationality, Culture, and Structure*, Mark I. Lichbach and Alan S. Zuckerman, eds (Cambridge: Cambridge University Press, 1997), p. 25.

13. Giovanni Capoccia and R. Daniel Keleman, "The Study of Critical Junctures: Theory, Narrative, and Counterfactuals in Historical Institutionalism," *World Politics*, Vol. 59, No. 3 (April 2007), p. 343.

14. Paul Pierson, *Politics in Time* (Princeton, NJ: Princeton University Press, 2004), p. 135.

15. Jessica L. P. Weeks, *Dictators at War and Peace* (Ithaca, NY: Cornell University Press, 2014), p. 5.

16. I have explored these and related developments in *Troubled Waters: Insecurity in the Persian Gulf* (Ithaca, NY: Cornell University Press, 2018).

2. STATES, INSTITUTIONS, AND POLITICAL ATROPHY

1. Kathleen Thelen, "Historical Institutionalism in Comparative Politics," *Annual Review of Political Science*, Vol. 2 (1999), p. 370.

2. See, for example, Kathleen Thelen, *How Institutions Evolve: The Political Economy of Skills in Germany, Britain, the United States, and Japan* (Cambridge: Cambridge University Press, 2004); and Gretchen Helmke and Steven Levitsky, "Introduction," in *Informal Institutions and Democracy: Lessons from Latin America*, Gretchen Helmke and Steven Levitsky, eds (Baltimore, MD: Johns Hopkins University Press, 2006), pp. 1–30.

3. This is not to imply, of course, that significant scholarship from a largely institutional perspective has not been produced in relation to the Middle East in recent years. A small sample includes: Nazih Ayubi,

Over-stating the Arab State: Politics and Society in the Middle East (London: I. B. Tauris, 1999); Abdo Baaklini, Guilain Denoeux, and Robert Springborg, *Legislative Politics in the Arab World: The Resurgence of Democratic Institutions* (Boulder, CO: Lynne Rienner Publishers, 1999); Steven Heydemann, ed., *War, Institutions, and Social Change in the Middle East* (Berkeley, CA: University of California Press, 2000); Marsha Pripstein Posusney and Michele Penner Angrist, eds, *Authoritarianism in the Middle East: Regimes and Resistance* (Boulder, CO: Lynne Rienner Publishers, 2005); and Charles Tilly, "War and State Power," *Middle East Report*, No. 171 (July/August 1991), pp. 38–40.

4. Giovanni Capoccia and R. Daniel Keleman, "The Study of Critical Junctures: Theory, Narrative, and Counterfactuals in Historical Institutionalism," *World Politics*, Vol. 59, No. 3 (April 2007), p. 341.

5. James Mahoney, "Path Dependence in Historical Sociology," *Theory and Society*, Vol. 29 (2000), p. 513.

6. Douglass C. North, *Institutions, Institutional Change and Economic Performance* (Cambridge: Cambridge University Press, 1990), pp. 7–8.

7. For more on state capacity in the Arab world, see below, Chapter 6.

8. Douglass C. North, "Institutional Change and Economic Growth," *Journal of Economic History*, Vol. 31, No. 1 (1971), p. 123–124.

9. Avner Greif, "Historical and Comparative Institutional Analysis," *American Economic Review*, Vol. 88, No. 2 (1998), p. 80.

10. Ibid., p. 82.

11. Mahoney, "Path Dependence in Historical Sociology," p. 507.

12. Thelen, *How Institutions Evolve*, p. 31. Margaret Levi's analogy of a tree with branches is a bit more apt: "Path dependence has to mean, if it is to mean anything, that once a country or region has started down a track, the costs of reversal are very high. There will be other choice points, but the entrenchments of certain institutional arrangements obstruct an easy reversal of the initial choice. Perhaps the better metaphor is a tree, rather than a path. From the same trunk, there are many different branches and smaller branches. Although it is possible to turn around and to clamber from one to the other—and essential if the chosen branch dies—the branch on which a climber begins is the one she tends to follow." Margaret Levi, "A Model, a Method, and a Map: Rational Choice in Comparative and Historical Analysis," in *Comparative Politics: Rationality, Culture, and Structure*, Mark I. Lichbach and Alan S. Zuckerman, eds (Cambridge: Cambridge University Press, 1997), p. 28.

13. Thelen, *How Institutions Evolve*, p. 31.

14. Ibid., p. xiii.

15. Paul Pierson, "Increasing Returns, Path Dependence, and the Study of

Politics," *American Political Science Review*, Vol. 94, No. 2 (2000), p. 252. Original emphasis.

16. Kathleen Thelen, "How Institutions Evolve: Insights from Comparative Historical Analysis," in *Comparative Historical Analysis in the Social Sciences*, James Mahoney and Dietrich Rueschemeyer, eds (Cambridge: Cambridge University Press, 2003), p. 225.

17. Ibid., p. 226.

18. S. N. Sangmpam, "Politics Rules: The False Primacy of Institutions in Developing Countries," *Political Studies*, Vol. 55, No. 1 (2007), pp. 204–5.

19. Ian Greener, "The Potential of Path Dependence in Political Studies," *Politics*, Vol. 25, No. 1 (2005), p. 64.

20. Greener, "The Potential of Path Dependence in Political Studies," p. 66. Greener's arguments were influenced by those developed by Margaret Archer. See Margaret S. Archer, *Realist Social Theory: The Morphogenetic Approach* (Cambridge: Cambridge University Press, 1995), pp. 308–12.

21. Ibid., p. 68.

22. H. E. Chehabi, and Juan J. Linz, "A Theory of Sultanism 1: A Type of Nondemocratic Rule," in *Sultanistic Regimes*, H. E. Chehabi and Juan J. Linz, eds (Baltimore, MD: Johns Hopkins University Press, 1998).

23. For one of the more fascinating treatments of the colonial legacy of the Middle East, see Karl E. Meyer and Shareen Blair Brysac, *Kingmakers: The Invention of the Modern Middle East* (New York: Norton, 2008).

24. David Waldner calls this category of states "mediated," whereby many state functions and services are mediated through local notable elites; as compared to "unmediated states," in which instead of notable elites "a diverse array of institutions connect centralized public authority to society and economy." David Waldner, *State Building and Late Development* (Ithaca, NY: Cornell University Press, 1999), p. 22.

25. Eric Nordlinger, *Soldiers in Politics: Military Coups and Governments* (Englewood Cliffs, NJ: Prentice Hall, 1977), pp. 22–7.

26. Imad Harb, "The Egyptian Military in Politics: Disengagement or Accommodation?" *Middle East Journal*, Vol. 57, No. 2 (Spring 2003), p. 278.

27. Ibid.

28. Steven Heydemann, "Social Pacts and the Persistence of Authoritarianism in the Middle East," in *Debating Arab Authoritarianism: Dynamics and Durability in Nondemocratic Regimes*, Oliver Schlumberger, ed. (Stanford, CA: Stanford University Press, 2007), p. 25.

29. Daniel Brumberg, "Authoritarian Legacies and Reform Strategies in

the Arab World," in *Political Liberalization and Democratization in the Arab World: Vol. 1, Theoretical Perspectives*, Rex Brynen, Bahgat Korany, and Paul Noble, eds (Boulder, CO: Lynne Rienner Publishers, 1995), p. 233.

30. Heydemann, "Social Pacts and the Persistence of Authoritarianism in the Middle East," p. 22.

31. Saad Eddin Ibrahim, "Liberalization and Democratization in the Arab World: An Overview," in *Political Liberalization and Democratization in the Arab World: Vol. 1, Theoretical Perspectives*, Rex Brynen, Bahgat Korany, and Paul Noble, eds (Boulder, CO: Lynne Rienner Publishers, 1995), p. 36.

32. James A. Bill and Robert Springborg, *Politics in the Middle East*, 5th edn (New York: Addison Wesley Longman, 2000), pp. 112–20.

33. Shadi Hamid, "Political Party Development Before and After the Arab Spring," in *Beyond the Arab Spring*, Mehran Kamrava, ed. (New York: Oxford University Press, 2014), p. 132.

34. Roger Owen, *The Rise and Fall of Arab Presidents for Life* (Cambridge, MA: Harvard University Press, 2012), p. 3.

35. Ibid., p. 56.

36. Ibrahim, "Liberalization and Democratization in the Arab World," pp. 48–9.

37. Michele Dunne and Tarek Radwan, "Egypt: Why Liberalism Still Matters," in *Democratization and Authoritarianism in the Arab World*, Larry Diamond and Marc F. Plattner, eds (Baltimore, MD: Johns Hopkins University Press, 2014), p. 250.

38. Owen, *The Rise and Fall of Arab Presidents for Life*, p. 72.

39. Eva Bellin, "Coercive Institutions and Coercive Leaders," in *Authoritarianism in the Middle East: Regimes and Resistance* (Boulder, CO: Lynne Rienner Publishers, 2005), pp. 26–7.

40. Zoltan Barany, "The Role of the Military," in *Democratization and Authoritarianism in the Arab World*, Larry Diamond and Marc F. Plattner, eds (Baltimore, MD: Johns Hopkins University Press, 2014), p. 163.

41. Philippe Droz-Vincent, "The Military amidst Uprisings and Transitions in the Arab World," in *The New Middle East: Protest and Revolution in the Arab World*, Fawaz A. Gerges, ed. (Cambridge: Cambridge University Press, 2014), p. 189.

42. Ibid., p. 194.

43. Roger Owen, "Egypt and Tunisia: From the Revolutionary Overthrow of Dictatorships to the Struggle to Establish a New Constitutional Order," in *The New Middle East: Protest and Revolution in the Arab World*, Fawaz A. Gerges, ed. (Cambridge: Cambridge University Press, 2014), pp. 261, 263.

44. Droz-Vincent, "The Military amidst Uprisings and Transitions in the

Arab World," p. 188. This was not a challenge that the states of the Arabian Peninsula faced, as most did not have armed forces that could be considered "national." In Bahrain, for example, the Defense Forces and the Interior Ministry forces are staffed by foreign commanders and soldiers from countries such as Pakistan and Jordan and all are Sunni. The UAE and Qatar, and to a lesser extent Kuwait, are also largely reliant on foreign-born troops for their armed forces, many of them from Yemen or Baluchis from Pakistan. On this point, see Droz-Vincent, "The Military amidst Uprisings and Transitions in the Arab World," pp. 194–5; and Barany, "The Role of the Military," p. 169.

45. Owen, *The Rise and Fall of Arab Presidents for Life*, p. 37.
46. Wael Ghonim, *Revolution 2.0: The Power of the People is Greater than the People in Power: A Memoir*, (Boston, MA: Houghton Mifflin Harcourt, 2012), p. 2.
47. Owen, *The Rise and Fall of Arab Presidents for Life*, p. 78.
48. Ghonim, *Revolution 2.0*, p. 28.
49. Brumberg, "Authoritarian Legacies and Reform Strategies in the Arab World," pp. 235–6.
50. Fadhel Kaboub, "The End of Neoliberalism? An Institutional Analysis of the Arab Uprisings," *Journal of Economic Issues*, Vol. 67, No. 2 (June 2013), p. 535.
51. Joel Beinin, *Workers and Thieves: Labor Movements and Popular Uprisings in Tunisia and Egypt* (Stanford, CA: Stanford University Press, 2016), p. 59.
52. Kaboub, "The End of Neoliberalism?" p. 537.
53. Massoud Karshenas, Valentine M. Moghadam, and Randa Alami, "Social Policy after the Arab Spring: States and Social Rights in the MENA Region," *World Development*, Vol. 64 (2014), p. 731.
54. Tunisia and the GCC states were exceptions in this regard. Ibid., p. 733.
55. Ibid., p. 734.
56. Owen, *The Rise and Fall of Arab Presidents for Life*, p. 35.
57. The observations of Jean-Pierre Filiu in this regard are worth remembering: "Nasser, Boumediene, and Assad were far from being the most talented rulers, but they were ruthless survivors in an implacable environment of intrigues, coups and treachery. They learnt to kill before being killed. Their obsession with security defined the fate of the nation. After hijacking the gains of independence, they made the whole nation hostage to their ambitions." Jean-Pierre Filiu, *From Deep State to Islamic State: The Arab Counter-Revolution and its Jihadi Legacy* (New York: Oxford University Press, 2015), p. 48.
58. Owen, *The Rise and Fall of Arab Presidents for Life*, p. 38.

59. Ibid., p. 32.
60. Ibid., p. 5.
61. On "soft authoritarianism," see Nadine Sika, "The Arab State and Social Contestation," in *Beyond the Arab Spring*, Mehran Kamrava, ed. (New York: Oxford University Press, 2014), p. 95. On Assad's mode of governance in Syria, see Joshua Stacher, *Adaptable Autocrats: Regime Power in Egypt and Syria* (Stanford, CA: Stanford University Press, 2012), p. 14.
62. Marie Duboc, "Challenging the Trade Union, Reclaiming the Nation: The Politics of Labor Protest in Egypt, 2006–11," in *Beyond the Arab Spring*, Mehran Kamrava, ed. (New York: Oxford University Press, 2014), p. 237.
63. This was, at least, a popular perception in Egypt, regardless of Mubarak's actual intentions. Fawaz A. Gerges, "Introduction," in *The New Middle East: Protest and Revolution in the Arab World*, Fawaz A. Gerges, ed. (Cambridge: Cambridge University Press, 2014), p. 5.
64. Sika, "The Arab State and Social Contestation," p. 91.
65. Owen, *The Rise and Fall of Arab Presidents for Life*, pp. 5–6.
66. Lisa Anderson, "Authoritarian Legacies and Regime Change: Toward Understanding Political Transition in the Arab World," in *The New Middle East: Protest and Revolution in the Arab World*, Fawaz A. Gerges, ed. (Cambridge: Cambridge University Press, 2014), pp. 48–9.
67. Owen, *The Rise and Fall of Arab Presidents for Life*, pp. 174–5.
68. Julia Choucair-Vizoso, "Illusive Reform: Jordan's Stubborn Stability," in *Beyond the Façade: Political Reform in the Arab World*, Marina Ottaway and Julia Choucair-Vizoso, eds (Washington, DC: Carnegie Endowment for International Peace, 2008), p. 46.
69. Charles Tripp, *The Power and the People: Paths of Resistance in the Middle East* (Cambridge: Cambridge University Press, 2013), p. 314.
70. See, for example, Bellin, "Coercive Institutions and Coercive Leaders," pp. 21–41; Eva Bellin, "The Robustness of Authoritarianism in the Middle East: Exceptionalism in Comparative Perspective," *Comparative Politics*, Vol. 36, No. 2 (January 2004), pp. 139–57; and Eva Bellin, "Reconsidering the Robustness of Authoritarianism in the Middle East: Lessons from the Arab Spring," *Comparative Politics*, Vol. 44, No. 2 (January 2012), pp. 127–49.
71. For my own elaboration of the concept of "civic myth monarchies" and other typologies of Middle Eastern states in the late 1990s, see Mehran Kamrava, "Non-Democratic States and Political Liberalization in the Middle East: A Structural Analysis," *Third World Quarterly*, Vol. 19, No. 1 (Spring 1998), pp. 63–85.
72. This is discussed more extensively below, in Chapter 6. See also

Rachid Yalouh, "The Discourse of Change in Morocco," *Policy Analysis*, Doha Institute, Arab Center for Research and Policy Studies (2011).

73. Sean L. Yom and F. Gregory Gause, III, "Resilient Royals: How Arab Monarchies Hang On," in *Democratization and Authoritarianism in the Arab World*, Larry Diamond and Marc F. Plattner, eds (Baltimore, MD: Johns Hopkins University Press, 2014), pp. 113–14.

74. Ibid., p. 119.

75. Heydemann, "Social Pacts and the Persistence of Authoritarianism in the Middle East," p. 26.

76. Stacher, *Adaptable Autocrats*, pp. 21–2.

77. Marina Ottoway and Meredith Riley, "Morocco: Top-Down Reform Without Democratic Transition," in *Beyond the Façade: Political Reform in the Arab World*, Marina Ottaway and Julia Choucair-Vizoso, eds (Washington, DC: Carnegie Endowment for International Peace, 2008), pp. 166–9.

78. Rachid Yalouh, "The Discourse of Change in Morocco," *Policy Analysis*, Doha Institute, Arab Center for Research and Policy Studies (2011), p. 1.

79. Sarah Phillips, "Yemen: The Centrality of the Process," in *Beyond the Façade: Political Reform in the Arab World*, Marina Ottaway and Julia Choucair-Vizoso, eds (Washington, DC: Carnegie Endowment for International Peace, 2008), p. 233.

80. Stacher, *Adaptable Autocrats*, p. 23.

81. Ibid., pp. 17–18.

82. Heydemann, "Social Pacts and the Persistence of Authoritarianism in the Middle East," p. 32.

83. Joseph Sassoon, *Anatomy of Authoritarianism in the Arab Republics* (Cambridge: Cambridge University Press, 2016), p. 253–8.

84. Ibid., p. 145.

85. There are multiple ways to categorize states into ideal types. Stepan and Linz, as an example, have come up with six: democratic, author-itarian, totalitarian, post-totalitarian, sultanistic, and, a more recent addition, an authoritarian-democratic hybrid. Alfred Stepan and Juan J. Linz, "Democratization Theory and the 'Arab Spring,'" in *Democratization and Authoritarianism in the Arab World*, Larry Diamond and Marc F. Plattner, eds (Baltimore, MD: Johns Hopkins University Press, 2014), p. 85.

3. CHALLENGING THE STATE

1. I have expounded on the conditions for and varieties of revolution in Mehran Kamrava, "Revolution Revisited: Revolutionary Types and the

Structuralist–Voluntarist Debate," *Canadian Journal of Political Science*, Vol. 32, No. 2 (1999), pp. 1–29.

2. This genesis of spontaneous revolutions deep within and because of social dynamics leads John Foran to argue that the 2011 Arab uprisings may be better labeled as "radical social change" rather than as revolutions. John Foran, "Global Affinities: The New Cultures of Resistance Behind the Arab Spring," in *Beyond the Arab Spring*, Mehran Kamrava, ed. (New York: Oxford University Press, 2014), p. 51.

3. For a useful and descriptive summary of events before and after the uprisings in the countries affected, see Michael B. Bishku, "Is it Arab Spring or Business as Usual? Recent Changes in the Arab World in Historical Context," *Journal of Third World Studies*, Vol. 30, No. 1 (2013), pp. 55–71.

4. James DeFronzo defines a social movement as "a persistent, organized effort by a relatively large number of people either to bring about *social change* or to resist it." James DeFronzo, *Revolutions and Revolutionary Movements*, 5th edn (Boulder, CO: Westview, 2015), p. 9. Emphasis added. I see this definition as somewhat constricting, as social movements may revolve around the attainment of policy or political objectives as well.

5. Sidney Tarrow maintains that "contentious politics is triggered when changing political opportunities and constraints create incentives to take action for actors who lack resources on their own. People contend through known repertoires of contention and expand them by creating innovations at the margins. When backed by well-structured social networks and galvanized by culturally resonant, action-oriented symbols, contentious politics leads to sustained interaction with opponents—to social movements." Sidney G. Tarrow, *Power in Movement: Social Movements and Contentious Politics*, 3rd edn (Cambridge: Cambridge University Press, 2011), p. 6.

6. Sidney Tarrow, *Strangers at the Gates: Movements and States in Contentious Politics* (Cambridge: Cambridge University Press, 2012), p. 1.

7. Ibid., pp. 77–8.

8. Charles Tilly and Lesley J. Wood, *Social Movements, 1768–2012*, 3rd edn (Boulder, CO: Paradigm Publishers, 2013), p. 12.

9. Tarrow, *Power in Movement*, p. 11.

10. Ibid., pp. 28–9.

11. Tilly and Wood, *Social Movements, 1768–2012*, p. 13.

12. Tarrow, *Strangers at the Gates*, p. 3.

13. Tilly and Wood, *Social Movements, 1768–2012*, p. 98.

14. Ibid., p. 112.

15. Eric Selbin, *Revolution, Rebellion, Resistance: The Power of Story* (London: Zed Books, 2010), p. 4.

16. Tilly and Wood, *Social Movements, 1768–2012*, p. 15.
17. Asef Bayat, *Life as Politics: How Ordinary People Change the Middle East*, 2nd edn (Stanford, CA: Stanford University Press, 2013), p. 13.
18. Charles Tripp, *The Power and the People: Paths of Resistance in the Middle East* (Cambridge: Cambridge University Press, 2013), p. 133.
19. Foran, "Global Affinities," p. 59.
20. Charles Tripp, "The Politics of Resistance and the Arab Spring," in *The New Middle East: Protest and Revolution in the Arab World*, Fawaz A. Gerges, ed. (Cambridge: Cambridge University Press, 2014), p. 138.
21. Fawaz A. Gerges, "Introduction," in *The New Middle East: Protest and Revolution in the Arab World*, Fawaz A. Gerges, ed. (Cambridge: Cambridge University Press, 2014), p. 3.
22. Lisa Anderson, "Authoritarian Legacies and Regime Change: Toward Understanding Political Transition in the Arab World," in *The New Middle East: Protest and Revolution in the Arab World*, Fawaz A. Gerges, ed. (Cambridge: Cambridge University Press, 2014), pp. 51–3.
23. Hamid Dabashi, *The Arab Spring: The End of Postcolonialism* (London: Zed, 2012), pp. 166–7.
24. Ibid., p. 10. In Dabashi's words, the uprisings signaled "the end of colonially conditioned ideologies" and the "closure to all absolutist ideologies manufactured in dialogical contestation with European and American imperialisms." p. 13.
25. Ibid., p. 252.
26. Said Amir Arjomand, "Revolution and Constitution in the Arab World, 2011–2012," in *Beyond the Arab Spring*, Mehran Kamrava, ed. (New York: Oxford University Press, 2014), p. 154.
27. Abdullah Al-Arian, "Islamist Movements and the Arab Spring," in *Beyond the Arab Spring*, Mehran Kamrava, ed. (New York: Oxford University Press, 2014), p. 110.
28. Bahgat Korany, "A Microcosm of the Arab Spring: Sociology of Tahrir Square," in *Beyond the Arab Spring*, Mehran Kamrava, ed. (New York: Oxford University Press, 2014), p. 260.
29. Al-Arian, "Islamist Movements and the Arab Spring," p. 106. For more on post-Islamism, see below, Chapter 5.
30. Dilshod Achilov, "Revisiting Political Islam: Explaining the Nexus Between Political Islam and Contentious Politics in the Arab World," *Social Science Quarterly*, Vol. 97, No. 2 (June 2016), p. 267.
31. Al-Arian, "Islamist Movements and the Arab Spring," p. 101.
32. Joel Beinin and Frederic Vairel, "Introduction: The Middle East and North Africa Beyond Classical Social Movement Theory," in *Social Movements, Mobilization, and Contestation in the Middle East and North*

Africa, 2nd edn, Joel Beinin and Frederic Vairel, eds (Stanford, CA: Stanford University Press, 2013), p. 27.

33. Al-Arian, "Islamist Movements and the Arab Spring," p. 111.
34. Bayat, *Life as Politics*, pp. 5–6.
35. Ibid., p. 15.
36. Ibid., p. 9.
37. Beinin and Vairel, "Introduction: The Middle East and North Africa Beyond Classical Social Movement Theory," pp. 26–7. Beinin and Vairel label these unemployed or underemployed professionals as "lumpen intellectuals" whose socioeconomic predicaments and unfulfilled aspirations made them receptive to anti-regime sentiments.
38. Joel Beinin, *Workers and Thieves: Labor Movements and Popular Uprisings in Tunisia and Egypt* (Stanford, CA: Stanford University Press, 2016), p. 107.
39. Ibid., pp. 94–5. According to Beinin, from mid-2004 to mid-2008, Egyptian workers engaged in no less than 1,300 strikes and collective action forms. Joel Beinin, "New-Liberal Structural Adjustment, Political Demobilization and Neo-Authoritarianism in Egypt," in *The Arab State and Neo-Liberal Globalization: The Restructuring of State Power in the Middle East*, Laura Guazzone and Daniela Pioppi, eds (Reading, UK: Ithaca Press, 2012), p. 26.
40. Tripp, *The Power and the People*, p. 69.
41. Ibid., p. 51.
42. Tarrow, *Strangers at the Gates*, p. 129.
43. Valerie Bunce, "Conclusion: Rebellious Citizens and Resilient Authoritarians," in *The New Middle East: Protest and Revolution in the Arab World*, Fawaz Gerges, ed. (Cambridge: Cambridge University Press, 2014), pp. 448–9.
44. For this transition, see Wael Ghonim, *Revolution 2.0: The Power of the People is Greater than the People in Power: A Memoir* (Boston, MA: Houghton Mifflin Harcourt, 2012), pp. 100–101.
45. Selbin, *Revolution, Rebellion, Resistance*, p. 16.
46. Ibid.
47. Ibid., p. 75.
48. See, Ghonim, *Revolution 2.0*, pp. 184–7 for the Egyptian police's violent clearing of Tahrir Square on 25 January 2011.
49. Azmi Bishara, "On the Intellectual and the Revolution," Arab Center for Research and Policy Studies, Research Paper (June 2013), p. 20.
50. Ibid., pp. 16–17.
51. Tripp, "The Politics of Resistance and the Arab Spring," p. 138.
52. Ghonim, *Revolution 2.0*, pp. 58–9. Ghonim moderated a Facebook discussion group called "We Are All Said."

53. Chonghyun Christie Byun and Ethan J. Hollander, "Explaining the Intensity of the Arab Spring," *Digest of Middle East Studies*, Vol. 24, No. 1 (2015), p. 28.
54. Ibid., p. 26.
55. Ibid., p. 38.
56. Caitlin E. Werrell, Francesco Femia, and Troy Sternberg, "Did We See It Coming? State Fragility, Climate Vulnerability, and the Uprisings in Syria and Egypt," *SAIS Review*, Vol. 35, No. 1 (Winter–Spring 2015), p. 35.
57. Ibid., pp. 32–3.
58. Ibid., p. 43.
59. See, for example, Ghonim, *Revolution 2.0*, p. 271.
60. Gerges, "Introduction," p. 4.
61. Tripp, "The Politics of Resistance and the Arab Spring," pp. 136–7.
62. Michael McFaul, "Transitions from Postcommunism," *Journal of Democracy*, Vol. 16, No. 3 (July 2005), p. 12.
63. Philip N. Howard and Muzammil M. Hussain, "The Role of Digital Media," in *Democratization and Authoritarianism in the Arab World*, Larry Diamond and Marc F. Plattner, eds (Baltimore, MD: Johns Hopkins University Press, 2014), p. 195.
64. Sadik Al-Azm, "Arab Nationalism, Islamism, and the Arab Uprisings," in *The New Middle East: Protest and Revolution in the Arab World*, Fawaz A. Gerges, ed. (Cambridge: Cambridge University Press, 2014), pp. 276–7.
65. For more on the role of the media in the Arab Spring, see Suzi Mirgani, "The State of the Arab Media in the Wake of the Arab Uprisings," in *Bullets and Bulletins: Media and Politics in the Wake of the Arab Uprisings*, Mohamed Zayani and Suzi Mirgani, eds (New York: Oxford University Press, 2016), pp. 1–22.
66. Joshua Stacher, *Adaptable Autocrats: Regime Power in Egypt and Syria* (Stanford, CA: Stanford University Press, 2012), p. 4.
67. Similar to civil wars, discussed in the next chapter, the response of the armed forces to an uprising is critical to its success or failure. According to Zoltan Barany, the military's response to a revolution is influenced by four factors: the military establishment itself; its relations with other institutions of the state; its relations with the larger society; and the external environment. Similarly, the army's disposition toward the revolution is the most important predictor of the revolution's outcome, and the military's support is a necessary, if not sufficient, condition for the success of the revolution. Militaries are likely either to support uprisings, or suppress them, or be split by them.

Zoltan Barany, *How Armies Respond to Revolutions and Why* (Princeton, NJ: Princeton University Press, 2016), pp. 16–24.

68. Philippe Droz-Vincent, "The Military amidst Uprisings and Transitions in the Arab World," in *The New Middle East: Protest and Revolution in the Arab World*, Fawaz A. Gerges, ed. (Cambridge: Cambridge University Press, 2014), p. 180.

69. Robert Springborg, "Whither the Arab Spring? 1989 or 1848?" *International Spectator*, Vol. 46, No. 3 (September 2011), p. 8.

70. Anderson, "Authoritarian Legacies and Regime Change," p. 41.

71. Jason Brownlee, Tarek Masoud, and Andrew Reynolds, "Why the Modest Harvest?" in *Democratization and Authoritarianism in the Arab World*, Larry Diamond and Marc F. Plattner, eds (Baltimore, MD: Johns Hopkins University Press, 2014), p. 134.

72. Amin Allal, "Becoming Revolutionary in Tunisia, 2007–2011," in *Social Movements, Mobilization, and Contestation in the Middle East and North Africa*, 2nd edn, Joel Beinin and Frederic Vairel, eds (Stanford, CA: Stanford University Press, 2013), p. 203.

73. Quoted in, Ghonim, *Revolution 2.0*, p. 131.

74. Risa Brooks, "Abandoned at the Palace: Why the Tunisian Military Defected from the Ben Ali Regime in January 2011," *Journal of Strategic Studies*, Vol. 90, No. 2 (2013), p. 207.

75. Alfred Stepan, "Tunisia's Transition and the 'Twin Tolerations,'" in *Democratization and Authoritarianism in the Arab World*, Larry Diamond and Marc F. Plattner, eds (Baltimore, MD: Johns Hopkins University Press, 2014), p. 221.

76. Larbi Sadiki and Youcef Bouandel, "The Post Arab Spring Reform: The Maghreb at a Cross Roads," *Digest of Middle East Studies*, Vol. 25, No. 1 (2016), pp. 116–17.

77. Beinin, *Workers and Thieves*, p. 97.

78. Beinin and Vairel, "Introduction," p. 22.

79. Michele Dunne and Tarek Radwan, "Egypt: Why Liberalism Still Matters," in *Democratization and Authoritarianism in the Arab World*, Larry Diamond and Marc F. Plattner, eds (Baltimore, MD: Johns Hopkins University Press, 2014), p. 252.

80. Ghonim, *Revolution 2.0*, p. 123.

81. Korany, "A Microcosm of the Arab Spring," p. 251.

82. Ghonim, *Revolution 2.0*, p. 39.

83. Ibid., p. 133.

84. Dunne and Radwan, "Egypt: Why Liberalism Still Matters," p. 249.

85. Gerges, "Introduction," pp. 5–6.

86. Droz-Vincent, "The Military amidst Uprisings and Transitions in the Arab World," p. 182.

87. Tarek Massoud, "The Road to (and from) Liberation Square," in *Democratization and Authoritarianism in the Arab World*, Larry Diamond and Marc F. Plattner, eds (Baltimore, MD: Johns Hopkins University Press, 2014), p. 236.

88. Nathan Brown, "Egypt's Failed Transition," in *Democratization and Authoritarianism in the Arab World*, Larry Diamond and Marc F. Plattner, eds (Baltimore, MD: Johns Hopkins University Press, 2014), p. 268.

89. Droz-Vincent, "The Military amidst Uprisings and Transitions in the Arab World," pp. 183, 198.

90. Roger Owen, "Egypt and Tunisia: From the Revolutionary Overthrow of Dictatorships to the Struggle to Establish a New Constitutional Order," in *The New Middle East: Protest and Revolution in the Arab World*, Fawaz A. Gerges, ed. (Cambridge: Cambridge University Press, 2014), p. 264.

91. Droz-Vincent, "The Military amidst Uprisings and Transitions in the Arab World," p. 199.

92. Brown, "Egypt's Failed Transition," p. 264.

93. Alfred Stepan and Juan J. Linz, "Democratization Theory and the 'Arab Spring,'" in *Democratization and Authoritarianism in the Arab World*, Larry Diamond and Marc F. Plattner, eds (Baltimore, MD: Johns Hopkins University Press, 2014), p. 87.

94. Brown, "Egypt's Failed Transition," pp. 269–71.

95. Ibid., p. 264.

96. Stacher, *Adaptable Autocrats*, p. 13.

97. Steven Heydemann, "Syria and the Future of Authoritarianism," in *Democratization and Authoritarianism in the Arab World*, Larry Diamond and Marc F. Plattner, eds (Baltimore, MD: Johns Hopkins University Press, 2014), p. 303.

98. Ibid., p. 301.

99. Karim Mezran, "Libya in Transition: From *Jamahiriya* to *Jumhuriyyah?*" in *The New Middle East: Protest and Revolution in the Arab World*, Fawaz A. Gerges, ed. (Cambridge: Cambridge University Press, 2014), p. 310.

100. Tripp, *The Power and the People*, pp. 64–5.

101. Droz-Vincent, "The Military amidst Uprisings and Transitions in the Arab World," p. 202.

102. Gabriele Vom Bruck, Atiaf Alwazir, and Benjamin Wiacek, "Yemen: Revolution Suspended?" in *The New Middle East: Protest and Revolution in the Arab World*, Fawaz A. Gerges, ed. (Cambridge: Cambridge University Press, 2014), p. 290.

103. Laurent Bonnefoy and Marine Poirier, "Dynamics of the Yemeni Revolution: Contextualizing Mobilizations," in *Social Movements, Mobilization, and Contestation in the Middle East and North Africa*, 2nd

edn, Joel Beinin and Frederic Vairel, eds (Stanford, CA: Stanford University Press, 2013), p. 233.

104. Vom Bruck, Alwazir, and Wiacek, "Yemen," p. 292.
105. Ibid., p. 285.
106. April Longley Alley, "Yemen Changes Everything…And Nothing," in *Democratization and Authoritarianism in the Arab World*, Larry Diamond and Marc F. Plattner, eds. (Baltimore, MD: Johns Hopkins University Press, 2014), p. 277.
107. Vom Bruck, Alwazir and Wiacek, "Yemen," p. 306.
108. James L. Gelvin, *The Arab Uprisings: What Everyone Needs to Know* (New York: Oxford University Press, 2012), p. 138.
109. In the years immediately preceding the 2011 unrest, political space had been significantly narrowed and many NGOs were banned or dissolved. Jane Kinninmont, "Bahrain," in *Power and Politics in the Persian Gulf Monarchies*, Christopher Davidson, ed. (London: Hurst & Co., 2011), pp. 46–7.
110. Frederic Wehrey, "Bahrain's Decade of Discontent," in *Democratization and Authoritarianism in the Arab World*, Larry Diamond and Marc F. Plattner, eds (Baltimore, MD: Johns Hopkins University Press, 2014), p. 323.
111. Kinninmont, "Bahrain," p. 49.
112. Quinn Mecham, "Bahrain's Fractured Ruling Bargain: Political Mobilization, Regime Response, and the New Sectarianism," in *Beyond the Arab Spring*, Mehran Kamrava, ed. (New York: Oxford University Press, 2014), pp. 368–9.
113. Justin Gengler, "How Bahrain's crushed uprising spawned the Middle East's sectarianism," *Washington Post*, 13 February 2016, https://www.washingtonpost.com/news/monkey-cage/wp/2016/02/13/how-bahrains-crushed-uprising-spawned-the-middle-easts-sectarianism/.
114. Zoltan Barany, "The 'Arab Spring' in the Kingdoms," Arab Center for Research and Policy Studies, Research Paper (September 2012), p. 8.
115. Anderson, "Authoritarian Legacies and Regime Change," p. 54.
116. Ziad Abu-Rish, "Protests, Regime Stability, and State Formation in Jordan," in *Beyond the Arab Spring*, Mehran Kamrava, ed. (New York: Oxford University Press, 2014), p. 296.
117. Sean L. Yom and F. Gregory Gause, III. "Resilient Royals: How Arab Monarchies Hang On," in *Democratization and Authoritarianism in the Arab World*, Larry Diamond and Marc F. Plattner, eds (Baltimore, MD: Johns Hopkins University Press, 2014), pp. 113–14.
118. Rachid Yalouh, "The Discourse of Change in Morocco," *Policy Analysis* (Doha Institute, Arab Center for Research and Policy Studies, 2011), p. 10.

119. Ibid., p. 1.
120. Ibid., pp. 1–2, 8.
121. For more on reforms to the judiciary in the 2011 constitution, see Norman L. Greene, "Rule of Law in Morocco: A Journey Toward a Better Judiciary Through the Implementation of the 2011 Constitutional Reforms," *ILSA Journal of International and Comparative Law*, Vol. 18, No. 2 (2011–12), pp. 455–514.
122. Mohammed Hashas, "Moroccan Exceptionalism Examined: Constitutional Insights pre- and post-2011," Instituto Affari Internazionali, Working Paper 13–34 (December 2013), p. 12.
123. Sadiki and Bouandel, "The Post Arab Spring Reform," p. 118.
124. Ibid., p. 119.
125. Ibid., p. 122.
126. Roger Owen, *The Rise and Fall of Arab Presidents for Life* (Cambridge, MA: Harvard University Press, 2012), p. 177.
127. Frederic Volpi, "Algeria Versus the Arab Spring," in *Democratization and Authoritarianism in the Arab World*, Larry Diamond and Marc F. Plattner, eds (Baltimore, MD: Johns Hopkins University Press, 2014), pp. 330, 334.
128. Sadiki and Bouandel, "The Post Arab Spring Reform," pp. 124–5.
129. Decades before the Arab Spring, in 1977–8, the same lack of elite unity in Iran had doomed the country's monarchy, when the imperial armed forces refused orders to fire on street protesters, thereby paving the way for the success of the revolution.

4. NEW SETTINGS, OLD PATTERNS

1. See, for example, Theodore S. Hamerow, "History and the German Revolution of 1848," *American Historical Review*, Vol. 60, No. 1 (October 1954), pp. 27–44.
2. Daniel Byman, "Regime Change in the Middle East: Problems and Prospects," *Political Science Quarterly*, Vol. 127, No. 1 (2012), p. 26.
3. Ibid., p. 44.
4. Arshin Adib-Moghaddam, *On the Arab Revolts and the Iranian Revolution: Power and Resistance Today* (London: Bloomsbury Academic, 2013), pp. 24, 26.
5. Robert Springborg, "Whither the Arab Spring? 1989 or 1848?" *International Spectator*, Vol. 46, No. 3 (September 2011), p. 5.
6. Ibid., p. 6.
7. Daniel Brumberg, "Transforming the Arab World's Protection Racket Politics," in *Democratization and Authoritarianism in the Arab World*, Larry Diamond and Marc F. Plattner, eds (Baltimore, MD: Johns Hopkins University Press, 2014), p. 97.

8. Said Amir Arjomand, "Revolution and Constitution in the Arab World, 2011–2012," in *Beyond the Arab Spring*, Mehran Kamrava, ed. (New York: Oxford University Press, 2014), p. 152.

9. Paul Pierson, "The Limits of Design: Explaining Institutional Origins and Change," *Governance*, Vol. 13, No. 4 (October 2000), p. 491.

10. Peter J. Boettke, Christopher J. Coyne, and Peter T. Leeson, "Institutional Stickiness and the New Development Economics," *American Journal of Economics and Sociology*, Vol. 67, No. 2 (April 2008), pp. 332–333.

11. Robin Yassin-Kassab, "'I was terribly wrong'–writers look back at the Arab spring five years on," *The Guardian*, 23 January 2016, https://www.theguardian.com/books/2016/jan/23/arab-spring-five-years-on-writers-look-back.

12. Oussama Romdhani, "The Next Revolution: A Call for Reconciliation in the Arab World," *World Affairs* (November/December 2013), p. 91.

13. Joshua Stacher, *Adaptable Autocrats: Regime Power in Egypt and Syria* (Stanford, CA: Stanford University Press, 2012), p. 3.

14. Brumberg, "Transforming the Arab World's Protection Racket Politics," p. 97.

15. Steven Heydemann, "Syria and the Future of Authoritarianism," in *Democratization and Authoritarianism in the Arab World*, Larry Diamond and Marc F. Plattner, eds (Baltimore, MD: Johns Hopkins University Press, 2014), p. 302.

16. Ibid., p. 312.

17. Ibid., p. 306.

18. Juan J. Linz, *Totalitarian and Authoritarian Regimes* (Boulder, CO: Lynne Rienner Publishers, 2000), p. 159.

19. Ibid., p. 162.

20. Milan W. Svolik, *The Politics of Authoritarian Rule* (Cambridge: Cambridge University Press, 2012), p. 2.

21. Jennifer Gandhi, *Political Institutions under Dictatorship* (Cambridge: Cambridge University Press, 2010), p. 80.

22. Ibid., p. 79.

23. Steven Levitsky and Lucan A. Way, *Competitive Authoritarianism: Hybrid Regimes After the Cold War* (Cambridge: Cambridge University Press, 2010), pp. 27–8.

24. Ibid., p. 3.

25. Ibid., p. 79.

26. In addition to the survey below, see Larbi Sadiki and Youcef Bouandel, "The Post Arab Spring Reform: The Maghreb at a Cross Roads," *Digest of Middle East Studies*, Vol. 25, No. 1 (2016), pp. 109–31.

27. See Daniel Brumberg, "The Trap of Liberalized Autocracy," *Journal of Democracy*, Vol. 13, No. 4 (October 2002), pp. 56–68.

28. Giovanni Capoccia and R. Daniel Kelemen, "The Study of Critical Junctures: Theory, Narrative, and Counterfactuals in Historical Institutionalism," *World Politics*, Vol. 59, No. 3 (April 2007), pp. 341, 343.

29. Romdhani, "The Next Revolution," p. 91.

30. Idriss Jaberi, "Algeria's Discontented Middle Class," *Carnegie Endowment for International Peace*, 19 January 2017.

31. See, for example, Yousef Cherif, "Tunisia's Fledgling Gulf Relations," *Carnegie Endowment for International Peace*, 17 January 2017.

32. World Bank, "Poverty has Fallen in the Maghreb, but Inequality Persists," 17 October 2016, www.worldbank.org.

33. Massoud Karshenas, Valentine M. Moghadam, and Randa Alami, "Social Policy after the Arab Spring States and Social Rights in the MENA Region," *World Development*, Vol. 64 (2014), p. 728.

34. Fadhel Kaboub, "The End of Neoliberalism? An Institutional Analysis of the Arab Uprisings," *Journal of Economic Issues*, Vol. 67, No. 2 (June 2013), p. 538.

35. Philippe Droz-Vincent, "Prospects for 'Democratic Control of the Armed Forces'? Comparative Insights and Lessons for the Arab World in Transition," *Armed Forces and Society*, Vol. 40, No. 4 (2013), p. 718.

36. Hicham Bou Nassif, "Generals and Autocrats: How Coup-Proofing Predetermined the Military Elite's Behavior in the Arab Spring," *Political Science Quarterly*, Vol. 130, No. 2 (2015), p. 249.

37. Samuel E. Finer, *The Man on Horseback: The Role of the Military in Politics* (New Brunswick, NJ: Transaction Publishers, 2006), p. 4.

38. For a discussion of this role of Arab militaries behind the scenes, see Chapter 3. Joseph Sassoon has compiled a very useful list of state leaders in the Arab republics from military and non-military backgrounds: see his *Anatomy of Authoritarianism in the Arab Republics* (Cambridge: Cambridge University Press, 2016), pp. 75–7.

39. According to Finer, the advantages the armed forces have over civilians, especially in moments of crisis, include a marked superiority in organizational coherence and effectiveness, a highly "emotionalized symbolic status" in society, and a monopoly over arms. Finer, *The Man on Horseback*, pp. 30–56.

40. Samuel Huntington defines military professionalism in terms of expertise, responsibility, and corporateness. Samuel P. Huntington, *The Soldier and the State: The Theory and Politics of Civil–Military Relations* (Cambridge, MA: Harvard University Press, 1957), pp. 8–10.

41. This could serve as one explanation for the Egyptian military's relatively poor performance in the Sinai in its struggle to contain a brewing insurgency by Salafist-jihadi groups affiliated with Daesh or al-Qaʿida.

42. Jessica L. P. Weeks, *Dictators at War and Peace* (Ithaca, NY: Cornell University Press, 2014), p. 17.

43. Holger Albrecht, "The Myth of Coup-Proofing: Risks and Instances of Military Coups d'état in the Middle East and North Africa, 1950–2013," *Armed Forces and Society*, Vol. 41, No. 4 (2014), pp. 659–60, 664.

44. Ibid., p. 661.

45. Bou Nassif, "Generals and Autocrats," p. 256.

46. Ibid., p. 259.

47. Albrecht, "The Myth of Coup-Proofing," p. 660.

48. Sharon Erickson Nepstad, "Mutiny and nonviolence in the Arab Spring: Exploring military defections and loyalty in Egypt, Bahrain, and Syria," *Journal of Peace Research*, Vol. 50, No. 3 (2013), pp. 344–5.

49. Dorothy Ohl, Holger Albrecht, and Kevin Koehler, "For Money or Liberty? The Political Economy of Military Desertion and Rebel Recruitment in the Syrian Civil War," Carnegie Middle East Center (Beirut), 24 November 2015, p. 2.

50. Nepstad, "Mutiny and nonviolence in the Arab Spring," p. 338.

51. Sidney Tarrow, *War, States, and Contention: A Comparative Historical Study* (Ithaca, NY: Cornell University Press, 2015), p. 26.

52. Steven Heydemann, "War, Institutions, and Social Change in the Middle East," in *War, Institutions, and Social Change in the Middle East*, Steven Heydemann, ed. (Berkeley, CA: University of California Press, 2000), p. 15.

53. Sassoon, *Anatomy of Authoritarianism in the Arab Republics*, pp. 218–19.

54. All data here come from Yezid Sayigh, "Dilemmas of Reform: Policing in Arab Transitions," (Beirut: Carnegie Middle East Center, 2016), p. 11.

55. Ibid., pp. 13–14.

56. Ibid., p. 16.

57. Ibid., pp. 7, 10.

58. Ibid., pp. 9, 26.

59. Bou Nassif, "Generals and Autocrats," p. 247.

60. For a discussion of typologies of civil–military relations before the 2011 uprisings, see Mehran Kamrava, "Military Professionalization and Civil–Military Relations in the Middle East," *Political Science Quarterly*, Vol. 115, No. 1 (Spring 2000), pp. 67–87.

61. Alfred Stepan, *Rethinking Military Politics: Brazil and the Southern Cone* (Princeton, NJ: Princeton University Press, 1988), p. 30.

62. Another alternative scenario, which occurred in parts of South America in the mid-1980s, may be liberalization or civilianization by the military. See ibid., p. 31.

63. For a succinct discussion of the development of the Lebanese army, see Nayla Moussa, "Loyalties and Group Formation in the Lebanese

Officers Crops," Carnegie Middle East Center (Beirut), 27 January 2016.

64. Sayigh, "Dilemmas of Reform," p. 23.

65. Frederic Wehrey and Ariel I. Ahram, *Taming the Militias: Building National Guards in Fractured Arab States* (Washington, DC: Carnegie Endowment for International Peace, 2015), p. 1.

66. Sayigh, "Dilemmas of Reform," p. 8.

67. While Iranian involvement in the Iraqi and Syrian theaters has been well-documented, and is not denied by the Tehran government, the extent of its support for the Houthi rebels is not fully clear and is often downplayed by Iran. See, for example, Thomas Juneau, "Iran's policy towards the Houthis in Yemen: a limited return on a modest investment," *International Affairs*, Vol. 92, No. 3 (2016), pp. 647–63.

68. Abigail Hauslohner, "Gulf states that backed Syria's jihadists in an uneasy spot," *Washington Post*, 14 June 2014, p. 8.

69. The Preamble to Morocco's 2011 Constitution starts with stereotypically lofty language characteristic of constitutions: "With fidelity to its irreversible choice to construct a democratic State of Law, the Kingdom of Morocco resolutely pursues the process of consolidation and of reinforcement of the institutions of a modern State, having as its bases the principles of participation, of pluralism and of good governance. It develops a society of solidarity where all enjoy security, liberty, equality of opportunities, of respect for their dignity and for social justice, within the framework of the principle of correlation between the rights and the duties of the citizenry." Morocco's Constitution of 2011, available at https://www.constituteproject.org/constitution/Morocco_2011.pdf?lang=en.

70. Sabina Henneberg, "Comparing the first provisional administrations in Tunisia and Libya: some tentative conclusions," Paper presented at the Middle East Studies Association annual meeting, Boston, MA, November 2016, p. 1.

71. Dan Horowitz, "Dual Authority Polities," *Comparative Politics*, Vol. 14, No. 3 (April 1982), pp. 329–49.

72. Narrimane Benakcha, "The Algerian Regime: An Arab Spring Survivor," *Columbia Journal of International Affairs*, March 2012, https://jia.sipa.columbia.edu/online-articles/algerian-regime-arab-spring-survivor.

73. Personal interview with Lies Boukraa, Director General of the National Institute for Global Strategic Studies, Algiers, 31 July 2016.

74. George Jaffe, "National Reconciliation and General Amnesty in Algeria," in *The Politics of Violence, Truth and Reconciliation in the Arab Middle East*, Sune Haugbolle and Andres Hastrup, eds (London: Routledge, 2009), pp. 65–70.

75. For example, the Algerian president's brother, Said Bouteflika, officially his "advisor," is often accused of having amassed considerable wealth. Lahouari Addi, "Algeria and its Permanent Political Crisis," *IEMed, Mediterranean Yearbook 2015* (2015), p. 181.
76. Richard Nield, "Why Bouteflika dissolved Algeria's powerful spy agency?" *Al Jazeera*, 25 February 2016, http://www.aljazeera.com/indepth/features/2016/02/algeria-dissolved-powerful-spy-agency-160225171417842.html.
77. Ibid.
78. Addi, "Algeria and its Permanent Political Crisis," p. 182.
79. Ibid., p. 183.
80. Ibid., p. 180.
81. Mohammed Hashas, "Moroccan Exceptionalism Examined: Constitutional Insights pre- and post-2011," Instituto Affari Internazionali, Working Paper 13–34 (December 2013), p. 3.
82. Mohamed Daadaoui, "Party Politics and Elections in Morocco," *Middle East Institute Policy Brief*, No. 29 (May 2010), p. 2.
83. Carol Migdalovitz, "Morocco: Current Issues," *Congressional Research Service*, 7–5700 (4 December 2008), p. 2.
84. Daadaoui, "Party Politics and Elections in Morocco," p. 4.
85. Migdalovitz, "Morocco," p. 1.
86. Ibid., p. 2. Prior to 2011, the Moroccan king was able to resort to his own religious legitimacy as a means of deflating the appeal of the Islamist opposition. See Daadaoui, "Party Politics and Elections in Morocco," p. 5.
87. Mohammed Hashas, "Moroccan Exceptionalism Examined: Constitutional Insights pre- and post-2011," Instituto Affari Internazionali, Working Paper 13–34 (December 2013), p. 3.
88. Daadaoui, "Party Politics and Elections in Morocco," p. 3.
89. Hashas, "Moroccan Exceptionalism Examined," p. 13.
90. Traditionally thought of as the political inner circle and power elite, *Makhzen* "refers both to an administrative apparatus and to particular social and cultural symbols, as well as practices and rituals that have always buttressed functions of the state." Mohamed Daadaoui, *Moroccan Monarchy and the Islamist Challenge: Maintaining Makhzen Power* (New York: Palgrave, 2011), p. 47.
91. Hashas, "Moroccan Exceptionalism Examined," p. 13.
92. Ibid., p. 14.
93. Ibid., p. 17.
94. Hashas, "Moroccan Exceptionalism Examined," p. 17.
95. Nur Koprulu, "Monarchical Pluralism or De-democratization: Actors and Choices in Jordan," *Insight Turkey*, Vol. 14, No. 1 (2012), p. 72.

96. Hassan A. Barari, "The Limits of Political Reform in Jordan: The Role of External Actors," *Friedrich Ebert Stiftung* (December 2013), p. 1.

97. Ibid., p. 8.

98. Ziad Abu-Rish, "Protests, Regime Stability, and State Formation in Jordan," in *Beyond the Arab Spring*, Mehran Kamrava, ed. (New York: Oxford University Press, 2014), pp. 284–90.

99. Jean-Loup Samaan, "Jordan's New Geopolitics," *Survival*, Vol. 54, No. 2 (April–May 2012), p. 15.

100. Curtis R. Ryan, "The Armed Forces and the Arab Uprisings: The Case of Jordan," *Middle East Law and Governance*, Vol. 4 (2012), p. 160.

101. Samaan, "Jordan's New Geopolitics," p. 16.

102. Koprulu, "Monarchical Pluralism or De-democratization," p. 86.

103. Jeremy M. Sharp, "Jordan: Background and U.S. Relations," *Congressional Research Service*, 7–5700 (27 January 2016), p. 7.

104. Kristen Kao, "How Jordan's election revealed enduring weaknesses in its political system," *Washington Post*, 3 October 2016, https://www.washingtonpost.com/news/monkey-cage/wp/2016/10/03/how-jordans-election-revealed-enduring-weaknesses-in-its-political-system/?utm_term=.eddd15cc0fb5.

105. Barari, "The Limits of Political Reform in Jordan," p. 2.

106. Quoted in, Anja Wehler-Schoeck, "Parliamentary Elections in Jordan: A Competition of Mixed Messages," *Alsharq* (September 2016), http://www.alsharq.de/2016/mashreq/jordanien/parliamentary-elections-in-jordan-a-competition-of-mixed-messages/, p. 1.

107. Barari, "The Limits of Political Reform in Jordan," p. 3.

108. Kao, "How Jordan's election revealed enduring weaknesses in its political system."

109. Wehler-Schoeck, "Parliamentary Elections in Jordan," p. 2.

110. Barari, "The Limits of Political Reform in Jordan," p. 7.

111. Wehler-Schoeck, "Parliamentary Elections in Jordan," p. 2.

112. Kristen Kao, "Rigging Democracy: Maintaining Power Through Authoritarian Electoral Institutions," Paper presented at the annual meeting of the Middle East Studies Association, Boston, MA, November 2016, p. 2.

113. Kao, "How Jordan's election revealed enduring weaknesses in its political system."

114. Barari, "The Limits of Political Reform in Jordan," p. 3.

115. Kristen Kao, "How Jordan's election revealed enduring weaknesses in its political system."

116. Koprulu, "Monarchical Pluralism or De-democratization," p. 89.

117. Ibid., p. 82.

118. Wehler-Schoeck, "Parliamentary Elections in Jordan," p. 6.

119. Sharp, "Jordan," p. 14.
120. Ibid., p. 1.
121. Ibid., p. 2.
122. Samaan, "Jordan's New Geopolitics," pp. 21–2.
123. Quoted in, Sharp, "Jordan," p. 10.
124. Barari, "The Limits of Political Reform in Jordan," p. 7.
125. Nepstad, "Mutiny and nonviolence in the Arab Spring," p. 344.
126. Florence Gaub, "An Unhappy Marriage: Civil–Military Relations in Post-Saddam Iraq," Carnegie Middle East Center (Beirut), 13 January 2016, p. 2.
127. Ibid., p. 10.
128. Ibid., p. 3.
129. Derek Lutterbeck, "Arab Uprisings, Armed Forces, and Civil–Military Relations," *Armed Forces and Society*, Vol. 39, No. 1 (2013), p. 39.
130. Ibid., p. 40.
131. William C. Taylor, *Military Responses to the Arab Uprisings and the Future of Civil–Military Relations in the Middle East: Analysis from Egypt, Tunisia, Libya, and Syria* (New York: Palgrave Macmillan, 2014), p. 166.
132. Ibid., p. 171.
133. Henneberg, "Comparing the first provisional administrations in Tunisia and Libya," p. 24.
134. Ibid., p. 8.
135. Khedar Khaddour, *The Assad Regime's Hold on the Syrian State* (Washington, DC: Carnegie Endowment for International Peace, 2015), p. 1.
136. Ibid., p. 9.
137. Stacher, *Adaptable Autocrats*, p. 20.
138. Steven Heydemann, "Syria and the Future of Authoritarianism," in *Democratization and Authoritarianism in the Arab World*, Larry Diamond and Marc F. Plattner, eds (Baltimore, MD: Johns Hopkins University Press, 2014), p. 301.
139. Taylor, *Military Responses to the Arab Uprisings and the Future of Civil–Military Relations in the Middle East*, p. 110.
140. Ohl, Albrecht, and Koehler, "For Money or Liberty?" p. 4.
141. Ibid., p. 3.
142. Wehrey and Ahram, *Taming the Militias*, p. 5.
143. Ohl, Albrecht, and Koehler, "For Money or Liberty?" pp. 5–7.
144. Ibid., pp. 8–9.
145. Wehrey and Ahram, *Taming the Militias*, p. 9.
146. Victoria Clark, *Yemen: Dancing on the Heads of Snakes* (New Haven, CT: Yale University Press, 2010), p. 5.
147. Ibid., p. 269.

148. Philippe Droz-Vincent, "The Military in the Arab World, from Authoritarian regimes to Transitional Settings and New Regimes in the Making," *Singapore Middle East Papers*, No. 10/11 (27 March 2015), p. 21.

149. Ibid., p. 20.

150. For the likelihood of most post-revolutionary states resorting to coercion and violence, see Mehran Kamrava, *Revolutionary Politics* (Westport, CT: Praeger, 1992), pp. 77–83.

151. Amnesty International, *Amnesty International Report 2015/16: The State of the World's Human Rights* (London: Amnesty International, 2016), pp. 145–48.

152. Holger Albrecht and Dina Bishara, "Back on Horseback: the Military and Political Transformation in Egypt," *Middle East Law and Governance*, Vol. 3 (2011), p. 23.

153. Shana Marshall, *The Egyptian Armed Forces and the Remaking of an Economic Empire* (Washington, DC: Carnegie Endowment for International Peace, 2015), p. 1.

154. Albrecht and Bishara, "Back on Horseback," p. 15.

155. Taylor, *Military Responses to the Arab Uprisings and the Future of Civil–Military Relations in the Middle East*, p. 126.

156. Marshall, *The Egyptian Armed Forces and the Remaking of an Economic Empire*, p. 7.

157. Ibid., p. 1.

158. Ibid.

159. World Bank, "Egypt Economic Monitor: Paving the Way to a Sustainable Recovery," No. 96946 (Spring 2015), p. 4.

160. Ibid., p. 5.

161. Ibid., p. 3.

162. Marshall, *The Egyptian Armed Forces and the Remaking of an Economic Empire*, p. 4.

163. Ibid., p. 3.

164. Michele Dunne and Tarek Radwan, "Egypt: Why Liberalism Still Matters," in *Democratization and Authoritarianism in the Arab World*, Larry Diamond and Marc F. Plattner, eds (Baltimore, MD: Johns Hopkins University Press, 2014), p. 260.

165. Ibid., p. 261.

166. Springborg, "Whither the Arab Spring?" p. 8.

167. Roger Owen, "Egypt and Tunisia: From the Revolutionary Overthrow of Dictatorships to the Struggle to Establish a New Constitutional Order," in *The New Middle East: Protest and Revolution in the Arab World*, Fawaz A. Gerges, ed. (Cambridge: Cambridge University Press, 2014), p. 262.

168. Abdullah Al-Arian, "Islamist Movements and the Arab Spring," in *Beyond the Arab Spring*, Mehran Kamrava, ed. (New York: Oxford University Press, 2014), p. 114.
169. Henneberg, "Comparing the first provisional administrations in Tunisia and Libya," p. 4.
170. Ibid., p. 6.
171. Ibid., p. 11.
172. Querine Hanlon, *The Prospects for Security Sector Reform in Tunisia: A Year after the Revolution* (Carlisle, PA: US Army War College, 2012), p. 8.
173. Ibid., p. 13.
174. Droz-Vincent, "The Military in the Arab World," p. 11.
175. Hanlon, *The Prospects for Security Sector Reform in Tunisia*.
176. Taylor, *Military Responses to the Arab Uprisings and the Future of Civil–Military Relations in the Middle East*, p. 82.
177. Samer Matta, Simon Appleton, and Michael Bleaney, "The Impact of the Arab Spring on the Tunisian Economy," World Bank, *Policy Research Working Paper*, 7856 (October 2016), p. 2.
178. Ibid., p. 17.
179. At an international donors' conference in Tunis in November 2016, for example, numerous pledges of financial support were made to Tunisia, with the country hoping to raise as much as $4.3 billion in funds: Qatar promised $1.25 billion in financial support, and agreed to postpone Tunisia's repayment of $500 in debt; the European Investment Bank pledged to lend $2.65 billion by 2020; the Arab Economic and Social Development Fund another $1.5 billion over the same period; Saudi Arabia offered $800 million in loans and aid; Kuwait $500 million in loans; and Turkey $100 million. "Qatar Gives $1.25bn in help for Tunisia," *Gulf Times* (Doha), 30 November 2016, p. 1.
180. Hanlon, *The Prospects for Security Sector Reform in Tunisia*, p. 6.
181. Al-Arian, "Islamist Movements and the Arab Spring," p. 101.
182. John Foran, "Global Affinities: The New Cultures of Resistance behind the Arab Spring," in *Beyond the Arab Spring*, Mehran Kamrava, ed. (New York: Oxford University Press, 2014), p. 66.
183. Arshin Adib-Moghaddam, *On the Arab Revolts and the Iranian Revolution*, p. 3.
184. Zoltan Barany, *The Soldier and the Changing State: Building Democratic Armies in Africa, Asia, Europe, and the Americas* (Princeton, NJ: Princeton University Press, 2012), p. 3.
185. Romdhani, "The Next Revolution," p. 89.
186. David A. Bell, "Inglorious Revolutions," *The National Interest* (January/February 2014), p. 38.

187. Ibid., p. 31.

188. Valerie Bunce, "Conclusion: Rebellious Citizens and Resilient Authoritarians," in *The New Middle East: Protest and Revolution in the Arab World*, Fawaz A. Gerges, ed. (Cambridge: Cambridge University Press, 2014), p. 468.

189. Moreover, where linkages to the West were weaker, pressures for democratization tend to be less. Where state structures were less developed and lacked cohesion, regimes are less stable. Levitsky and Way, *Competitive Authoritarianism*, pp. 21–3.

190. Bell, "Inglorious Revolutions," p. 36.

5. THE CONTESTED TERRAIN

1. On Shia sectarianism, see Elisheva Machlis, *Shiʻi Sectarianism in the Middle East: Modernisation and the Quest for Islamic Universalism* (London: I. B. Tauris, 2014). On doctrinal changes within (Iranian) Shiism, see Mehran Kamrava, *Iran's Intellectual Revolution* (Cambridge: Cambridge University Press, 2008).

2. Roel Meijer, "Political Citizenship and Social Movements in the Arab World," in *Handbook of Political Citizenship and Social Movements*, Hein-Anton van der Heijden, ed. (Cheltenham, UK: Edward Elgar, 2014), p. 628. See also Roel Meijer and Nils Butenschøn, "Introduction," in *The Crisis of Citizenship in the Arab World*, Roel Meijer and Nils Butenschøn, eds (Leiden: Brill, 2017), p. 2; and Roel Meijer, "Liberalism in the Middle East and the Issue of Citizenship Rights," in *Arab Liberal Thought after 1967: Old Dilemmas, New Perceptions*, Meir Hatina and Christoph Schumann, eds (New York: Palgrave Macmillan, 2015), p. 63.

3. Mark R. Beissinger, Amaney A. Jamal, and Kevin Mazur, "Explaining Divergent Revolutionary Coalitions: Regime Strategies and the Structuring of Participation in the Tunisian and Egyptian Revolutions," *Comparative Politics*, Vol. 48, No. 1 (October 2015), p. 2.

4. Abdou Filali-Ansary, "The Languages of the Arab Revolutions," in *Democratization and Authoritarianism in the Arab World*, Larry Diamond and Marc F. Plattner, eds (Baltimore, MD: Johns Hopkins University Press, 2014), p. 7.

5. Meijer and Butenschøn, *The Crisis of Citizenship in the Arab World*, p. 6. This is not to imply that any of these concepts were necessarily new to the intellectual discourse of the Arab world. Their resurgent popularity at the time of the 2011 uprisings, nevertheless, tells us much about the specific demands of the protesters and the intellectual context that informed their actions.

6. Meijer, "Political Citizenship and Social Movements in the Arab World," p. 635.

7. Meijer, "Liberalism in the Middle East and the Issue of Citizenship Rights," pp. 71–2.
8. Meijer, "Political Citizenship and Social Movements in the Arab World," p. 634.
9. Nils A. Butenschøn, "State, Power, and Citizenship in the Middle East: A Theoretical Introduction," in *Citizenship and the State in the Middle East: Approaches and Applications*, Nils A. Butenschøn, Uri Davis, and Manuel Hassassian, eds (Syracuse, NY: Syracuse University Press, 2000), p. 11.
10. Meijer, "Political Citizenship and Social Movements in the Arab World," p. 635.
11. Ibid., pp. 645–51.
12. Zahra Babar, "Enduring 'Contested Citizenship' in the Gulf Cooperation Council," in *The Middle East in Transition: The Centrality of Citizenship*, Roel Meijer and Nils A. Butenschøn, eds. (Cheltenham, UK: Edward Elgar Publishing Ltd, 2018), pp. 11–13.
13. Steven Heydemann, "War, Institutions, and Social Change in the Middle East," in *War, Institutions, and Social Change in the Middle East*, Steven Heydemann, ed. (Berkeley, CA: University of California Press, 2000), p. 19.
14. Meijer, "Political Citizenship and Social Movements in the Arab World," p. 645.
15. Joel Beinin, *Workers and Thieves: Labor Movements and Popular Uprisings in Tunisia and Egypt* (Stanford, CA: Stanford University Press, 2016), p. 114.
16. Rachid Yalouh, "The Discourse of Change in Morocco," *Policy Analysis*, Doha Institute, Arab Center for Research and Policy Studies (2011), pp. 3–6.
17. According to Yalouh, the Moroccan *Makhzen* "exerts its legitimacy from historical postulates that are incapable of progress and are closer to being historical sacred relics." Ibid., p. 3.
18. Larbi Sadiki and Youcef Bouandel, "The Post Arab Spring Reform: The Maghreb at a Cross Roads," *Digest of Middle East Studies*, Vol. 25, No. 1 (2016), p. 110.
19. Throughout the late 1990s and early 2000s, President Bouteflika steadily demilitarized the Algerian system and instead relied on non-state actors such as voluntary associations, the Sufi orders, state-run television, and the civil administration, while at the same time keeping competition in check and opening up the formal political sphere. The president also tried to rationalize authoritarian government and to reconstitute, or at least reorient, Algerian national identity. Hugh Roberts, "Demilitarizing Algeria," in *Beyond the Façade: Political Reform in the Arab World*, Marina Ottaway and Julia Choucair-Vizoso, eds

(Washington, DC: Carnegie Endowment for International Peace, 2008), pp. 151–3.

20. Uzi Rabi, "Introduction," in *Tribes and State in a Changing Middle East*, Uzi Rabi, ed. (New York: Oxford University Press, 2016), p. 7.

21. Dawn Chatty, "Bedouin Tribes in Contemporary Syria: Alternative Perceptions of Authority, Management, and Control," in *Tribes and State in a Changing Middle East*, Uzi Rabi, ed. (New York: Oxford University Press, 2016), p. 171.

22. Juan Cole, *The New Arabs: How the Millennial Generation is Changing the Middle East* (New York: Simon & Schuster, 2014), p. 7.

23. Ibid., pp. 122–3. Below, I shall have more to say about the social characteristics and cultural preferences of contemporary Arab populations.

24. Beissinger, Jamal, and Mazur, "Explaining Divergent Revolutionary Coalitions," pp. 2–3. By contrast, this study shows that Egyptian protesters were disproportionately drawn from the middle classes, mostly organized by civil society organizations, and many were from the professional classes. The differences, according to the authors, were a product of the different strategies of rule by the Mubarak and Ben Ali regimes. Whereas in Egypt state retreat from the economy created openings for civil society, in Tunisia Ben Ali's corporatism undermined civil society and instead heightened disparities across regions and social groups.

25. Thierry Desrues, "Moroccan Youth and the Forming of a New Generation: Social Change, Collective Action and Political Activism," *Mediterranean Politics*, Vol. 17, No. 1 (March 2012), pp. 26–9.

26. Oussama Romdhani, "North Africa Beyond Jihadist Radicalization," *World Affairs* (January/February 2015), p. 64.

27. Seymour Martin Lipset, "Some Social Requisites of Democracy: Economic Development and Political Legitimacy," *American Political Science Review*, Vol. 53, No. 1 (March 1959), p. 86.

28. Peter G. Stillman, "The Concept of Legitimacy," *Polity*, Vol. 7, No. 1 (Autumn 1974), p. 39.

29. Michael C. Hudson, *Arab Politics: The Search for Legitimacy* (New Haven, CT: Yale University Press, 1977), p. ix.

30. Thomas R. Bates, "Gramsci and the Theory of Hegemony," *Journal of the History of Ideas*, Vol. 36, No. 2 (April–June 1975), p. 352.

31. Hudson, *Arab Politics*, pp. 83–4.

32. Ibid., p. 83.

33. On Libya, see Sami G. Hajjar, "The Jamahiriya Experiment in Libya: Qadhafi and Rousseau," *Journal of Modern African Studies*, Vol. 18, No. 2 (June 1980), pp. 181–200. For more on Iraq, see Kanan Makiya, *The Republic of Fear: The Politics of Modern Iraq* (Berkeley, CA: University of

California Press, 1998). The Battle of Qadisiyyah, fought in 636 CE, was the decisive battle in which Arab-Muslim armies defeated Sassanid forces and conquered Iran. For Saddam's use (and abuse) of history, see D. Gershon Lewental, "'Saddam's Qadisiyyah': Religion and History in the Service of State Ideology in Baʿthi Iraq," *Middle Eastern Studies*, Vol. 50, No. 6 (2014), pp. 891–910.

34. Rabi, "Introduction," p. 4.
35. Yoav Alon, "From Abdullah (I) to Abdullah (II): The Monarchy, The Tribes and the Shaykhly Families in Jordan, 1920–2012," in *Tribes and State in a Changing Middle East*, Uzi Rabi, ed. (New York: Oxford University Press, 2016), pp. 34–5.
36. Ibid., p. 11.
37. Nathan J. Brown, *Arguing Islam after the Revival of Arab Politics* (New York: Oxford University Press, 2017), pp. 166–8.
38. Ibid., p. 172.
39. Ibid., pp. 173–5. In the new draft, article 219 of the 2012 constitution was dropped but a lessened constitutional role for Al-Azhar was retained.
40. Hudson, *Arab Politics*, p. 107.
41. Brown, *Arguing Islam after the Revival of Arab Politics*, p. 12.
42. Arab Center for Research and Policy Studies, *The 2016 Arab Opinion: How the Arabs Saw the World in 2016* (Doha: ACRPS, 2016), p. 38.
43. Brown, *Arguing Islam after the Revival of Arab Politics*, p. 12.
44. Mark Tessler, Amaney Jamal, and Michael Robbins, "New Findings on Arab Democracy," in *Democratization and Authoritarianism in the Arab World*, Larry Diamond and Marc F. Plattner, eds (Baltimore, MD: Johns Hopkins University Press, 2014), p. 54. This topic will be explored in more detail below.
45. Ibid., pp. 57, 60.
46. Brown, *Arguing Islam after the Revival of Arab Politics*, p. 55.
47. Appendix 1 provides details about the methodology used in gathering the data for *The 2016 Arab Opinion* survey. Additional information on the methodology used for the survey is available in Arabic at http://www.dohainstitute.org/release/a91ff972–235c–4638–9bd2–27888c44fc68. I am grateful to Mohammad Almasri of the Arab Center for Research and Policy Studies for clarifying the methodology used in collecting the data for the annual survey in order to ensure its accuracy and representativeness of the populations of the countries in which the surveys were conducted.
48. Arab Center for Research and Policy Studies, *The 2016 Arab Opinion*, p. 76.
49. In this and subsequent tables, when percentages do not add up to 100,

the remainder of the respondents either refused to answer or did not know the answer.

50. Ibid., p. 16.
51. Ibid., p. 18.
52. Ibid., p. 19.
53. Ibid., p. 21.
54. Ibid., p. 22.
55. Ibid., p. 27.
56. Ibid., p. 32.
57. Ibid., p. 81.
58. Ibid., p. 34.
59. Ibid., p. 36.
60. Daniel Brumberg, "Transforming the Arab World's Protection Racket Politics," in *Democratization and Authoritarianism in the Arab World*, Larry Diamond and Marc F. Plattner, eds (Baltimore, MD: Johns Hopkins University Press, 2014), p. 96.
61. Arab Center for Research and Policy Studies, *The 2016 Arab Opinion*, p. 30.
62. Ibid., p. 39.
63. Ibid., p. 40.
64. Ibid., p. 42.
65. Ibid., p. 58.
66. Ibid., p. 59.
67. Hudson, *Arab Politics*, p. 162.
68. Stillman, "The Concept of Legitimacy," p. 43.
69. Ibid.
70. Asef Bayat, *Life as Politics: How Ordinary People Change the Middle East*, 2nd edn (Stanford, CA: Stanford University Press, 2013), p. 8.
71. Cole, *The New Arabs*, p. 17.
72. Ibid., pp. 19–22.
73. Tessler, Jamal, and Robbins, "New Findings on Arab Democracy," p. 62.
74. Hamid Dabashi, *The Arab Spring: The End of Postcolonialism* (London: Zed Books, 2012), p. 13.
75. Olivier Roy, "The Transformation of the Arab World," in *Democratization and Authoritarianism in the Arab World*, Larry Diamond and Marc F. Plattner, eds (Baltimore, MD: Johns Hopkins University Press, 2014), p. 27.
76. Bayat, *Life as Politics*, p. 8.
77. Asef Bayat, *Making Islam Democratic: Social Movements and the Post-Islamist Turn* (Stanford, CA: Stanford University Press, 2007), p. 11.
78. In Iranian politics, "reformists" are the best representatives of the post-Islamist current in society. For more on the country's changing fac-

tional landscape, see Naghmeh Sohrabi, "Reading the Tea Leaves: Iranian Domestic Politics and the Presidential Election of 2013," *Middle East Brief*, Crown Center for Middle East Studies, Brandies University, No. 65 (July 2012).

79. Malik Mufti, "Democratizing Potential of the 'Arab Spring': Some Early Observations," *Government and Opposition*, Vol. 50, No. 3 (2015), pp. 405–6.

80. Nathan J. Brown and Amr Hamzawy, *Between Religion and Politics* (Washington, DC: Carnegie Endowment for International Peace, 2010), pp. 181–2.

81. Ibid., p. 181.

82. May Abdullah, "The Results of the 'Arab Spring' and the Obstacles of Change," *Communication and Development*, No. 8 (2013), p. 4.

83. Cole, *The New Arabs*, pp. 20–21.

84. Roy, "The Transformation of the Arab World," p. 16.

85. Al-Arian, "Islamist Movements and the Arab Spring," in *Beyond the Arab Spring*, Mehran Kamrava, ed. (New York: Oxford University Press, 2014), p. 126–7.

86. Mahias Rohe and Jakob Skovgaard-Petersen, "The Ambivalent Embrace of Liberalism: The Draft Program of the Freedom and Justice Party in Egypt," in *Arab Liberal Thought after 1967: Old Dilemmas, New Perceptions*, Meir Hatina and Christoph Schumann, eds (New York: Palgrave Macmillan, 2015), pp. 201–2.

87. Ibid., p. 203.

88. As Nathan Brown put it, the overall impression of the constitutional debate over religion is that there were plenty of emotions but little motion, with few textual changes to the role of religion in the post-uprising constitution. Brown, *Arguing Islam after the Revival of Arab Politics*, p. 176.

89. Roy, "The Transformation of the Arab World," pp. 18–20.

90. Hicham Ben Abdallah El Alaoui, "The Split in Arab Culture," in *Democratization and Authoritarianism in the Arab World*, Larry Diamond and Marc F. Plattner, eds (Baltimore, MD: Johns Hopkins University Press, 2014), p. 70.

91. For many Salafists and other Islamists, lack of familiarity with constructive, critical dialogue starts at a young age, in primary school. Religious curricula in Arab schools are often replete with rote learning, repetition, and memorization, and "the prevalent discourse is one of retribution and intimidation rather than love, tolerance, and disciplined freedom." Religious topics in the curricula are detached from contemporary concerns, with emphasis on memorization and minimal impact on skills, values, and behavior. Critical thought and constructive

dialogue are devalued and treated as unimportant. According to one study, there is in the Arab world a "breakdown of Islamic education curricula." See Najoua Fezzaa Ghriss, "The Role of Education in Individual Sustainable Development," in *Arab Human Development in the Twenty-first Century: The Primacy of Empowerment*, Bahgat Korany, ed. (Cairo: American University of Cairo Press, 2014), p. 255–6.

92. Dilshod Achilov, "Revisiting Political Islam: Explaining the Nexus Between Political Islam and Contentious Politics in the Arab World," *Social Science Quarterly*, Vol. 97, No. 2 (June 2016), p. 266.

93. Romdhani, "North Africa Beyond Jihadist Radicalization," p. 64.

94. Documents captured by the US forces in Iraq in 2007, for instance, showed that al-Qa'ida in Iraq was made up of Yemenis (8%), Algerians (7%), Moroccans (6%), Tunisians (5.5%), and Saudis. Romdhani, "North Africa Beyond Jihadist Radicalization," p. 63.

95. Ibid., p. 62–3.

96. Ibid., pp. 61–2.

97. Fawaz A. Gerges, *ISIS: A History* (Princeton, NJ: Princeton University Press, 2016), pp. 22–3.

98. Daesh is the transliteration of the Arabic acronym of the group known in English as the Islamic State of Iraq and Syria (ISIS), *al-Dowla al-Islaamiyya fii-il-I'raaq wa-ash-Shaam*.

99. For a summary list of Daesh's global affiliates, see Karen Leigh, Jason French, and Jovi Juan, "Islamic State and its Affiliates," *Wall Street Journal*, http://graphics.wsj.com/islamic-state-and-its-affiliates/.

100. On 1 July 2014, soon after declaring the establishment of a caliphate in territories under its control, Daesh changed its name to Islamic State, *al-Dowla al-Islaamiyya*. In what follows, I use ISIS, Daesh, and IS interchangeably.

101. Two such studies on which I have relied extensively here are Abdel Bari Atwan, *Islamic State: The Digital Caliphate* (Berkeley, CA: University of California Press, 2015); and Gerges, *ISIS*.

102. Gerges, *ISIS*, p. 109.

103. Ibid., p. 132.

104. Atwan, *Islamic State*, p. 112.

105. Ibid., p. 119.

106. Ibid., p. 50.

107. Gerges, *ISIS*, p. 10.

108. Atwan, *Islamic State*, p. 50.

109. Ibid., p. 55.

110. Gerges, *ISIS*, p. 10.

111. David Cook, *Understanding Jihad*, 2nd edn (Berkeley, CA: University of California Press, 2015), p. 177.

112. Gerges, *ISIS*, p. 34.

113. Atwan, *Islamic State*, p. 156.
114. Gerges, *ISIS*, p. 36.
115. Atwan, *Islamic State*, p. 161.
116. Ibid., p. 125.
117. Cook, *Understanding Jihad*, p. 168.
118. Gerges, *ISIS*, p. 28.
119. Cook, *Understanding Jihad*, p. 169.
120. Atwan, *Islamic State*, p. 87.
121. Cook, *Understanding Jihad*, p. 224.
122. Atwan, *Islamic State*, p. 12.
123. Estimates of the size of IS vary. At its height, the Caliphate was estimated to have numbered as many as 200,000.
124. Atwan, *Islamic State*, p. 138.
125. Ibid., p. 147.
126. Ibid., p. 149.
127. Ibid., p. 146.
128. Gerges, *ISIS*, p. 42.
129. Atwan, *Islamic State*, p. 133.
130. Gerges, *ISIS*, p. 27.
131. Olivier Roy, "Who are the new jihadis?" *The Guardian*, 13 April 2017, https://www.theguardian.com/news/2017/apr/13/who-are-the-new-jihadis.
132. Meijer, "Political Citizenship and Social Movements in the Arab World," p. 636.
133. Before the 2011 uprisings, Browers observes that more pragmatic and moderate strands of the different ideological currents began to form strategic alliances and accommodations, in order to focus on opposing the regime in power. Historically opposed ideological trends converged not so much because of common understandings of basic political and social concepts, but because they had mutual enemies. Michaelle L. Browers, *Political Ideology in the Arab World: Accommodation and Transformation* (Cambridge: Cambridge University Press, 2009), p. 176.
134. Gerges, *ISIS: A History*, p. x.
135. Jean-Pierre Filiu, *From Deep State to Islamic State: The Arab Counter-Revolution and its Jihadi Legacy* (Oxford: Oxford University Press, 2015), p. 251.
136. Hudson, *Arab Politics*, p. 392.

6. ADAPTIVE POLITICS IN THE ARABIAN PENINSULA

1. Throughout this chapter I use the terms GCC states, petro-states, and the states of the Arabian Peninsula interchangeably, referring to Bahrain,

Kuwait, Oman, Qatar, Saudi Arabia, and the United Arab Emirates. Iran, Iraq, and Yemen are not included in the discussion here, although technically Yemen also belongs to the Arabian Peninsula.

2. For more on the consequences of the resource curse on institutions see, Victor Menaldo, *The Institutions Curse: Natural Resources, Politics, and Development*, (Cambridge: Cambridge University Press, 2016).

3. Khaldoun Al-Naqeeb has traced the evolution of what he calls the "natural state" in the Arabian Peninsula after the fall of Baghdad, pointing to the "dynamic matrix of the socio-economic structure, the political forces, and the distinguishing characteristics of the social relationships" prevailing in the region, and "the way in which the social forces and relationships were shaped in the division of labour at the social level". Khaldoun Hassan Al-Naqeeb, *Society and State in the Gulf and Arab Peninsula: A Different Perspective*, L. M. Kenny, trans., (London: Routledge, 1990), p. 6.

4. These definitions are employed here as they relate to the specific cases under discussion and are not meant to be definitive conceptualizations of the three phenomena, each of which has been subject to countless scholarly debates and multiple definitions. For more on legitimacy see, Mattei Dogan, "Conceptions of Legitimacy," in *Encyclopedia of Government and Politics*, *Volume 1*, Mary Hawkesworth and Maurice Kogan, eds. (London: Routledge, 1992), pp. 116–126. For clientelism see, Rene Lemarchand and Keith Legg, "Political Clientelism and Development: A Preliminary Analysis," *Comparative Politics*, Vol. 4, No. 2 (January 1972), pp. 149–178. And for rentierism see, Michael Herb, "No Representation without Taxation? Rents, Development, and Democracy," *Comparative Politics*, Vol. 37, No. 3 (April 2005), pp. 297–316.

5. Gregory Gause, *Oil Monarchies: Domestic and Security Challenges in the Arab Gulf States*, (New York: Council on Foreign Relations Press, 1994), p. 25.

6. As an example see, Muhammad Bin Zayid Al Nahyan, *With United Strength: H. H. Shaikh Zayid Bin Sultan Al Nahyan, The Leader and the Nation*, 3rd ed. (Abu Dhabi: The Emirates Center for Strategic Studies and Research, 2013).

7. Gause, *Oil Monarchies*, p. 26.

8. Ibid., p. 23.

9. For a treatment of this phenomenon in specific relation to Qatar see, Mehran Kamrava, "State-Business Relations and Clientelism in Qatar," *Journal of Arabian Studies*, Vol. 7, No. 1, (April 2017), pp. 1–27.

10. Steffen Hertog, *Princes, Brokers, and Bureaucrats: Oil and the State in Saudi Arabia*, (Ithaca, NY: Cornell University Press, 2010), p. 5.

11. Peter Evans, *Embedded Autonomy: States and Industrial Transformation*, (Princeton, NJ: Princeton University Press, 1995), p. 22.
12. Terry Lynn Karl, *The Paradox of Plenty: Oil Booms and Petro-States*, (Berkeley, CA: University of California Press, 1997), p. 57.
13. Hertog, *Princes, Brokers, and Bureaucrats*, pp. 28–9.
14. Omer Ali and Ibrahim Elbadawi, "The Political Economy of Public Sector Employment in Resource-dependent Countries," in *Understanding and Avoiding the Oil Curse in Resource-Rich Arab Economies*, Ibrahim Elbadawi and Hoda Selim, eds. (Cambridge: Cambridge University Press, 2016), p. 103. Ali and Elbadawi present a model explaining expansive public sector employment in resource dependent economies (pp. 108–113).
15. Michael Herb, *Wages of Oil: Parliaments and Economic Development in Kuwait and the UAE*, (Ithaca, NY: Cornell University Press, 2014), p. 184.
16. Ingo Forstenlechner and Emilie Rutledge, "Unemployment in the Gulf: Time to Update the 'Social Contract,'" *Middle East Policy*, Vol. 17, No. 2, (Summer 2010), p. 38.
17. Herb, *Wages of Oil*, p. 134.
18. Ibid., p. 140.
19. Hertog, *Princes, Brokers, and Bureaucrats*, p. 19.
20. "Finance minister says bureaucracy hinders growth," *Gulf States News*, Vol. 37, No. 956, (17 October 2013), p. 10.
21. Hend Al-Sheikh and S. Nuri Erbas, "The Oil Curse and Labor Markets: The Case of Saudi Arabia," in *Understanding and Avoiding the Oil Curse in Resource-Rich Arab Economies*, Ibrahim Elbadawi and Hoda Selim, eds. (Cambridge: Cambridge University Press, 2016), p. 181.
22. Martin Sommer, et al. "Learning to Live with Cheaper Oil: Policy Adjustments in Oil-Exporting Countries of the Middle East and Central Asia," The International Monetary Fund, 2016, p. 36.
23. Herb, *Wages of Oil*, p. 7.
24. Hertog, *Princes, Brokers, and Bureaucrats*, p. 25.
25. Herb, *Wages of Oil*, p. 14.
26. Laura El-Katiri, Bassam Fattouh, and Paul Segal, "Anatomy of an oil-based welfare state: Rent distribution in Kuwait," Research Paper, Kuwait Program on Development, Governance and Globalization in the Gulf States, London School of Economics, (2011), pp. 7–24.
27. Herb, *Wages of Oil*, p. 5.
28. Ibid., pp. 22–4.
29. Ibid., pp. 32–3.
30. Madawi Al-Rasheed, "Theorizing the Arabian Peninsula Roundtable: Knowledge In the Time of Oil," *Jadaliyya*, (22 April 2013), p. 1,

http://www.jadaliyya.com/pages/index/11297/theorizing-the-arabian-peninsula-roundtable_perspe.

31. Miriam R. Lowi, *Oil Wealth and the Poverty of Politics: Algeria Compared*, (Cambridge: Cambridge University Press, 2009), p. 43.

32. OPEC, "Oil Prices, OPEC Reference Basket," http://asb.opec.org/index.php/interactive-charts/oil-prices.

33. Hootan Shambayati, "The Rentier State, Interest Groups, and the Paradox of Autonomy: State and Business in Turkey and Iran," *Comparative Politics*, Vol. 26, No. 3, (April 1994), p. 308.

34. Ibid., p. 310.

35. Gause, *Oil Monarchies*, p. 11.

36. For the example of Qatar see, Mehran Kamrava, *Qatar: Small State, Big Politics*, (Ithaca, NY: Cornell University Press, 2015), pp. 118–122.

37. Juan J. Linz, *Totalitarian and Authoritarian Regimes*, (Boulder, CO: Lynne Rienner Publishers, 2000), p. 152.

38. Ibid., p. 162.

39. Baqir al-Najjar, "Foreign Labor and Questions of Identity in the Arabian Gulf," Arab Center for Research and Policy Studies, Research Paper (August 2013), p. 6.

40. Faisal Al-Marzouqi, "Excuse me…what's happening in Qatar museum's authority?," *Al-Arab Al-Qataria* (Doha), (25 August 2013).

41. al-Najjar, "Foreign Labor and Questions of Identity in the Arabian Gulf," p. 13.

42. Mohamed Ozwain, "Qatar Adopts Reforms to Protect the Arabic Language," *Aljazeera Note*, (2 December 2016), http://www.aljazeera.net/news/cultureandart.

43. Abdullah Ghanem Albinali Mohannadi, "'Christmas' and Happy New Year," *Al-Watan* (Doha), (21 May 2016).

44. Sean Foley, *The Arab Gulf States: Beyond Oil and Islam*, (Boulder, CO: Lynne Rienner, 2010), p. 4.

45. Herb, *Wages of Oil*, p. 122.

46. Quoted in, ibid., p. 4.

47. Ibid., p. 120.

48. Foley, *The Arab Gulf States*, p. 153.

49. al-Najjar, "Foreign Labor and Questions of Identity in the Arabian Gulf," p. 14.

50. Foley, *The Arab Gulf States*, p. 152.

51. Herb, *Wages of Oil*, p. 115.

52. Ibid., p. 11.

53. For more on second generation Arab migrant communities in the Arab petro-states see the collection of essays in, Zahra Babar, ed. *Arab Migrant Communities in the GCC* (New York: Oxford University Press, 2017).

54. al-Najjar, "Foreign Labor and Questions of Identity in the Arabian Gulf," p. 12.
55. Zahra Babar, "The Cost of Belonging: Citizenship Construction in the State of Qatar," *The Middle East Journal*, Vol. 68, No. 3, (Summer 2014), pp. 403–420. See also, Zahra Babar, "Population, Power, and Distributional Politics in Qatar," *Journal of Arabian Studies*, Vol. 5, No. 2, (2015), pp. 141–143.
56. For a small sample of works on the topic see, Madawi Al-Rasheed, *Muted Modernists: The Struggle Over Divine Politics in Saudi Arabia*, (Oxford: Oxford University Press, 2015); David Cummins, *Islam in Saudi Arabia*, (Ithaca, NY: Cornell University Press, 2015); and, Thomas Hegghammer, *Jihad in Saudi Arabia: Violence and Pan-Islamism since 1979*, (Cambridge: Cambridge University Press, 2010).
57. Gause, *Oil Monarchies*, p. 15. Significantly, many of the *ulama* in countries such as Qatar and the UAE are usually not nationals. Moreover, the GCC states have long tightly controlled traditional religious schools, *alkotaab*, and have even shut them down and instead opened state-sponsored religious schools. This has seriously impacted the emergence of a local crop of religious scholars.
58. Ibid., p. 31.
59. Cole Bunzel, *The Kingdom and the Caliphate: Duel of the Islamic States*, (Washington, DC: Carnegie Endowment for International Peace, 2016), pp. 15–17.
60. Ibid.
61. "Salafists move to the frontlines of Hadi-Saudi strategy," *Gulf States News*, Vol. 40, No. 1,013, (21 April 2016), p. 3.
62. Courtney Freer, "The Changing Islamist Landscape of the Gulf Arab States," The Arab Gulf Institute in Washington, (21 November 2016), p. 3.
63. Toby C. Jones, "Counterrevolution in the Gulf," *United States Institute of Peace Brief*, No. 89, (15 April 2011), p. 1.
64. Herb, *Wages of Oil*, p. 138.
65. Youseff Harb, "Bahraini monarchy manufactures demographic changes," *Al-Akhbar English*, (5 April 2014), http://english.al-akhbar.com/node/19301.
66. Al-Rasheed, "Theorizing the Arabian Peninsula Roundtable: Knowledge In the Time of Oil," *Jadaliyya*, p. 3.
67. "Writer sentenced for criticising ex-PM," *Gulf States News*, Vol. 37, No. 956, (17 October 2013), p. 7; "Kuwait vows to target 'rogue citizens,'" *Gulf States News*, Vol. 40, No. 1,013, (21 April 2016), p. 1.
68. "More hefty corruption sentences," *Gulf States News*, Vol. 38, No. 966, (20 March 2014), p. 17.

69. Average Annual OPEC Crude Oil Prices from 1960 to 2017, https://www.statista.com/statistics/262858/change-in-opec-crude-oil-prices-since-1960/.
70. Ibid.
71. PwC, *An introduction to Value Added Tax in the GCC*, January 2017, https://www.pwc.com/m1/en/tax/documents/what-is-vat-faq-on-vat-in-the-gcc.pdf.
72. For a comprehensive review of the concept of state capacity, and of different ways of measuring it, see, Luciana Cingolani, "The State of State Capacity: a review of concepts, evidence and measures," *UNU-MERIT Working Paper*, 2013.
73. Karl, *The Paradox of Plenty*, p. 45. In what has now become a classic analysis of the topic, Kugler and Domke offer a similar definition: "a government's ability to mold and adapt to socioeconomic conditions that expand the societal pool of resources but also erect constraints and obstacles to governmental access." Jacek Kugler and William Domke, "Comparing the Strength of Nations," *Comparative Political Studies*, Vol. 19, No. 1, (April 1986), p. 66.
74. Cullen S. Hendrix, "Measuring state capacity: Theoretical and empirical implications for the study of civil conflict," *Journal of Peace Research*, Vol. 43, No. 3, (2010), pp. 273–285; Jonathan Hanson and Rachel Sigman, "Leviathan's Latent Dimensions: Measuring State Capacity for Comparative Political Research," The World Bank Political Economy Group, March 21, 2013.
75. See, especially, Hendrix, "Measuring state capacity".
76. Mehran Kamrava, "The Political Economy of Rentierism in the Persian Gulf," in *The Political Economy of Oil in the Persian Gulf*, Mehran Kamrava, ed. (New York: Oxford University Press, 2012), p. 46.
77. Karl, *The Paradox of Plenty*, p. 46.
78. Evans, *Embedded Autonomy*, p. 59.
79. Ibid., p. 12.
80. Ibid., p. 72.
81. Ibid., p. 61.
82. Herb, *Wages of Oil*, p. 107. As Herb reminds us (p. 112), the GCC ruling families are already fabulously wealthy. By default, for example, the ruler owns all reclaimed land in the country, among other things, therefore benefiting from another major source of wealth.
83. In his fist address as Emir to the country's Shura Council, in November 2013, before the start of the oil slump, Qatar's Sheikh Tamim said the following: "despite the high standard of living we can provide, we must deal responsibly with our resources and our economy. This is not only about the next generation, but also the type of man we are keen on

grooming at the present. Is he productive or just a consumer?" "Emir's Address to Shura Council: Balanced development vital for building a modern state," *The Peninsula* (Doha), (6 November 2013), p. 9. See also, "Qatar urged to tackle 'culture of consumption,'" *Gulf Times* (Doha), (2 November 2016), pp. 1, 31.

84. "Quantifying a 'taboo' subject: Saudi Arabia counts the cost of Yemen war," *Gulf Studies News*, p. 5.

85. "No let-up for Bahrain's economy, as debt costs build, political discord continues," *Gulf States News*, Vol. 40, No. 1,019, (14 June 2016), p. 1.

86. Sultan Al Qassemi, "The Gulf's New Social Contract". *The Middle East Institute*, (8 February 2016), http://www.mei.edu/content/article/gulfs-new-social-contract.

87. Ibid.

88. Michael Ewers, Glnar Eskabder, and Bethany Shockley, "Public Acceptance of Taxation in Qatar," *SESRI Policy Brief*, No. 4, (June 2016), p. 1.

89. Ibid., p. 2.

90. Ibid., pp. 2–3.

91. The brief document can be accessed at http://www.mdps.gov.qa/en/qnv1/Pages/default.aspx.

92. Freer, "The Changing Islamist Landscape of the Gulf Arab States," p. 17.

93. Ibid., p. 15.

94. Ibid.

95. Ibid., p. 17.

96. Ibid., p. 16.

97. Sheikha Mayassa's high-profile acquisitions of Western works of art for the Qatar National Museum is a case in point. In 2013 she was identified by the international media as the world's most powerful woman in the world of art, spending more than £600m a year on art. But her art purchases met with some public skepticism at home, even resistance, and did not in any way engage the general public. See, Mark Brown, "Qatari royal tops international list of powerful people in art," *The Guardian* (London), (24 October 2013), p. 17; and, "Can Mayassa's bold art really change the Qatari landscape?" *Gulf States News*, Vol. 37, No. 956, (17 October 2013), p. 17.

98. "Qatar: Managing the limits of economic growth," *Gulf States News*, Vol. 37, No. 956, (17 October 2013), p. 12

99. This popularity shot up in the wake of the land and air blockade of Qatar by its three neighbors, when, through private and quite spontaneous initiatives, portraits of the emir with inscriptions reading

"Tamim the Magnificent" and "We Are All Tamim" became ubiquitous on cars, buildings, shops, and private residences.

100. Nada Abdelkader Benmansour, "Citizen and Resident Satisfaction with Public Services in Qatar," *SESRI Policy Brief*, No. 1, (March 2016), p. 2.

101. Freer, "The Changing Islamist Landscape of the Gulf Arab States," p. 15.

102. Ibid., p. 18.

103. Ibid., p. 19.

104. Ibid., p. 20.

105. Herb, *Wages of Oil*, p. 119.

106. Freer, "The Changing Islamist Landscape of the Gulf Arab States," p. 5.

107. The issue does, of course, receive state attention. According to *The UAE 2021 Vision*, the Emirati state "strives to preserve a cohesive society proud of its identity and sense of belonging". See, https://www.vision2021.ae/en/national-priority-areas/cohesive-society-and-preserved-identity. Thus, it promotes an inclusive environment that integrates all segments of society while preserving the UAE's unique culture, heritage and traditions and reinforces social and family cohesion.

108. Martin Hvidt, "The Dubai Model: An Outline of Key Development-Process Elements in Dubai," *International Journal of Middle East Studies*, Vol. 41, No. 3, (2009), p. 400.

109. Ibid., p. 401.

110. "Dubai real estate slump leads to bouts of realism and denial," *Gulf Studies News*, Vol. 40, No. 1,017, (16 June 2016), p. 10.

111. Herb, *Wages of Oil*, p. 116.

112. Ibid., p. 130.

113. "Small steps forward in elections for UAE's 'gradualist' democracy," *Gulf States News*, Vol. 39, No. 1,002, (15 October 2015), p. 1.

114. "Rising death toll in Yemen raises tough domestic questions for Abu Dhabi," *Gulf States News*, Vol. 40, No. 1,022, (22 September 2016), p. 6.

115. Kenneth Katzman, "Kuwait: Governance, Security, and U.S. Policy," *Congressional Research Service*, 5–5700, (29 September 2016), p. 3.

116. Ibid., p. 7.

117. Ibid. In March 2017, the emir agreed to reinstate the citizenship of those whose citizenships were revoked in 2014.

118. "Election law amendment represents fresh blow to Kuwaiti opposition group," *Gulf States News*, Vol. 40, No. 1,020, (28 July 2016), p. 1.

119. Herb, *Wages of Oil*, p. 105.

120. "Election law amendment represents fresh blow to Kuwaiti opposition group," p. 1.
121. Herb, *Wages of Oil*, p. 60.
122. Ibid., p. 185.
123. El-Katiri, Fattouh, and Segal, "Anatomy of an oil-based welfare state," p. 1.
124. Ibid.
125. Ibid., p. 24.
126. Herb, *Wages of Oil*, p. 4.
127. Katzman, "Kuwait," p. 7.
128. Freer, "The Changing Islamist Landscape of the Gulf Arab States," p. 13.
129. "Authorities focus on enhanced security fearing new IS attacks," *Gulf States News*, Vol. 40, No. 1,016, (2 June 2016), p. 5. Kuwait has about 100,000 bidoon, who are not allowed to have citizenship. Also, about 30 percent of Kuwaitis are Shia.
130. "Authorities focus on enhanced security fearing new IS attacks," *Gulf States News*, p. 5.
131. Katzman, "Kuwait," p. 19.
132. The Bahrain Defence Force, for example, which is a highly professional, well-equipped, and effective army, is closed to the Shia. Zoltan Barany, "The Bahrain Defence Force: The Monarchy's Second to Last Line of Defense," Center for Strategic and International Studies (Washington, DC), (9 December 2016), p. 3.
133. "Spending flows show how domestic security remains Bahrain's top priority," *Gulf States News*, Vol. 40, No. 1,013, (21 April 2016), p. 1.
134. Freer, "The Changing Islamist Landscape of the Gulf Arab States," p. 10.
135. "Bahrain doubles down on opposition as Al-Wafeq closed and usual suspects held," *Gulf States News*, Vol. 40, No. 1,017, (16 June 2016), p. 1.
136. Freer, "The Changing Islamist Landscape of the Gulf Arab States," p. 7.
137. Ibid., p. 8.
138. Barany, "The Bahrain Defence Force," pp. 6–7.
139. Ibid., p. 3. Original emphasis.
140. See, for example, Abdullah Juma Alhaj, "The Political Elite and the Introduction of Political Participation in Oman," *Middle East Policy*, Vol. 7, No. 3, (June 2000), p. 103.
141. Kenneth Katzman, "Oman: Reform, Security, and U.S. Policy," *Congressional Research Service*, 7–5700, (April 26, 2016), p. 3.
142. "Small pool of potential successors to Sultan Qaboos," *Gulf States News*, Vol. 37, No. 957, (17 October 2013), p. 3.

143. Alhaj, "The Political Elite and the Introduction of Political Participation in Oman," p. 97.

144. The letter, dated 4 September 2015, criticized both King Salman and his son, Mohammed. But it did not call for the overthrow of the ruling family altogether. It merely criticized the seeming inexperience and political excesses of the kingdom's new crop of rulers. See, Bel Trew, "Saudi royals want to overthrow king and embrace democracy," *The Time* (London), (1 October 2015), p. 32.

145. Paul Aarts and Carolien Roelants, "The Perils of transfer of power in the Kingdom of Saudi Arabia," *Contemporary Arab Affairs*, Vol. 9, No. 4, (2016), p. 3.

146. Hertog, *Princes, Brokers, and Bureaucrats*, p. 31.

147. Christopher M. Blanchard, "Saudi Arabia: Background and U.S. Relations," *Congressional Research Service*, 5–5700, (20 September 2016), p. 8. Aarts and Roelants go so far as to claim that reforms are essential to the monarchy's survival. Aarts and Roelants, "The Perils of transfer of power in the Kingdom of Saudi Arabia," p. 6.

148. Blanchard, "Saudi Arabia," p. 8. Like so many other ambitious initiatives, the credit for the kingdom's 'Vision 2030' actually goes to King Salman's son, Mohammad bin Salman (b. 1985), who officially holds multiple positions, including those of deputy crown prince and minister of defense. Saudi Arabia's 'Vision 2030' document can be accessed at http://vision2030.gov.sa/en. *The National Transformation Program 2020* is available through http://vision2030.gov.sa/sites/default/files/NTP_En.pdf.

149. "Saudi Arabia to push for more taxation, but no representation," *Gulf Studies News*, Vol. 40, No. 1,017, (16 June 2016), p. 4.

150. Ibid., p. 7.

151. For more on this see, Mehran Kamrava, "The Arab Spring and the Saudi-Led Counterrevolution," *Orbis*, Vol. 56, No. 1, (Winter 2012), pp. 96–104.

152. Aarts and Roelants, "The Perils of transfer of power in the Kingdom of Saudi Arabia," p. 7.

153. Sensitivity to overreliance has not translated itself to the kingdom's weapons purchases from the US. Between late 2012 and September 2016, Saudi Arabia purchased more than $42 billion in weapons from the United States. Christopher M. Blanchard, "Saudi Arabia: Background and U.S. Relations," *Congressional Research Service*, 5–5700, (20 September 2016), p. 1.

154. Leigh Nolan, "Managing Reform? Saudi Arabia and the King's Dilemma," *Brooking Doha Center*, Policy Briefing, (May 2011), p. 1.

155. Hala Aldosari, "Saudi Arabia's Virtual Quest for Citizenship and Identity," Washington Institute for Near East Policy, (2016), p. 6.

156. Silvia Colombo, "The GCC Countries and the Arab Spring: Between Outreach, Patronage and Repression," Instituto Affari Internazionali Working Paper, 12–09, (March 2012), pp. 5–6.

157. Aldosari, "Saudi Arabia's Virtual Quest for Citizenship and Identity," p. 2.

158. "Reserves questions resurface as Aramco pumps on from mature fields," *Gulf States News*, Vol. 40, No. 1,016, (2 June 2016), pp. 1, 11. Long assumed to have the world's largest oil reserves, in 2016 Saudi oil reserves were estimated as 212 billion barrels, behind those of the US at 264 billion barrels and perhaps even those of Russia.

159. Khaled al-Jayoussi, "Faced with 'austerity' measures and announcing 'bankruptcy' in Saudi Arabia, citizens are shocked…" *Rai al-Youm*, (7 November 2016), http://www.raialyoum.com/?p=558100.

160. Ibid.

161. Blanchard, "Saudi Arabia," p. 30.

162. Aarts and Roelants, "The Perils of transfer of power in the Kingdom of Saudi Arabia," p. 7. According to a report by the *Congressional Research Service*, "financial support for terrorism from Saudi individuals remains a threat to the kingdom and the international community." Blanchard, "Saudi Arabia," p. 13.

163. Nolan, "Managing Reform?" p. 2.

164. Blanchard, "Saudi Arabia," pp. 12–13.

165. Ibid., p. 12.

166. "Saudi Arabia to push for more taxation, but no representation," *Gulf Studies News*, p. 9.

167. "Quantifying a 'taboo' subject: Saudi Arabia counts the cost of Yemen war," *Gulf Studies News*, Vol. 40, No. 1,025, (3 November 2016), p. 1. According to this report, largely because of its mounting costs and its unpopularity, Crown Prince Mohammed bin Nayef has distanced himself from the Yemen war, something that even the war's chief architect, Mohammed bin Salman, has done as well (p. 6).

168. "Death toll in Yemen conflict passes 10,000," *Al Jazeera*, (January 17, 2017), http://www.aljazeera.com/news/2017/01/death-toll-yemen-conflict-passes-10000–170117040849576.html.

169. Quoted in, "Quantifying a 'taboo' subject: Saudi Arabia counts the cost of Yemen war," p. 7.

170. Ibid., p. 3.

171. "Estimating the financial costs of the Yemeni conflict," *Gulf Studies News*, Vol. 40, No. 1,025, (3 November 2016), p. 4.

172. "Quantifying a 'taboo' subject: Saudi Arabia counts the cost of Yemen war," *Gulf Studies News*, p. 1.

173. Jeffrey D. Sachs, "How to Handle the Macroeconomics of Wealth" in

Escaping the Resource Curse, Macartan Humphreys, Jeffrey D. Sachs, and Joseph E. Stiglitz, eds. (New York: Columbia University Press, 2007), p. 191.

174. Paul Collier, "Savings and Investment Decisions from Natural Resource Revenues: Implications for Arab Development," in *Understanding and Avoiding the Oil Curse in Resource-Rich Arab Economies*, Ibrahim Elbadawi and Hoda Selim, eds. (Cambridge: Cambridge University Press, 2016), p. 286.

CONCLUSION

1. Ariel I. Ahram and Ellen Lust, "The Decline and Fall of the Arab State," *Survival*, Vol. 58, No. 2 (April–May 2016), p. 25.
2. Ibid., pp. 23–4.

BIBLIOGRAPHY

Aarts, Paul and Carolien Roelants. "The perils of transfer of power in the Kingdom of Saudi Arabia." *Contemporary Arab Affairs*, Vol. 9, No. 4 (2016), pp. 596–606.

Abu-Rish, Ziad. "Protests, Regime Stability, and State Formation in Jordan," in *Beyond the Arab Spring*, Mehran Kamrava, ed. New York: Oxford University Press, 2014, pp. 284–90.

Abu-'Uksa, Wael. "Liberal Renewal of the *Turath*: Constructing the Egyptian Past in Sayyid al-Qimni's Works," in *Arab Liberal Thought after 1967: Old Dilemmas, New Perceptions*, Meir Hatina and Christoph Schumann, eds. New York: Palgrave Macmillan, 2015, pp. 101–17.

Achilov, Dilshod. "Revisiting Political Islam: Explaining the Nexus Between Political Islam and Contentious Politics in the Arab World." *Social Science Quarterly*, Vol. 97, No. 2 (June 2016), pp. 252–70.

Addi, Lahouari. "Algeria and its Permanent Political Crisis." *IEMed, Mediterranean Yearbook 2015* (2015).

Adib-Moghaddam, Arshin. *On the Arab Revolts and the Iranian Revolution: Power and Resistance Today*. London: Bloomsbury Academic, 2013.

Ahram, Ariel I. and Ellen Lust. "The Decline and Fall of the Arab State." *Survival*, Vol. 58, No. 2 (April–May 2016), pp. 7–34.

Al-Arian, Abdulla. "Islamist Movements and the Arab Spring," in *Beyond the Arab Spring*, Mehran Kamrava, ed. New York: Oxford University Press, 2014, pp. 99–129.

Al Bana, Khalil. *To the Arab Nation, A Salutation (Ila Al-Umma Al-Arabia, Ma' Tahia)*. Amman: Amwaj, 2011.

Albrecht, Holger. "The Myth of Coup-Proofing: Risks and Instances of Military Coups d'état in the Middle East and North Africa, 1950–2013." *Armed Forces and Society*, Vol. 41, No. 4 (2014), pp. 659–87.

Albrecht, Holger and Dina Bishara. "Back on Horseback: the Military and

Political Transformation in Egypt." *Middle East Law and Governance*, Vol. 3 (2011), pp. 13–23.

Aldosari, Hala. "Saudi Arabia's Virtual Quest for Citizenship and Identity." Washington Institute for Near East Policy (Washington, DC), 2016.

Ali, Omer and Ibrahim Elbadawi. "The Political Economy of Public Sector Employment in Resource-Dependent Countries," in *Understanding and Avoiding the Oil Curse in Resource-Rich Arab Economies*, Ibrahim Elbadawi and Hoda Selim, eds. Cambridge: Cambridge University Press, 2016, pp. 103–48.

Allal, Amin. "Becoming Revolutionary in Tunisia, 2007–2011," in *Social Movements, Mobilization, and Contestation in the Middle East and North Africa*, 2nd edn, Joel Beinin and Frederic Vairel, eds. Stanford, CA: Stanford University Press, 2013, pp. 185–204.

Alley, April Longley. "Yemen Changes Everything…And Nothing," in *Democratization and Authoritarianism in the Arab World*, Larry Diamond and Marc F. Plattner, eds. Baltimore, MD: Johns Hopkins University Press, 2014, pp. 277–88.

Al Nahyan, Muhammad Bin Zayid. *With United Strength: H. H. Shaikh Zayid Bin Sultan Al Nahyan, The Leader and the Nation*, 3rd edn. Abu Dhabi: Emirates Center for Strategic Studies and Research, 2013.

al-Najjar, Baqir. "Foreign Labor and Questions of Identity in the Arabian Gulf." Arab Center for Research and Policy Studies (Doha), Research Paper, August 2013.

Al-Naqeeb, Khaldoun Hassan. *Society and State in the Gulf and Arab Peninsula: A Different Perspective*. L. M. Kenny, trans. London: Routledge, 1990.

Alon, Yoav. "From Abdullah (I) to Abdullah (II): The Monarchy, the Tribes and the Shaykhly Families in Jordan, 1920–2012," in *Tribes and State in a Changing Middle East*, Uzi Rabi, ed. New York: Oxford University Press, 2016, pp. 11–35.

Al-Rasheed, Madawi. *Muted Modernists: The Struggle Over Divine Politics in Saudi Arabia*. Oxford: Oxford University Press, 2015.

————. "Theorizing the Arabian Peninsula Roundtable: Knowledge in the Time of Oil." *Jadaliyya*, 22 April 2013. http://www.jadaliyya.com/pages/index/11297/theorizing-the-arabian-peninsula-roundtable_perspe.

Al-Sheikh, Hend and S. Nuri Erbas, "The Oil Curse and Labor Markets: The Case of Saudi Arabia," in *Understanding and Avoiding the Oil Curse in Resource-Rich Arab Economies*, Ibrahim Elbadawi and Hoda Selim, eds. Cambridge: Cambridge University Press, 2016, pp. 149–86.

Al-Shubashi, Sharif. *Egypt's Future After the Revolution (Mustaqbal Misr Ba'd Al-Thawra)*. Cairo: National Library and Archives Scientific Centers, 2012.

Al-Thawr, Sabira. "Ending Persistent Poverty: Pathways to Reform and Empowerment," in *Arab Human Development in the Twenty-first Century: The*

BIBLIOGRAPHY

Primacy of Empowerment, Bahgat Korany, ed. Cairo: American University of Cairo Press, 2014, pp. 139–65.

Althusser, Louis. "Ideology and Ideological State Apparatuses," in *Literary Theory: An Anthology*, 2nd edn. Julie Rivkin and Michael Ryan, eds. Maiden, MA: Blackwell, 2004, pp. 693–702.

Amnesty International. *Amnesty International Report 2015/16: The State of the World's Human Rights*. London: Amnesty International, 2016.

Anderson, Lisa. "Authoritarian Legacies and Regime Change," in *The New Middle East: Protest and Revolution in the Arab World*, Fawaz A. Gerges, ed. Cambridge: Cambridge University Press, 2014, pp. 41–59.

Arab Center for Research and Policy Studies, *The 2016 Arab Opinion: How the Arabs Saw the World in 2016*. Doha: ACRPS, 2016.

Aras, Bülent and Richard Falk, "Authoritarian 'geopolitics' of survival in the Arab Spring." *Third World Quarterly*, Vol. 36, No. 2 (2015), pp. 322–36.

Archer, Margaret S. *Realist Social Theory: The Morphogenetic Approach*. Cambridge: Cambridge University Press, 1995.

Arjomand, Said Amir. "Revolution and Constitution in the Arab World, 2011–2012," in *Beyond the Arab Spring*, Mehran Kamrava, ed. New York: Oxford University Press, 2014, pp. 151–88.

Askari, Hossein. *Collaborative Colonialism: The Political Economy of Oil in the Persian Gulf*. New York: Palgrave Macmillan, 2013.

Atwan, Abdel Bari. *Islamic State: The Digital Caliphate*. Berkeley, CA: University of California Press, 2015.

Ayubi, Nazih. *Over-stating the Arab State: Politics and Society in the Middle East*. London: I. B. Tauris, 1999.

Baaklini, Abdo, Guilain Denoeux, and Robert Springborg. *Legislative Politics in the Arab World: The Resurgence of Democratic Institutions*. Boulder, CO: Lynne Rienner Publishers, 1999.

Babar, Zahra, ed. *Arab Migrant Communities in the GCC*. New York: Oxford University Press, 2017.

————. "Population, Power, and Distributional Politics in Qatar." *Journal of Arabian Studies*, Vol. 5, No. 2 (2015), pp. 138–55.

————. "The Cost of Belonging: Citizenship Construction in the State of Qatar." *Middle East Journal*, Vol. 68, No. 3 (Summer 2014), pp. 403–20.

Barany, Zoltan. "The Bahrain Defence Force: The Monarchy's Second to Last Line of Defense." Center for Strategic and International Studies (Washington, DC), 9 December 2016.

————. "The Role of the Military," in *Democratization and Authoritarianism in the Arab World*, Larry Diamond and Marc F. Plattner, eds. Baltimore, MD: Johns Hopkins University Press, 2014, pp. 162–73.

————. *The Soldier and the Changing State: Building Democratic Armies in Africa, Asia, Europe, and the Americas*. Princeton, NJ: Princeton University Press, 2012.

BIBLIOGRAPHY

————. "The 'Arab Spring' in the Kingdoms." Arab Center for Research and Policy Studies (Doha), Research Paper, September 2012.

Barari, Hassan A. "The Limits of Political Reform in Jordan: The Role of External Actors." *Friedrich Ebert Stiftung*, December 2013.

Bates, Thomas R. "Gramsci and the Theory of Hegemony." *Journal of the History of Ideas*, Vol. 36, No. 2 (April–June 1975), pp. 351–66.

Bayat, Asef. *Life as Politics: How Ordinary People Change the Middle East*, 2nd edn. Stanford, CA: Stanford University Press, 2013.

Beinin, Joel. *Workers and Thieves: Labor Movements and Popular Uprisings in Tunisia and Egypt*. Stanford, CA: Stanford University Press, 2016.

————. "New-Liberal Structural Adjustment, Political Demobilization and Neo-Authoritarianism in Egypt," in *The Arab State and Neo-Liberal Globalization: The Restructuring of State Power in the Middle East*, Laura Guazzone and Daniela Pioppi, eds. Reading, UK: Ithaca Press, 2012, pp. 19–46.

Beinin, Joel and Frederic Vairel. "Introduction: The Middle East and North Africa Beyond Classical Social Movement Theory," in *Social Movements, Mobilization, and Contestation in the Middle East and North Africa*, 2nd edn. Joel Beinin and Frederic Vairel, eds. Stanford, CA: Stanford University Press, 2013, pp. 1–29.

Beissinger, Mark R., Amaney A. Jamal, and Kevin Mazur. "Explaining Divergent Revolutionary Coalitions: Regime Strategies and the Structuring of Participation in the Tunisian and Egyptian Revolutions." *Comparative Politics*, Vol. 48, No. 1 (October 2015), pp. 1–21.

Bell, David A. "Inglorious Revolutions." *The National Interest* (January/February 2014), pp. 31–8.

Bellin, Eva. "Reconsidering the Robustness of Authoritarianism in the Middle East: Lessons from the Arab Spring." *Comparative Politics*, Vol. 44, No. 2 (January 2012), pp. 127–49.

————. "Coercive Institutions and Coercive Leaders," in *Authoritarianism in the Middle East: Regimes and Resistance*, Marsha Pripstein Posusney and Michele Penner Angrist, eds. Boulder, CO: Lynne Rienner Publishers, 2005, pp. 21–41.

————. "The Robustness of Authoritarianism in the Middle East: Exceptionalism in Comparative Perspective." *Comparative Politics*, Vol. 36, No. 2 (January 2004), pp. 139–57.

Benakcha, Narrimane. "The Algerian Regime: An Arab Spring Survivor." *Columbia Journal of International Affairs* (March 2012). https://jia.sipa.columbia.edu/online-articles/algerianregime-arab-spring-survivor.

Benmansour, Nada Abdelkader. "Citizen and Resident Satisfaction with Public Services in Qatar." *SESRI Policy Brief*, No. 1 (March 2016).

Bill, James A. and Robert Springborg. *Politics in the Middle East*, 5th edn. New York: Addison Wesley Longman, 2000.

BIBLIOGRAPHY

Bishara, Azmi. "On the Intellectual and the Revolution." Arab Center for Research and Policy Studies Studies (Doha), Research Paper, June 2013.

Bishku, Michael B. "Is It Arab Spring or Business as Usual? Recent Changes in the Arab World in Historical Context." *Journal of Third World Studies*, Vol. 30, No. 1 (2013), pp. 55–71.

Blanchard, Christopher M. "Saudi Arabia: Background and U.S. Relations." *Congressional Research Service*, 5–5700, 20 September 2016.

Boettke, Peter J., Christopher J. Coyne, and Peter T. Leeson, "Institutional Stickiness and the New Development Economics." *American Journal of Economics and Sociology*, Vol. 67, No. 2 (April 2008), pp. 331–58.

Bonnefoy, Laurent and Marine Poirier. "Dynamics of the Yemeni Revolution: Contextualizing Mobilizations," in *Social Movements, Mobilization, and Contestation in the Middle East and North Africa*, 2nd edn, Joel Beinin and Frederic Vairel, eds. Stanford, CA: Stanford University Press, 2013, pp. 228–45.

Bou Nassif, Hicham. "Generals and Autocrats: How Coup-Proofing Predetermined the Military Elite's Behavior in the Arab Spring." *Political Science Quarterly*, Vol. 130, No. 2 (2015), pp. 245–75.

Brooks, Risa. "Abandoned at the Palace: Why the Tunisian Military Defected from the Ben Ali Regime in January 2011." *Journal of Strategic Studies*, Vol. 90, No. 2 (2013), pp. 205–20.

Browers, Michaelle L. *Political Ideology in the Arab World: Accommodation and Transformation*. Cambridge: Cambridge University Press, 2009.

Brown, Nathan. *Arguing Islam after the Revival of Arab Politics*. New York: Oxford University Press, 2017.

————. "Egypt's Failed Transition," in *Democratization and Authoritarianism in the Arab World*, Larry Diamond and Marc F. Plattner, eds. Baltimore, MD: Johns Hopkins University Press, 2014, pp. 263–76.

Brown, Nathan J. and Amr Hamzawy. *Between Religion and Politics*. Washington, DC: Carnegie Endowment for International Peace, 2010.

Brownlee, Jason, Tarek Masoud, and Andrew Reynolds. "Why the Modest Harvest?" in *Democratization and Authoritarianism in the Arab World*, Larry Diamond and Marc F. Plattner, eds. Baltimore, MD: Johns Hopkins University Press, 2014, pp. 137–42.

Brumberg, Daniel. "Transforming the Arab World's Protection Racket Politics," in *Democratization and Authoritarianism in the Arab World*, Larry Diamond and Marc F. Plattner, eds. Baltimore, MD: Johns Hopkins University Press, 2014, pp. 96–111.

————. "The Trap of Liberalized Autocracy." *Journal of Democracy*, Vol. 13, No. 4 (October 2002), pp. 56–68.

————. "Authoritarian Legacies and Reform Strategies in the Arab World," in *Political Liberalization and Democratization in the Arab World: Vol. 1, Theoretical*

Perspectives, Rex Brynen, Bahgat Korany, and Paul Noble, eds. Boulder, CO: Lynne Rienner Publishers, 1995, pp. 229–59.

Bunce, Valerie. "Conclusion: Rebellious Citizens and Resilient Authoritarians," in *The New Middle East: Protest and Revolution in the Arab World*, Fawaz A. Gerges, ed. Cambridge: Cambridge University Press, 2014, pp. 446–68.

Bunzel, Cole. *The Kingdom and the Caliphate: Duel of the Islamic States*, Washington, DC: Carnegie Endowment for International Peace, 2016.

Butenschøn, Nils A. "State, Power, and Citizenship in the Middle East: A Theoretical Introduction," in *Citizenship and the State in the Middle East: Approaches and Applications*, Nils A. Butenschøn, Uri Davis, and Manuel Hassassian, eds. Syracuse, NY: Syracuse University Press, 2000, pp. 3–27.

Byman, Daniel. "Regime Change in the Middle East: Problems and Prospects." *Political Science Quarterly*, Vol. 127, No. 1 (2012), pp. 25–46.

Byun, Chonghyun Christie, and Ethan J. Hollander. "Explaining the Intensity of the Arab Spring." *Digest of Middle East Studies*, Vol. 24, No. 1 (2015), pp. 26–46.

Capoccia, Giovanni and R. Daniel Keleman. "The Study of Critical Junctures: Theory, Narrative, and Counterfactuals in Historical Institutionalism." *World Politics*, Vol. 59, No. 3 (April 2007), pp. 341–69.

Chatty, Dawn. "Bedouin Tribes in Contemporary Syria: Alternative Perceptions of Authority, Management, and Control," in *Tribes and State in a Changing Middle East*, Uzi Rabi, ed. New York: Oxford University Press, 2016, pp. 145–71.

Chehabi, H. E. and Juan J. Linz. "A Theory of Sultanism 1: A Type of Nondemocratic Rule," in *Sultanistic Regimes*, H. E. Chehabi and Juan J. Linz, eds. Baltimore, MD: Johns Hopkins University Press, 1998, pp. 3–25.

Cherif, Yousef. "Tunisia's Fledgling Gulf Relations." *Carnegie Endowment for International Peace*, 17 January 2017.

Choucair-Vizoso, Julia. "Illusive Reform: Jordan's Stubborn Stability," in *Beyond the Façade: Political Reform in the Arab World*, Marina Ottaway and Julia Choucair-Vizoso, eds. Washington, DC: Carnegie Endowment for International Peace, 2008, pp. 45–70.

Christie, Kenneth, and Mohammad Masad. *State Formation and Identity in the Middle East and North Africa*. New York: Palgrave Macmillan, 2013.

Cingolani, Luciana. "The State of State Capacity: a review of concepts, evidence and measures," UNU-MERIT Working Paper, 2013.

Clark, Victoria. *Yemen: Dancing on the Heads of Snakes*. New Haven, CT: Yale University Press, 2010.

Cole, Juan. *The New Arabs: How the Millennial Generation is Changing the Middle East*. New York: Simon & Schuster, 2014.

Collier, Paul. "Savings and Investment Decisions from Natural Resource

BIBLIOGRAPHY

Revenues: Implications for Arab Development," in *Understanding and Avoiding the Oil Curse in Resource-Rich Arab Economies*, Ibrahim Elbadawi and Hoda Selim, eds. Cambridge: Cambridge University Press, 2016, pp. 284–300.

Colombo, Silvia. "The GCC Countries and the Arab Spring: Between Outreach, Patronage and Repression." Instito Affari Internazionali (Rome), Working Paper 12–09, March 2012.

Connell, John. "Nauru: The First Failed Pacific State?" *Round Table*, Vol. 95, No. 383 (January 2006), pp. 47–63.

Constitution of Kingdom of Morocco, 2011. Ruchti, Jefri J., trans. https://www.constituteproject.org/constitution/Morocco_2011.pdf?lang=en.

Cook, Steven A. *False Dawn: Protest, Democracy, and Violence in the New Middle East*. New York: Oxford University Press, 2017.

Cronin, Stephanie. *Armies and State-Building in the Modern Middle East: Politics, Nationalism and Military Reform*. London: I. B. Tauris, 2014.

Crotty, William, ed. *Political Science: Looking to the Future, Vol. Two: Comparative Politics, Policy, and International Relations*. Evanston, IL: Northwestern University Press, 1991.

Cummins, David. *Islam in Saudi Arabia*. Ithaca, NY: Cornell University Press, 2015.

Daadaoui, Mohamed. *Moroccan Monarchy and the Islamist Challenge: Maintaining Makhzen Power*. New York: Palgrave, 2011.

————. "Party Politics and Elections in Morocco," *Middle East Institute Policy Brief*, No. 29, May 2010.

Dabashi, Hamid. *The Arab Spring: The End of Postcolonialism*. London: Zed Books, 2012.

Davis, Diane E. and Anthony W. Pereira. *Irregular Armed Forces and their Role in Politics and State Formation*. Cambridge: Cambridge University Press, 2003.

DeFronzo, James. *Revolutions and Revolutionary Movements*, 5th edn. Boulder, CO: Westview, 2015.

Dekmejian, R. Hrair. *Egypt Under Nasir: A Study in Political Dynamics*. Albany, NY: SUNY Press, 1971.

Desrues, Thierry. "Moroccan Youth and the Forming of a New Generation: Social Change, Collective Action and Political Activism." *Mediterranean Politics*, Vol. 17, No. 1 (March 2012), pp. 23–40.

Diamond, Larry, Marc F. Plattner, and Nate Grubman. "Introduction," in *Democratization and Authoritarianism in the Arab World*, Larry Diamond and Marc F. Plattner, eds. Baltimore, MD: Johns Hopkins University Press, 2014, pp. ix-xxxiii.

Diop, Ndiame and Jaime de Melo. "Dutch Disease in the Services Sector: Evidence from Oil Exporters in the Arab Region," in *Understanding and Avoiding the Oil Curse in Resource-Rich Arab Economies*, Ibrahim Elbadawi and

BIBLIOGRAPHY

Hoda Selim, eds. Cambridge: Cambridge University Press, 2016, pp. 82–102.

Dogan, Mattei. "Conceptions of Legitimacy," in *Encyclopedia of Government and Politics*, *Vol. 1*, Mary Hawkesworth and Maurice Kogan, eds. London: Routledge, 1992, pp. 116–26.

Donini, Antonio, Norah Niland, and Karin Wermester. *Nation-Building Unraveled? Aid, Peace and Justice in Afghanistan*. Bloomfield, CT: Kumarian Press, 2004.

Droz-Vincent, Philippe. "The Military in the Arab World, from Authoritarian Regimes to Transitional Settings and New Regimes in the Making." *Singapore Middle East Papers*, No. 10/11, 27 March 2015.

———. "The Military amidst Uprisings and Transitions in the Arab World," in *The New Middle East: Protest and Revolution in the Arab World*, Fawaz A. Gerges, ed. Cambridge: Cambridge University Press, 2014, pp. 180–208.

———. "Prospects for 'Democratic Control of the Armed Forces'? Comparative Insights and Lessons for the Arab World in Transition." *Armed Forces and Society*, Vol. 40, No. 4 (2013), pp. 696–723.

———. "A Return of Armies to the Forefront of Arab Politics?" Instituto Affari Internazionali (Rome), Working Paper 11–21, July 2011.

Duboc, Marie. "Challenging the Trade Union, Reclaiming the Nation: The Politics of Labor Protest in Egypt, 2006–11," in *Beyond the Arab Spring*, Mehran Kamrava, ed. New York: Oxford University Press, 2014, pp. 223–48.

Dunne, Michele and Tarek Radwan. "Egypt: Why Liberalism Still Matters," in *Democratization and Authoritarianism in the Arab World*, Larry Diamond and Marc F. Plattner, eds. Baltimore, MD: Johns Hopkins University Press, 2014, pp. 248–62.

Ehteshami, Anoushiravan. *After Khomeini: The Iranian Second Republic*. London: Routledge, 1995.

El Alaoui, Hicham Ben Abdallah. "The Split in Arab Culture," in *Democratization and Authoritarianism in the Arab World*, Larry Diamond and Marc F. Plattner, eds. Baltimore, MD: Johns Hopkins University Press, 2014, pp. 69–80.

Elbadawi, Ibrahim and Hoda Selim. "Overview of Context, Issues and Summary," in *Understanding and Avoiding the Oil Curse in Resource-Rich Arab Economies*, Ibrahim Elbadawi and Hoda Selim, eds. Cambridge: Cambridge University Press, 2016, pp. 1–15.

Elbadawi, Ibrahim and Raimundo Soto, "Resource Rents, Political Institutions and Economic Growth," in *Understanding and Avoiding the Oil Curse in Resource-Rich Arab Economies*, Ibrahim Elbadawi and Hoda Selim, eds. Cambridge: Cambridge University Press, 2016, pp. 187–224.

Evans, Peter. "The Eclipse of the State? Reflections on Stateness in an Era of Globalization." *World Politics*, Vol. 50, No. 1 (October 1997), pp. 62–87.

BIBLIOGRAPHY

————. *Embedded Autonomy: States and Industrial Transformation*. Princeton, NJ: Princeton University Press, 1995.

————. "The State as Problem and Solution: Predation, Embedded Autonomy, and Structural Change," in *The Politics of Economic Development*, Stephan Haggard and Robert R. Kaufman, eds. Princeton, NJ: Princeton University, Press, 1992, pp. 139–82.

Evans, Peter B., Dietrich Rueschemeyer, and Theda Skocpol, eds. *Bringing the State Back In*. Cambridge: Cambridge University Press, 1985.

Ewers, Michael, Glnar Eskander, and Bethany Shockley. "Public Acceptance of Taxation in Qatar." *SESRI Policy Brief*, No. 4, June 2016.

Filali-Ansary, Abdou. "The Languages of the Arab Revolutions," in *Democratization and Authoritarianism in the Arab World*, Larry Diamond and Marc F. Plattner, eds. Baltimore, MD: Johns Hopkins University Press, 2014, pp. 3–14.

Filbert, Andrew. "The Consequences of Forced State Failure in Iraq." *Political Science Quarterly*, Vol. 128, No. 1 (2013), pp. 67–95.

Filiu, Jean-Pierre. *From Deep State to Islamic State: The Arab Counter-Revolution and its Jihadi Legacy*. Oxford: Oxford University Press, 2015.

Finer, Samuel E. *The Man on Horseback: The Role of the Military in Politics*. New Brunswick, NJ: Transaction Publishers, 2006.

Foley, Sean. *The Arab Gulf States: Beyond Oil and Islam*. Boulder, CO: Lynne Rienner Publishers, 2010.

Foran, John. "Global Affinities: The New Cultures of Resistance Behind the Arab Spring," in *Beyond the Arab Spring*, Mehran Kamrava, ed. New York: Oxford University Press, 2014, p. 47–71.

Forstenlechner, Ingo and Emilie Rutledge. "Unemployment in the Gulf: Time to Update the 'Social Contract.'" *Middle East Policy*, Vol. 17, No. 2 (Summer 2010), pp. 38–51.

Freer, Courtney. "The Changing Islamist Landscape of the Gulf Arab States." *Arab Gulf Institute in Washington*, 21 November 2016.

Fukuyama, Francis, ed. *Nation-Building: Beyond Afghanistan and Iraq*. Baltimore, MD: Johns Hopkins University Press, 2006.

————. *State-Building: Governance and World Order in the 21ˢᵗ Century*. Ithaca, NY: Cornell University Press, 2004.

Gandhi, Jennifer. *Political Institutions under Dictatorship*. Cambridge: Cambridge University Press, 2010.

Gaub, Florence. "An Unhappy Marriage: Civil–Military Relations in Post-Saddam Iraq." Carnegie Middle East Center (Beirut), 13 January 2016.

Gause, F. Gregory, III. *Oil Monarchies: Domestic and Security Challenges in the Arab Gulf States*. New York: Council on Foreign Relations Press, 1994.

Gelvin, James L. *The Arab Uprisings: What Everyone Needs to Know*. New York: Oxford University Press, 2012.

BIBLIOGRAPHY

Gengler, Justin. "How Bahrain's crushed uprising spawned the Middle East's sectarianism." *Washington Post*, 13 February 2016. https://www.washingtonpost.com/news/monkey-cage/wp/2016/02/13/how-bahrains-crushed-uprising-spawned-the-middle-easts-sectarianism/.

Gerges, Fawaz A. *ISIS: A History*. Princeton, NJ: Princeton University Press, 2016.

————. "Introduction," in *The New Middle East: Protest and Revolution in the Arab World*, Fawaz A. Gerges, ed. Cambridge: Cambridge University Press, 2014, pp. 1–38.

Ghonim, Wael. *Revolution 2.0: The Power of the People is Greater than the People in Power: A Memoir*. Boston, MA: Houghton Mifflin Harcourt, 2012.

Ghriss, Najoua Fezzaa. "The Role of Education in Individual Sustainable Development," in *Arab Human Development in the Twenty-first Century: The Primacy of Empowerment*, Bahgat Korany, ed. Cairo: American University of Cairo Press, 2014, pp. 245–84.

Gledhill, John. "Competing for Change: Regime Transition, Intrastate Competition, and Violence." *Security Studies*, Vol. 21 (2012), pp. 43–82.

Gongora, Thierry. "War Making and State Power in the Contemporary Middle East." *International Journal of Middle East Studies*, Vol. 29, No. 3 (1997), pp. 323–40.

Greene, Norman L. "Rule of Law in Morocco: A Journey Toward a Better Judiciary Through the Implementation of the 2011 Constitutional Reforms." *ILSA Journal of International and Comparative Law*, Vol. 18, No. 2 (2011–12), pp. 455–514.

Greener, Ian. "The Potential of Path Dependence in Political Studies." *Politics*, Vol. 25, No. 1 (2005), pp. 62–72.

Greif, Avner. "Historical and Comparative Institutional Analysis." *American Economic Review*, Vol. 88, No. 2 (1998), pp. 80–84.

Guazzone, Laura and Daniela Pioppi, eds. *The Arab State and Neo-Liberal Globalization: The Restructuring of State Power in the Middle East*. Reading, UK: Ithaca Press, 2012.

Hajjar, Sami G. "The Jamahiriya Experiment in Libya: Qadhafi and Rousseau." *Journal of Modern African Studies*, Vol. 18, No. 2 (June 1980), pp. 181–200.

Halliday, Fred. *Nation and Religion in the Middle East*. Boulder, CO: Lynne Rienner Publishers, 2000.

Hameiri, Shahar. "Failed states or a failed paradigm? State capacity and the limits of institutionalism." *Journal of International Relations and Development*, Vol. 10 (2007), pp. 122–49.

Hamerow, Theodore S. "History and the German Revolution of 1848." *American Historical Review*, Vol. 60, No. 1 (October 1954), pp. 27–44.

Hamid, Shadi. "Political Party Development Before and After the Arab Spring," in *Beyond the Arab Spring*, Mehran Kamrava, ed. New York: Oxford University Press, 2014, pp. 131–50.

BIBLIOGRAPHY

Hanieh, Adam. *Capitalism and Class in the Gulf Arab States*. New York: Palgrave Macmillan, 2011.

Hanlon, Querine. *The Prospects for Security Sector Reform in Tunisia: A Year after the Revolution*. Carlisle, PA: US Army War College, 2012.

Hanson, Jonathan and Rachel Sigman, "Leviathan's Latent Dimensions: Measuring State Capacity for Comparative Political Research," World Bank Political Economy Group, 21 March 2013.

Harb, Imad. "The Egyptian Military in Politics: Disengagement or Accommodation?" *Middle East Journal*, Vol. 57, No. 2 (Spring 2003), pp. 269–90.

Harik, Iliya and Denis J. Sullivan, eds. *Privatization and Liberalization in the Middle East*. Bloomington, IN: Indiana University Press, 1992.

Harmer, Christopher. *Iranian Naval and Maritime Strategy*. Washington, DC: Institute for the Study of War, 2013.

Hashas, Mohammed. "Moroccan Exceptionalism Examined: Constitutional Insights pre- and post-2011." Instituto Affari Internazionali (Rome), Working Paper 13–34, December 2013.

Hatina, Meir. "Arab Liberal thought in Historical Perspective," in *Arab Liberal Thought after 1967: Old Dilemmas, New Perceptions*, Meir Hatina and Christoph Schumann, eds. New York: Palgrave Macmillan, 2015, pp. 23–40.

Hauslohner, Abigail. "Gulf states that backed Syria's jihadists in an uneasy spot." *Washington Post*, 14 June 2014.

Hechter, Michael and Satoshi Kanazawa. "Sociological Rational Choice Theory." *Annual Review of Sociology*, Vol. 23 (1997), pp. 191–214.

Hegghammer, Thomas. *Jihad in Saudi Arabia: Violence and Pan-Islamism since 1979*. Cambridge: Cambridge University Press, 2010.

Hehir, Aidan. "The Myth of the Failed State and the War on Terror: A Challenge to the Conventional Wisdom." *Journal of Intervention and Statebuilding*, Vol. 1, No. 3 (November 2007), pp. 307–32.

Helmke, Gretchen and Steven Levitsky. "Introduction," in *Informal Institutions and Democracy: Lessons from Latin America*, Gretchen Helmke and Steven Levitsky, eds. Baltimore, MD: Johns Hopkins University Press, 2006, pp. 1–30.

Hendrix, Cullen S. "Measuring state capacity: Theoretical and empirical implications for the study of civil conflict." *Journal of Peace Research*, Vol. 43, No. 3 (2010), pp. 273–85.

Henneberg, Sabina. "Comparing the first provisional administrations in Tunisia and Libya: some tentative conclusions." Paper presented at the Middle East Studies Association annual meeting, Boston, MA, November 2016.

Herb, Michael. *The Wages of Oil: Parliaments and Economic Development in Kuwait and the UAE*. Ithaca, NY: Cornell University Press, 2014.

———. "No Representation without Taxation? Rents, Development, and Democracy." *Comparative Politics*, Vol. 37, No. 3 (April 2005), pp. 297–316.

BIBLIOGRAPHY

Hertog, Steffen. *Princes, Brokers, and Bureaucrats: Oil and the State in Saudi Arabia.* Ithaca, NY: Cornell University Press, 2010.

Heydemann, Steven. "Syria and the Future of Authoritarianism," in *Democratization and Authoritarianism in the Arab World*, Larry Diamond and Marc F. Plattner, eds. Baltimore, MD: Johns Hopkins University Press, 2014, pp. 300–314.

———. "Social Pacts and the Persistence of Authoritarianism in the Middle East," in *Debating Arab Authoritarianism: Dynamics and Durability in Nondemocratic Regimes*, Oliver Schlumberger, ed. Stanford, CA: Stanford University Press, 2007, pp. 21–38.

———. "War, Institutions, and Social Change in the Middle East," in *War, Institutions, and Social Change in the Middle East*, Steven Heydemann, ed. Berkeley, CA: University of California Press, 2000, pp. 1–30.

Hopwood, Derek. *Egypt: Politics and Society 1945–1981.* London: George Allen & Unwin, 1982.

Horowitz, Dan. "Dual Authority Polities." *Comparative Politics*, Vol. 14, No. 3 (April 1982), pp. 329–49.

Howard, Philip N. and Muzammil M. Hussain. "The Role of Digital Media," in *Democratization and Authoritarianism in the Arab World*, Larry Diamond and Marc F. Plattner, eds. Baltimore, MD: Johns Hopkins University Press, 2014, pp. 186–99.

Hudson, Michael C. *Arab Politics: The Search for Legitimacy.* New Haven, CT: Yale University Press, 1977.

Humphreys, Macartan, Jeffrey D. Sachs, and Joseph E. Stiglitz. "Introduction: What is the Problem with Natural Resource Wealth?" in *Escaping the Resource Curse*, Macartan Humphreys, Jeffrey D. Sachs, and Joseph E. Stiglitz, eds. New York: Columbia University Press, 2007, pp. 1–20.

Huntington, Samuel P. *The Soldier and the State: The Theory and Politics of Civil–Military Relations.* Cambridge, MA: Harvard University Press, 1957.

Hvidt, Martin. "The Dubai Model: An Outline of Key Development-Process Elements in Dubai." *International Journal of Middle East Studies*, Vol. 41, No. 3 (2009), pp. 397–418.

Ibrahim, Saad Eddin. "Liberalization and Democratization in the Arab World: An Overview," in *Political Liberalization & Democratization in the Arab World: Vol. 1, Theoretical Perspectives*, Bahgat Korany and Paul Noble, eds. Boulder, CO: Lynne Rienner Publishers, 1995, pp. 29–57.

Iqbal, Zaryab, and Harvey Starr. "Bad Neighbors: Failed States and their Consequences." *Conflict Management and Peace Science*, Vol. 23 (2008), pp. 315–31.

Ismael, Jacqueline. *Kuwait: Dependency and Class in a Rentier State.* Gainesville, FL: University Press of Florida, 1993.

Jaberi, Idriss. "Algeria's Discontented Middle Class." *Carnegie Endowment for International Peace*, 19 January 2017.

Jarzabek, Jaroslaw. "G.C.C. Military Spending in Era of Low Oil Prices." *MEI Policy Focus 2016–19*, August 2016.

Joffe, George. "National Reconciliation and General Amnesty in Algeria," in *The Politics of Violence, Truth and Reconciliation in the Arab Middle East*, Sune Haugbolle and Andres Hastrup, eds. London: Routledge, 2009, pp. 63–78.

Jones, Branwen Gruffydd. "'Good governance' and 'state failure': genealogies of imperial discourse." *Cambridge Review of International Affairs*, Vol. 26, No. 1 (2013), pp. 49–70.

Jones, Toby C. "Counterrevolution in the Gulf." *United States Institute of Peace Brief*, No. 89, 15 April 2011.

Juneau, Thomas. "Iran's policy towards the Houthis in Yemen: a limited return on a modest investment." *International Affairs*, Vol. 92, No. 3 (2016), pp. 647–63.

Kaboub, Fadhel. "The End of Neoliberalism? An Institutional Analysis of the Arab Uprisings." *Journal of Economic Issues*, Vol. 67, No. 2 (June 2013), pp. 533–43.

Kamrava, Mehran. *Troubled Waters: Insecurity in the Persian Gulf*. Ithaca, NY: Cornell University Press, 2018.

———. *The Modern Middle East: A Political History Since the First World War*, 3rd edn. Berkeley, CA: University of California Press, 2013.

———. "The Arab Spring and the Saudi-Led Counterrevolution," *Orbis*. Vol. 56, No. 1 (Winter 2012), pp. 96–104.

———. "The Political Economy of Rentierism in the Persian Gulf," in *The Political Economy of Oil in the Persian Gulf*, Mehran Kamrava, ed. New York: Oxford University Press, 2012, pp. 39–68.

———. *Iran's Intellectual Revolution*. Cambridge: Cambridge University Press, 2008.

———. "Military Professionalization and Civil–Military Relations in the Middle East." *Political Science Quarterly*, Vol. 115, No. 1 (Spring 2000), pp. 67–87.

———. "Revolution Revisited: Revolutionary Types and the Structuralist–Voluntarist Debate." *Canadian Journal of Political Science*, Vol. 32, No. 2 (1999), pp. 1–29.

———. "Non-Democratic States and Political Liberalization in the Middle East: A Structural Analysis." *Third World Quarterly*, Vol. 19, No. 1 (Spring 1998), pp. 63–85.

———. *Revolutionary Politics*. Westport, CT: Praeger, 1992.

———. *Revolution in Iran: The Roots of Turmoil*. London: Routledge, 1990.

Kao, Kristen. "Rigging Democracy: Maintaining Power Through Authoritarian Electoral Institutions." Paper presented at the annual meeting of the Middle East Studies Association, Boston, MA, November 2016.

———. "How Jordan's election revealed enduring weaknesses in its political system." *Washington Post*, 3 October 2016. https://www.washingtonpost.com/news/monkey-cage/wp/2016/10/03/how-jordans-election-revealed-enduring-weaknesses-in-its-political system/?utm_term=.1d57 83c990e9.

Kaplan, Seth. "Identity in Fragile State: Social cohesion and state building." *Development*, Vol. 52, No. 4 (2009), pp. 466–72.

Karl, Terry Lynn. "Ensuring Fairness: The Case for a Transparent Social Contract," in *Escaping the Resource Curse*, Macartan Humphreys, Jeffrey D. Sachs, and Joseph E. Stiglitz, eds. New York: Columbia University Press, 2007, pp. 256–85.

————. *The Paradox of Plenty: Oil Booms and Petro-States*. Berkeley, CA: University of California Press, 1997.

Karshenas, Massoud, Valentine M. Moghadam, and Randa Alami. "Social Policy after the Arab Spring: States and Social Rights in the MENA Region." *World Development*, Vol. 64 (2014), pp. 726–39.

Kassab, Elizabeth Suzanne. *Contemporary Arab Thought: Cultural Critique in Comparative Perspective*. New York: Columbia University Press, 2010.

Katzman, Kenneth. "Oman: Reform, Security, and U.S. Policy." *Congressional Research Service*, 7–5700, 26 April 2016.

Keddie, Nikki. *Modern Iran: Roots and Results of the Revolution*. New Haven, CT: Yale University Press, 2003.

Khaddour, Khedar. *The Assad Regime's Hold on the Syrian State*. Washington, DC: Carnegie Endowment for International Peace, 2015.

Khatib, Lina. "Transforming the Media: From Tool of the Rulers to Tool of Empowerment," in *Arab Human Development in the Twenty-first Century: The Primacy of Empowerment*, Bahgat Korany, ed. Cairo: American University of Cairo Press, 2014, pp. 67–104.

King, Stephen J. *The New Authoritarianism in the Middle East and North Africa*. Bloomington, IN: Indiana University Press, 2009.

Kinninmont, Jane. "Bahrain," in *Power and Politics in the Persian Gulf Monarchies*, Christopher Davidson, ed. London: Hurst & Co., 2011, pp. 31–62.

Koprulu, Nur. "Monarchical Pluralism or De-democratization: Actors and Choices in Jordan." *Insight Turkey*, Vol. 14, No. 1 (2012), pp. 71–92.

Korany, Bahgat. "A Microcosm of the Arab Spring: Sociology of Tahrir Square," in *Beyond the Arab Spring*, Mehran Kamrava, ed. New York: Oxford University Press, 2014, pp. 249–76.

————. ed. *Arab Human Development in the Twenty-first Century: The Primacy of Empowerment*. Cairo: American University in Cairo Press, 2014.

Korany, Bahgat, Rez Brynen, and Paul Noble. *Political Liberalization and Democratization in the Arab World: Vol. 2, Comparative Experiences*. Boulder, CO: Lynne Rienner Publishers, 1998.

Kosmatopoulos, Nikolas. "Toward an Anthropology of 'State Failure'." *Social Analysis*, Vol. 55, No. 3 (Winter 2011), pp. 115–42.

BIBLIOGRAPHY

Krasner, Stephen D. "Approaches to the State: Alternative Conceptions and Historical Dynamics." *Comparative Politics*, Vol. 16, No. 2 (1984), pp. 223–46.

Kugler, Jacek and William Domke, "Comparing the Strength of Nations." *Comparative Political Studies*, Vol. 19, No. 1 (April 1986), pp. 39–69.

Lemarchand, Rene and Keith Legg. "Political Clientelism and Development: A Preliminary Analysis." *Comparative Politics*, Vol. 4, No. 2 (January 1972), pp. 149–78.

Lemay-Hébert, Nicolas. "Statebuilding without Nation-building? Legitimacy, State Failure and the Limits of the Institutionalist Approach." *Journal of Intervention and Statebuilding*, Vol. 3, No. 1 (March 2009), pp. 21–45.

Levi, Margaret. "A Model, a Method, and a Map: Rational Choice in Comparative and Historical Analysis," in *Comparative Politics: Rationality, Culture, and Structure*, Mark I. Lichbach and Alan S. Zuckerman, eds. Cambridge: Cambridge University Press, 1997, pp. 19–41.

———. "Theories of Historical and Institutional Change." *PS: Political Science & Politics*, Vol. 20, No. 3 (1987), pp. 684–8.

Levitsky, Steven and Lucan A. Way. *Competitive Authoritarianism: Hybrid Regimes After the Cold War*. Cambridge: Cambridge University Press, 2010.

Lewental, D. Gershon. "'Saddam's Qadisiyyah': Religion and History in the Service of State Ideology in Baʿthi Iraq." *Middle Eastern Studies*, Vol. 50, No. 6 (2014), pp. 891–910.

Lichbach, Mark Irving and Alan S. Zuckerman, eds. *Comparative Politics: Rationality, Culture, and Structure*. Cambridge: Cambridge University Press, 1997.

Lindell, Ulf and Stefan Persson. "The Paradox of Weak State Power: A Research and Literature Overview." *Cooperation and Conflict*, Vol. 21 (1986), pp. 79–97.

Linz, Juan J. *Totalitarian and Authoritarian Regimes*. Boulder, CO: Lynne Rienner Publishers, 2000.

Linz, Juan and Alfred Stepan. *Problems of Democratic Transition and Consolidation: Southern Europe, South America, and Post-Communist Europe*. Baltimore, MD: Johns Hopkins University Press, 1996.

Lipset, Seymour Martin. "Some Social Requisites of Democracy: Economic Development and Political Legitimacy." *American Political Science Review*, Vol. 53, No. 1 (March 1959), pp. 69–105.

Lowi, Miriam R. *Oil Wealth and the Poverty of Politics: Algeria Compared*. Cambridge: Cambridge University Press, 2009.

Lust-Okar, Ellen and Saloua Zerhouni, eds. *Political Participation in the Middle East*. Boulder, CO: Lynne Rienner Publishers, 2008.

Lutterbeck, Derek. "Arab Uprisings, Armed Forces, and Civil-Military Relations." *Armed Forces and Society*, Vol. 39, No. 1 (2013), pp. 28–52.

Lynch, Marc. *The New Arab Wars: Uprisings and Anarchy in the Middle East*. New York: Public Affairs, 2016.

Machlis, Elisheva. *Shi'i Sectarianism in the Middle East: Modernisation and the Quest for Islamic Universalism*. London: I. B. Tauris, 2014.

Mahoney, James. "Path Dependence in Historical Sociology." *Theory and Society*, Vol. 29 (2000), pp. 507–48.

Mahoney, James and Dietrich Rueschemeyer, eds. *Comparative Historical Analysis in the Social Sciences*. Cambridge: Cambridge University Press, 2003.

Mahoney, James and Kathleen Thelen, eds. *Advances in Comparative-Historical Analysis*. Cambridge: Cambridge University Press, 2015.

Makiya, Kanan. *The Republic of Fear: The Politics of Modern Iraq*. Berkeley, CA: University of California Press, 1998.

Malki, Mhamed. "From the Law of the Ruler to the Rule of Law," in *Arab Human Development in the Twenty-first Century: The Primacy of Empowerment*, Bahgat Korany, ed. Cairo: American University of Cairo Press, 2014, pp. 27–66.

Marshall, Shana. *The Egyptian Armed Forces and the Remaking of an Economic Empire*. Washington, DC: Carnegie Endowment for International Peace, 2015.

Martin, Thomas. "Social Institutions: A Reformulation of the Concept." *Pacific Sociological Review*, Vol. 11, No. 2 (1968), pp. 100–109.

Martin, Vanessa. *Creating an Islamic State: Khomeini and the Making of a New Iran*. London: I. B. Tauris. 2003.

Martinez, Luis. *The Violence of Petro-Dollar Regimes: Algeria, Iraq and Libya*. Cynthia Schoch, trans. London: Hurst & Co., 2012.

Massoud, Tarek. "The Road to (and from) Liberation Square," in *Democratization and Authoritarianism in the Arab World*, Larry Diamond and Marc F. Plattner, eds. Baltimore, MD: Johns Hopkins University Press, 2014, pp. 233–47.

Matta, Samer, Simon Appleton, and Michael Bleaney. "The Impact of the Arab Spring on the Tunisian Economy." World Bank, Policy Research Working Paper, 7856, October 2016.

McFaul, Michael. "Transitions from Postcommunism." *Journal of Democracy*, Vol. 16, No. 3 (July 2005), pp. 5–19.

Mcloughlin, Claire. *Topic Guide on Fragile States*. Birmingham: Governance and Social Development Resource Centre, University of Birmingham, UK, 2012.

Mecham, Quinn. "Bahrain's Fractured Ruling Bargain: Political Mobilization, Regime Response, and the New Sectarianism," in *Beyond the Arab Spring*, Mehran Kamrava, ed. New York: Oxford University Press, 2014, pp. 341–71.

BIBLIOGRAPHY

Meijer, Roel. "Liberalism in the Middle East and the Issue of Citizenship Rights," in *Arab Liberal Thought after 1967: Old Dilemmas, New Perceptions*, Meir Hatina and Christoph Schumann, eds. New York: Palgrave Macmillan, 2015, pp. 63–81.

—————. "Political Citizenship and Social Movements in the Arab World," in *Handbook of Political Citizenship and Social Movements*, Hein-Anton van der Heijden, ed. Cheltenham, UK: Edward Elgar, 2014, pp. 628–60.

Meijer, Roel and Nils Butenschøn, eds. *The Crisis of Citizenship in the Arab World*. Leiden: Brill, 2017.

Menaldo, Victor. *The Institutions Curse: Natural Resources, Politics, and Development*. Cambridge: Cambridge University Press, 2016.

Menoret, Pascal. "Repression and Protest in Saudi Arabia," *Middle East Brief*, Crown Center for Middle East Studies, Brandeis University, No. 101, August 2016.

Meyer, Karl E. and Shareen Blair Brysac. *Kingmakers: The Invention of the Modern Middle East*. New York: Norton, 2008.

Mezran, Karim. "Libya in Transition: From *Jamahiriya* to *Jumhuriyyah*?" in *The New Middle East: Protest and Revolution in the Arab World*, Fawaz A. Gerges, ed. Cambridge: Cambridge University Press, 2014, pp. 309–31.

Migdal, Joel S. *State in Society: Studying How States and Societies Transform and Constitute One Another*. Cambridge: Cambridge University Press, 2001.

Migdal, Joel S., Atul Kohli, and Vivienne Shue, eds. *State Power and Social Forces: Domination and Transformation in the Third World*. Cambridge: Cambridge University Press, 1994.

Migdalovitz, Carol. "Morocco: Current Issues." *Congressional Research Service*, 7–5700, 4 December 2008.

Mirgani, Suzi. "The State of the Arab Media in the Wake of the Arab Uprisings," in *Bullets and Bulletins: Media and Politics in the Wake of the Arab Uprisings*, Mohamed Zayani and Suzi Mirgani, eds. New York: Oxford University Press, 2016, pp. 1–22.

Mitchell, Timothy. *Carbon Democracy: Political Power in the Age of Oil*. London: Verso, 2011.

Moussa, Nayla. "Loyalties and Group Formation in the Lebanese Officers Crops." Carnegie Middle East Center (Beirut), 27 January 2016.

Mufti, Malik. "Democratizing Potential of the 'Arab Spring': Some Early Observations." *Government and Opposition*, Vol. 50, No. 3 (2015), pp. 394–419.

Nepstad, Sharon Erickson. "Mutiny and nonviolence in the Arab Spring: Exploring military defections and loyalty in Egypt, Bahrain, and Syria." *Journal of Peace Research*, Vol. 50, No. 3 (2013), pp. 337–49.

Newman, Edward. "Failed States and International Order: Constructing a Post-Westphalian World." *Contemporary Security Policy*, Vol. 30, No. 3 (2009), pp. 421–43.

BIBLIOGRAPHY

Nield, Richard. "Why Bouteflika dissolved Algeria's powerful spy agency?" *Al Jazeera*, 25 February 2016. http://www.aljazeera.com/indepth/features/2016/02/algeria-dissolved-powerful-spy-agency-160225171417842.html.

Nolan, Leigh. "Managing Reform? Saudi Arabia and the King's Dilemma." *Brookings Doha Center*, Policy Briefing, May 2011.

Nordlinger, Eric. *Soldiers in Politics: Military Coups and Governments*. Englewood Cliffs, NJ: Prentice Hall, 1977.

North, Douglass C. *Institutions, Institutional Change and Economic Performance*. New York: Cambridge University Press, 1990.

————. "Institutional Change and Economic Growth." *Journal of Economic History* Vol. 31, No. 1 (1971), pp. 118–25.

Ohl, Dorothy, Holger Albrecht, and Kevin Koehler. "For Money or Liberty? The Political Economy of Military Desertion and Rebel Recruitment in the Syrian Civil War." Carnegie Middle East Center (Beirut), 24 November 2015.

Ostrom, Elinor. *Understanding Institutional Diversity*. Princeton, NJ: Princeton University Press, 2005.

Ottaway, Marina and Meredith Riley, "Morocco: Top-Down Reform Without Democratic Transition," in *Beyond the Façade: Political Reform in the Arab World*, Marina Ottaway and Julia Choucair-Vizoso, eds. Washington, DC: Carnegie Endowment for International Peace, 2008, pp. 161–85.

Owen, Roger. "Egypt and Tunisia: From the Revolutionary Overthrow of Dictatorships to the Struggle to Establish a New Constitutional Order," in *The New Middle East: Protest and Revolution in the Arab World*, Fawaz A. Gerges, ed. Cambridge: Cambridge University Press, 2014, pp. 257–72.

————. *The Rise and Fall of Arab Presidents for Life*. Cambridge, MA: Harvard University Press, 2012.

————. *State, Power and Politics in the Making of the Modern Middle East*, 2nd edn. London: Routledge, 2000.

Palmer, Monte. *The Politics of the Middle East*. Itasca, IL: E. E. Peacock, 2002.

Parolin, Gianluca P. *Citizenship in the Arab World: Kin, Religion and Nation-State*. Amsterdam: Amsterdam University Press, 2009.

Paul, T. V., ed. *Accommodating Rising Powers: Past, Present, and Future*. Cambridge: Cambridge University Press, 2016.

Pelham, Nicolas. *Holy Lands: Reviewing Pluralism in the Middle East*. New York: Columbia Global Reports, 2016.

Phillips, Sarah. "Yemen: The Centrality of the Process," in *Beyond the Façade: Political Reform in the Arab World*, Marina Ottaway and Julia Choucair-Vizoso, eds. Washington, DC: Carnegie Endowment for International Peace, 2008, pp. 231–59.

Pierson, Paul. *Politics in Time*. Princeton, NJ: Princeton University Press, 2004.

BIBLIOGRAPHY

————. "Increasing Returns, Path Dependence, and the Study of Politics." *American Political Science Review* Vol. 94, No. 2 (2000), pp. 251–67.

————. "The Limits of Design: Explaining Institutional Origins and Change." *Governance*, Vol. 13, No. 4 (October 2000), pp. 475–99.

Pousney, Marsha Pripstein and Michele Penner Angrist, eds. *Authoritarianism in the Middle East: Regimes and Resistance*. Boulder, CO: Lynne Rienner Publishers, 2005.

PwC, *An introduction to Value Added Tax in the GCC*, January 2017. https://www.pwc.com/m1/en/tax/documents/what-is-vat-faq-on-vat-in-the-gcc.pdf.

Rabi, Uzi. "Introduction," in *Tribes and State in a Changing Middle East*, Uzi Rabi, ed. New York: Oxford University Press, 2016, pp. 1–10.

Rivlin, Paul. *Arab Economies in the Twenty-First Century*. Cambridge: Cambridge University Press, 2009.

Roberts, Hugh. "Demilitarizing Algeria," in *Beyond the Façade: Political Reform in the Arab World*, Marina Ottaway and Julia Choucair-Vizoso, eds. Washington, DC: Carnegie Endowment for International Peace, 2008, pp. 137–59.

Rohe, Mahias and Jakob Skovgaard-Petersen. "The Ambivalent Embrace of Liberalism: The Draft Program of the Freedom and Justice Party in Egypt," in *Arab Liberal Thought after 1967: Old Dilemmas, New Perceptions*, Meir Hatina and Christoph Schumann, eds. New York: Palgrave Macmillan, 2015, pp. 195–214.

Romdhani, Oussama. "The Next Revolution: A Call for Reconciliation in the Arab World." *World Affairs* (November/December 2013), pp. 89–96.

Rosman-Stollman, Elisheva and Aharon Kampinsky, eds. *Civil–Military Relations in Israel: Essays in Honor of Stuart A. Cohen*. Lanham, MD: Lexington Books, 2014.

Ross, Michael L. *The Oil Curse: How Petroleum Wealth Shapes the Development of Nations*. Princeton, NJ: Princeton University Press, 2012.

Rougier, Eric. "'Fire in Cairo': Authoritarian-Redistributive Social Contracts, Structural Change, and the Arab Spring." *World Development*, Vol. 78 (2016), pp. 148–71.

Roy, Olivier. "The Transformation of the Arab World," in *Democratization and Authoritarianism in the Arab World*, Larry Diamond and Marc F. Plattner, eds. Baltimore, MD: Johns Hopkins University Press, 2014, pp. 15–28.

Ryan, Curtis R. "The Armed Forces and the Arab Uprisings: The Case of Jordan." *Middle East Law and Governance*, Vol. 4 (2012), pp. 153–67.

Sachs, Jeffrey D. "How to Handle the Macroeconomics of Wealth," in *Escaping the Resource Curse*, Macartan Humphreys, Jeffrey D. Sachs, and Joseph E. Stiglitz, eds. New York: Columbia University Press, 2007, pp. 173–193.

Sadiki, Larbi, ed. *Routledge Handbook of the Arab Spring: Rethinking Democratization*. London: Routledge, 2015.

Sadiki, Larbi and Youcef Bouandel. "The Post Arab Spring Reform: The Maghreb at a Cross Roads." *Digest of Middle East Studies*, Vol. 25, No. 1 (2016), pp. 109–31.

Salamé, Ghassan, ed. *The Foundations of the Arab State*. London: Croom Helm, 1987.

Samaan, Jean-Loup. "Jordan's New Geopolitics." *Survival*, Vol. 54, No. 2 (April–May 2012), pp. 15–26.

Sangmpam, S. N. "Politics Rules: The False Primacy of Institutions in Developing Countries." *Political Studies*, Vol. 55, No. 1 (2007), pp. 201–24.

Saouli, Adham. *The Arab State: Dilemmas of late formation*. London: Routledge, 2012.

Sassoon, Joseph. *Anatomy of Authoritarianism in the Arab Republics*. Cambridge: Cambridge University Press, 2016.

Sayigh, Yezid. "Dilemmas of Reform: Policing in Arab Transitions." Beirut: Carnegie Middle East Center, 2016.

Schirazi, Asghar. *The Constitution of Iran: Politics and the State in the Islamic Republic*. John O'Kane, trans. London: I. B. Tauris, 1997.

Schlumberger, Oliver, ed. *Debating Arab Authoritarianism: Dynamics and Durability in Nondemocratic Regimes*. Stanford, CA: Stanford University Press, 2007.

Schmidt-Hebbel, Klaus. "Fiscal Institutions in Resource-rich Economies: Lessons from Chile and Norway," in *Understanding and Avoiding the Oil Curse in Resource-Rich Arab Economies*, Ibrahim Elbadawi and Hoda Selim, eds. Cambridge: Cambridge University Press, 2016, pp. 225–83.

Schmitz, Charles. *Building a Better Yemen*. Washington, DC: Carnegie Endowment for International Peace, 2012.

Schwarz, Rolf. "The political economy of state-formation in the Arab Middle East: Rentier states, economic reform, and democratization." *Review of International Political Economy*, Vol. 15, No. 4 (October 2008), pp. 599–621.

Scott, James C. *Seeing Like a State: How Certain Schemes to Improve the Human Condition Have Failed*. New Haven, CT: Yale University Press, 1998.

———. *Weapons of the Weak: Everyday Forms of Peasant Resistance*. New Haven, CT: Yale University Press, 1985.

Selbin, Eric. *Revolution, Rebellion, Resistance: The Power of Story*. London: Zed Books, 2010.

Shambayati, Hootan. "The Rentier State, Interest Groups, and the Paradox of Autonomy: State and Business in Turkey and Iran." *Comparative Politics*, Vol. 26, No. 3 (1994), pp. 307–31.

BIBLIOGRAPHY

Sharabi, Hisham. *Neopatriarchy: A Theory of Distorted Change in Arab Society*. New York: Oxford University Press, 1988.

Sharp, Jeremy M. "Jordan: Background and U.S. Relations." *Congressional Research Service*, 7–5700, 27 January 2016.

Sika, Nadine. "The Arab State and Social Contestation," in *Beyond the Arab Spring*, Mehran Kamrava, ed. New York: Oxford University Press, 2014, pp. 73–97.

Smith, Benjamin. "Oil Wealth and Regime Survival in the Developing World, 1960–1999." *American Journal of Political Science*, Vol. 48, No. 2 (April 2004), pp. 232–46.

Sohrabi, Naghmeh. "Reading the Tea Leaves: Iranian Domestic Politics and the Presidential Election of 2013," *Middle East Brief*, Crown Center for Middle East Studies, Brandies University, No. 65 (July 2012).

Sommer, Martin, et al. "Learning to Live with Cheaper Oil: Policy Adjustments in Oil-Exporting Countries of the Middle East and Central Asia." International Monetary Fund, 2016.

Sonn, Tamara. *Between Qur'an and Crown: The Challenge of Political Legitimacy in the Arab World*. Boulder, CO: Westview Press, 1990.

Soto, Raimundo and Ilham Haouas. "Has the UAE Escaped the Oil Curse?" in *Understanding and Avoiding the Oil Curse in Resource-Rich Arab Economies*, Ibrahim Elbadawi and Hoda Selim, eds. Cambridge: Cambridge University Press, 2016, pp. 373–420.

Springborg, Robert. "Whither the Arab Spring? 1989 or 1848?" *International Spectator*, Vol. 46, No. 3 (September 2011), pp. 5–12.

Stacher, Joshua. *Adaptable Autocrats: Regime Power in Egypt and Syria*. Stanford, CA: Stanford University Press, 2012.

Stepan, Alfred. "Tunisia's Transition and the 'Twin Tolerations,'" in *Democratization and Authoritarianism in the Arab World*, Larry Diamond and Marc F. Plattner, eds. Baltimore, MD: Johns Hopkins University Press, 2014, pp. 218–32.

———. *Rethinking Military Politics: Brazil and the Southern Cone*. Princeton, NJ: Princeton University Press, 1988.

Stepan Alfred and Juan J. Linz, "Democratization Theory and the 'Arab Spring,'" in *Democratization and Authoritarianism in the Arab World*, Larry Diamond and Marc F. Plattner, eds. Baltimore, MD: Johns Hopkins University Press, 2014, pp. 81–95.

Stewart, Patrick. "Weak States and Global Threats: Assessing Evidence of 'Spillovers.'" Center for Global Development Working Paper, No. 73 (January 2006), pp. 1–31.

Stiglitz, Joseph. "What is the Role of the State?" in *Escaping the Resource Curse*. Macartan Humphreys, Jeffrey D. Sachs, and Joseph E. Stiglitz, eds. New York: Columbia University Press, 2007, pp. 23–52.

Stillman, Peter G. "The Concept of Legitimacy." *Polity*, Vol. 7, No. 1 (Autumn 1974), pp. 32–56.

Stokes, Susan C., Thad Dunning, Marcelo Nazareno, and Valeria Brusco. *Brokers, Voters, and Clientelism: The Puzzle of Distributive Politics.* Cambridge: Cambridge University Press, 2013.

Svolik, Milan W. *The Politics of Authoritarian Rule.* Cambridge: Cambridge University Press, 2012.

Takeyh, Ray. *Guardians of the Revolution: Iran and the World in the Age of the Ayatollahs.* Oxford: Oxford University Press, 2009.

Talmadge, Caitlin. *The Dictator's Army: Battlefield Effectiveness in Authoritarian Regimes.* Ithaca, NY: Cornell University Press, 2015.

Tarrow, Sidney G. *War, States, and Contention: A Comparative Historical Study.* Ithaca, NY: Cornell University Press, 2015.

——————. *Strangers at the Gates: Movements and States in Contentious Politics.* Cambridge: Cambridge University Press, 2012.

——————. *Power in Movement: Social Movements and Contentious Politics*, 3rd edn. Cambridge: Cambridge University Press, 2011.

Taylor, William C. *Military Responses to the Arab Uprisings and the Future of Civil–Military Relations in the Middle East: Analysis from Egypt, Tunisia, Libya, and Syria.* New York: Palgrave Macmillan, 2014.

Tessler, Mark, Amaney Jamal, and Michael Robbins, "New Findings on Arab Democracy," in *Democratization and Authoritarianism in the Arab World*, Larry Diamond and Marc F. Plattner, eds. Baltimore, MD: Johns Hopkins University Press, 2014, pp. 54–68.

Thelen, Kathleen. *How Institutions Evolve: The Political Economy of Skills in Germany, Britain, the United States, and Japan.* Cambridge: Cambridge University Press, 2004.

——————. "How Institutions Evolve: Insights from Comparative Historical Analysis," in *Comparative Historical Analysis in the Social Sciences*, James Mahoney and Dietrich Rueschemeyer, eds. Cambridge: Cambridge University Press, 2003, pp. 208–40.

——————. "Historical Institutionalism in Comparative Politics." *Annual Review of Political Science*, Vol. 2 (1999), pp. 369–404.

Tilly, Charles. "War and State Power." *Middle East Report*, Vol. 171 (1991), pp. 38–40.

Tilly, Charles and Lesley J. Wood. *Social Movements: 1768–2012*, 3rd edn. Boulder, CO: Paradigm Publishers, 2013.

Tripp, Charles. "The Politics of Resistance and the Arab Spring," in *The New Middle East: Protest and Revolution in the Arab World*, Fawaz A. Gerges, ed. Cambridge: Cambridge University Press, 2014, pp. 135–54.

——————. *The Power and the People: Paths of Resistance in the Middle East.* Cambridge: Cambridge University Press, 2013.

BIBLIOGRAPHY

Tsebelis, George. *Nested Games: Rational Choice in Comparative Politics.* Berkeley, CA: University of California Press, 1990.

Vatikiotis, P. J. *Nasser and his Generation.* New York: St Martin's Press, 1978.

Volpi, Frederic. "Algeria Versus the Arab Spring," in *Democratization and Authoritarianism in the Arab World*, Larry Diamond and Marc F. Plattner, eds. Baltimore, MD: Johns Hopkins University Press, 2014, pp. 326–37.

Vom Bruck, Gabriele, Atiaf Alwazir, and Benjamin Wiacek. "Yemen: revolution suspended?" in *The New Middle East Protest and Revolution in the Arab World*, Fawaz A. Gerges, ed. Cambridge: Cambridge University Press, 2014, pp. 285–308.

Waldner, David. *State Building and Late Development.* Ithaca, NY: Cornell University Press, 1999.

Ward, Steven R. *Immortal: A Military History of Iran and its Armed Forces.* Washington, DC: Georgetown University Press, 2009.

Weeks, Jessica L. P. *Dictators at War and Peace.* Ithaca, NY: Cornell University Press, 2014.

Wehler-Schoeck, Anja. "Parliamentary Elections in Jordan: A Competition of Mixed Messages." *Alsharq*, September 2016. http://www.alsharq. de/2016/mashreq/jordanien/parliamentary-elections-in-jordan-a-competition-of-mixed-messages/

Wehrey, Frederic. "Bahrain's Decade of Discontent," in *Democratization and Authoritarianism in the Arab World*, Larry Diamond and Marc F. Plattner, eds. Baltimore, MD: Johns Hopkins University Press, 2014, pp. 315–25.

Wehrey, Frederic and Ariel I. Ahram. *Taming the Militias: Building National Guards in Fractured Arab State.* Washington, DC: Carnegie Endowment for International Peace, 2015.

Weiss, Linda. *The Myth of the Powerless State.* Ithaca, NY: Cornell University Press, 1998.

Werrell, Caitlin E. Francesco Femia, and Troy Sternberg. "Did We See It Coming? State Fragility, Climate Vulnerability, and the Uprisings in Syria and Egypt." *SAIS Review*, Vol. 35, No. 1 (Winter-Spring 2015), pp. 29–46.

Wheelock, Keith. *Nasser's New Egypt: A Critical Analysis.* Westport, CT: Greenwood, 1975.

Wolf, Anne. *Can Secular Parties Lead the New Tunisia?* Washington, DC: Carnegie Endowment for International Peace, 2014.

Woo-Cumings, Meredith, ed. *The Developmental State.* Ithaca, NY: Cornell University Press, 1999.

World Bank. "Poverty has Fallen in the Maghreb, but Inequality Persists," 17 October 2016. http://www.worldbank.org/en/news/feature/2016/10/17/poverty-has-fallen-in-the-maghreb-but-inequality-persists.

———. "Egypt Economic Monitor: Paving the Way to a Sustainable Recovery," No. 96946, Spring 2015.

BIBLIOGRAPHY

Yalouh, Rachid. "The Discourse of Change in Morocco." *Policy Analysis*, Doha Institute, Arab Center for Research and Policy Studies, 2011.

Yom, Sean L. and F. Gregory Gause, III. "Resilient Royals: How Arab Monarchies Hang On," in *Democratization and Authoritarianism in the Arab World*, Larry Diamond and Marc F. Plattner, eds. Baltimore, MD: Johns Hopkins University Press, 2014, pp. 112–26.

Zurayk, Rami and Anne Gough, "Bread and Olive Oil: The Agrarian Root of the Arab Uprising," in *The New Middle East: Protest and Revolution in the Arab World*, Fawaz A. Gerges, ed. Cambridge: Cambridge University Press, 2014, pp. 107–31.

INDEX